COMPLETE
WORKS OF
H. EMILIE
CADY

COMPLETE
WORKS OF
H. EMILIE
CADY

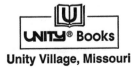

UNITY® Books

Unity Village, Missouri

Complete Works of H. Emilie Cady
First Edition 1995

Publishing information for each of the three volumes in this book can be obtained on the back of the individual title page for each volume.

To receive a catalog of all Unity publications (books, cassettes, and magazines) or to place an order, call the Customer Service Department: 1-800-669-0282 or (816) 251-3580. For information, address Unity Books, Publishers, Unity School of Christianity, 1901 NW Blue Parkway, Unity Village, MO 64065-0001.

"H. Emilie Cady: Physician and Metaphysician" was originally published in August/September 1975 *Unity Magazine*. "Dr. H. Emilie Cady: Author With Authority" originally appeared in June 1979 in *Unity Magazine*.

The New Revised Standard Version used for
all Bible verses, unless otherwise noted.

Cover design by Jill L. Ziegler
Cover is an adaptation of the original cover of *Lessons in Truth*

LIBRARY OF CONGRESS CATALOGING-IN-PUBLICATION DATA
Cady, H. Emilie (Harriet Emilie), 1848-1941.
   [works. 1955]
   Complete Works of H. Emilie Cady. — 1st ed.
     p. cm.
   Contents: Lessons in Truth — How I Used Truth — God a Present Help.
   1. Unity School of Christianity—Doctrines. 2. Cady, H. Emilie
(Harriet Emilie), 1848-1941. I. Title.
BX9890.U505 1995
289.9'7—dc20   95-5147
ISBN 0-87159-029-8 : $13.95
Canada GST R132529033

Unity Books feels a sacred trust to be a healing presence in the world. By printing with biodegradable soybean ink on recycled paper, we believe we are doing our part to be wise stewards of our Earth's resources.

Dedicated ...

to the many loving friends around
the world who have been
cheered and helped by these
simple messages.

EDITOR'S NOTE

In her 1930 letter to Lowell Fillmore, which is now the first chapter of *How I Used Truth*, Emilie Cady wrote: "You can see, dear Mr. Fillmore, that these children [her articles] born ... out of the very travail of my soul, are precious to me, and how I felt I would rather never see them again than to see them changed in any way. I thank the Fillmores that they have kept them as they were written, for they are God's own burning words to anyone suffering under like conditions, however simple they may seem to one not needing them."

This new edition of Emilie Cady's work has been a labor of love. Every effort has been made to restore her original writing; this effort will be particularly noticeable in *God a Present Help*. Editors must do their jobs, however, as benevolently as possible. In seventy-five to one hundred years, language and culture have changed so archaic words and inaccurate Bible translations are best replaced. We are confident that the reader will be pleased by what we've restored and how we've kept the best of the earlier editing. It is my sincerest hope that Dr. Cady would also be pleased, for we all owe her more than we can say.

Astute readers with either long memories or good libraries may realize that there are a few articles Emilie Cady wrote, published in *Unity Magazine, Weekly Unity,* and *Progress,* that are not included in this "complete works." Since the themes in these articles have already been thoroughly explored elsewhere in her work, we let them be.

Michael A. Maday
1995

CONTENTS

Book III GOD A PRESENT HELP

Introduction
H. EMILIE CADY:
PHYSICIAN AND METAPHYSICIAN

Hundreds of thousands of copies of Unity's textbook *Lessons in Truth*, by H. Emilie Cady, have been sold since its first publication in 1896. Inasmuch as each copy of a book of this kind is usually read by several people, over the years literally millions of people have read *Lessons in Truth.*

How famous, how widely known an author would be today if his or her book sold a million copies! That author would be on talk shows and television, lecturing in colleges, becoming more and more widely known every day. But it is safe to say that the thought of becoming widely known, famous, or rich never occurred to the author of *Lessons in Truth.* H. Emilie Cady just did not think in those terms.

For one thing, metaphysicians of her school of thought were very distrustful of what they called "personality." They desired that their reader's attention be directed, not toward them, but toward God, or Spirit. So well did Emilie Cady succeed in this respect that, as a person, little was known about her, even to officials of Unity School of Christianity. Because of their clear, simple, and effective teaching, linked with a distinctly religious element, her books gained wide circulation among church people, Unity students, and readers of New Thought and metaphysical Christian literature. She was invited to teach at Unity headquarters but never accepted the invitation. Even Charles and Myrtle

1

Fillmore, Unity's co-founders, never met her until they visited New York in either 1926 or 1927.

H. Emilie Cady was as good at shunning publicity and keeping herself in the background as she was at writing. And at writing, she was highly skilled. Her literary ability, her mastery of a clear, universal, almost timeless prose style, is evident. Her books were written in the nineteenth and early twentieth centuries, and most books of that era reflect the literary tastes and styles of their period. There may be flowery speech, words strange to our ears, classical allusions now lost on most of us. But Miss Cady, like the Fillmores, wrote "plain style" for readers of all time. How did she master this style? As she herself said, she was divinely commissioned to write. As a result, though not a line from her writings found its way into *Bartlett's Familiar Quotations*, her message found its way into many a human heart, there to influence human affairs for good, perhaps throughout eternity.

Many of those who found in her writings an answer to their life problems must have wondered about the author. Who was she? Where did she come from? Was she young or old, married or single? It happens that I can throw a little light on these questions because when I was minister of the Unity Church of Truth in Syracuse, New York, in 1949, a member of our church discovered Dr. Cady's grave at Dryden, a town south of Syracuse. Along with this member and two others, I made a "minipilgrimage" to Dryden, where we met Dr. Cady's niece, Carolyn E. Cady, who was employed by the public library.

We introduced ourselves to her, and she very kindly accompanied us to the cemetery. There I photographed her beside the large, beautifully polished family tombstone, which bore the following inscriptions: "Oliver B. Cady, 1815-1897. Cornelia A. Phillips, (his wife), 1819-1897. Helen Cady More, 1846-1920. Harriet E. Cady, 1848-1941." The latter, our author, had a long life, just seven years short of the century mark!

It appears that Dr. Cady, as a writer, disguised her family connections somewhat by stressing her middle name, Emilie, instead of Harriet, by which she was known to the family. We were fortunate to have her niece for our guide. She took us to the old Cady farmhouse where Emilie was born, lived as a child and returned to for vacations from her medical practice in New York City.

After visiting the old farm and also the one-room schoolhouse (at that time being used as a residence) where Emilie taught at one period of her life, Carolyn Cady invited us to her home, where she had some things of her aunt's. She was very friendly and was interested in our desire to know more about her aunt. There was a certain family resemblance in Carolyn to the photographic portrait of Dr. Cady, which had a prominent place in her living room.

Unlike Dr. Cady, however, who appeared from her picture to be a large, robust woman, Carolyn was small, almost frail in body; she had dark hair and eyes, and features tending toward ruggedness in a feminine way. Yet the independence of thought and adventurous disposition of Emilie Cady was apparent in her niece. She also shared her aunt's attitude toward publicity.

After my return to Syracuse, she became much concerned that the pictures I had taken might be published and draw curious seekers to her aunt's grave. I reassured her that the pictures would not be published, and they never were.

We learned from Carolyn that she and Dr. Cady had toured Europe together. One travel souvenir which she said Dr. Cady had purchased in Italy was a large hand-colored photograph of Mt. Etna in eruption. I remember wondering what the good doctor had found attractive in this. Perhaps as a teacher in the little country school, she had taught her pupils about volcanoes, and this had satisfied her desire for firsthand knowledge. Or—who knows—perhaps she visualized an "eruption" of Truth over the earth!

At any rate, to understand the person who later became a distinguished metaphysical author and healer, one should know her early background. She was born in rural upstate New York, a beautiful and prosperous part of the state. When she was born, James Knox Polk was the eleventh President of the United States, and she lived through the terms of twenty other Presidents, until at least the third term of Franklin Delano Roosevelt! What a life span! Evidently she shared the modern idea that the passage of time need not necessarily cause old age.

She was the daughter of a hardy pioneer. She tells us in *How I Used Truth* that her father was well known and respected in the neighborhood. He must have had, as a pioneer, a built-in ruggedness and persistence as well as ability to cope with whatever need developed. (I was told that some of the old rail fences in the neighborhood were constructed with wooden nails; there being no metal nails available, pegs whittled out of hardwood were used instead.)

The same adventurous, self-reliant, and "can do" spirit must have led Emilie Cady to choose a career in medicine in the 1880s. Even today, nearly a hundred years later, men still predominate in medicine. What a drive within her it must have taken to leave schoolteaching, one of the few callings other than marriage sanctioned for women at that time, and to brave the disapproval of society to become a doctor of homeopathic medicine in New York City!

And she succeeded. It was as an established and successful physician that she first appeared on the Unity scene. Quite on her own, she had written and published a booklet, called *Finding the Christ in Ourselves*. This came to the attention of Myrtle Fillmore, who was so impressed with it that she gave it to Charles Fillmore. He lost no time in asking permission to print and distribute the booklet and invited her to write for *Unity Magazine.*

As a result, beginning in January 1892, a number of articles by Dr. Cady appeared in the magazine. The first one, "Neither Do I Condemn Thee," later became a chapter in the book *Miscellaneous Writings* (later renamed *How I Used Truth*). Subsequent articles entitled "Oneness With God" and "God's Hand" were also included in this book.

A letter written by Dr. Cady, which appeared in the March 1892 issue of *Unity Magazine*, shows that she had already established in herself a superb confidence in Truth principles. She led a busy life of service, not only treating those who came to her for help in overcoming sickness, discouragement, or other personal problems, but seeking after office hours to aid persons in institutions, such as homes for delinquent young women.

In this letter, Dr. Cady tells how, after a busy day at her office, she gave a talk at one of these institutions to some twenty-five of those she calls "the younger sisters," giving them words of love and encouragement instead of reproaches. After this talk, when as she says she was "alone in her home with the Father," a feeling of discouragement came over her. Faithfully she released all the various cases to God.

To quote from her letter: "Dear Lord, I commit all these various cases to Thee. I do not know that I have helped any of these troubled hearts a bit, but thou knowest I have, in each case, given them the very best I knew how to give."

Then she says, "As I looked into His face, great tears trickled down my own at the thought of my weakness and insufficiency." How many times have you and I felt the same way, after our best efforts to help or heal another? How could we believe that we had helped them in any way? Here is one of the most outstanding metaphysicians of the early Truth movement overcome by the same feelings that often beset us.

How did Emilie Cady handle this? Actually she did not handle it, nor did she overcome it. God did it for her. She says: "Quick as a flash, He said unto me, 'Well done, good and faithful servant ... enter thou into the joy of thy lord' (Mt. 25:23 KJV). As much as to say, 'My child, you went forth with love and tried to do faithfully and unselfishly My work. Now do not waste one moment thinking it over, for I, all unseen by you, have poured the living bread and water through it to my fainting, famishing children. The work is Mine, not yours, and it is all well finished by Me.' "

Truth principles never change, do they? Some years ago, several scientists reported on their experiments with the power of prayer. One of the key principles established was that each time, after making a prayer or a treatment, there must be a complete transfer of the problem to God, a total relinquishing of it to the Supreme Power. Emilie Cady learned this a long time ago.

In her letter to Myrtle Fillmore, she goes on to say, "We are told 'delight thyself also in the Lord; and he shall give thee the desires of thine heart' (Ps. 37:4 KJV). It is not while we are worrying over results or failures that we get our desires, but while we are delighting ourselves in Him, just resting in Him, saying, 'Dear Father, while I am trusting Thou are working and Thou canst not fail.' Hold yourself in peace and quietness with Him. 'In quietness and in confidence shall be your strength' " (Is. 30:15 KJV).

Then she continues in language reminiscent of the chapter on "Finding the Secret Place" in *Lessons in Truth*: "The moment you are able to possess your soul in patience and in harmony, you will begin without effort to radiate health and harmony and all good, and whoever is looking to you for help will draw from you just the help they need, even if you never give a set treatment."

Though she was self-effacing, we nevertheless get glimpses from her writings that tell of her struggles in proving her Truth principles. Her whole emphasis was primarily on proving the Truth. In *How I Used Truth*, she tells us: "We ask no one to believe that which is here written simply because it is presented as Truth. 'Prove all things' for yourself; it is possible to prove every statement in this book. Every statement given was proved before it was written.... But results that one obtains from them will depend on how faithfully and persistently one uses the helps given."

The Master counseled persistency in his parable of the widow and the unjust judge, and Emilie Cady was his faithful disciple. We sometimes read that one should pray only once for any object or purpose, and thereafter give thanks. Yet Jesus prayed three times for the same purpose in the garden of Gethsemane and did he not say that men "need to pray always and not to lose heart" (Lk. 18:1)?

In her letter to Lowell Fillmore (which later became the first chapter of *How I Used Truth*), she says of the articles that make up the book: "Almost every one ... was born out of the travail of my soul after I had been weeks, months, sometimes years, trying by affirmations, by claiming the promises of Jesus, and by otherwise faithfully using all of the knowledge of Truth that I then possessed to secure deliverance for myself or others from some distressing bondage that thus far had defied all human help."

Think of it: weeks, months, sometimes years of continued prayer for one particular purpose, until the desired demonstration was made! Yes, Emilie Cady was truly persistent. And her persistence was always rewarded. Her elderly father was exiled from his home for five years, although innocent of a charge that she says was "the wicked machination of another man." All due processes of law had failed to clear him of the false accusation. Years of her own prayers were fruitless, until one day she made an impassioned plea to God for his deliverance and was told that she herself, acting as God's agent, must decree his freedom. Unquestioningly she obeyed. As if by magic, in a few days her father came home, a free man, his innocence clearly established. Persistence had triumphed!

Another case in point was that of the healing of a young friend from drinking. For weeks, Dr. Cady tells us, she watched with awful anxiety as she saw him drinking day by day, until she reached the point where she could "loose him and let him go." When she did gain to that place in consciousness where she completely transferred the problem to God and stood steadfast in spite of appearances, it required only a few hours before she saw him healed. So thoroughly was he set free that in forty years he had never again touched alcoholic liquors or indulged in any form of dissipation.

There was still another problem to be overcome, the problem of money supply. She herself had an established medical practice, with plenty of patients paying their bills monthly, so it was not her own supply that troubled her. Other cases whose means of support were exhausted, came to her for help. To the kindhearted physician, these cases were as distressing and painful as though the patients were afflicted with cancer or rheumatism. What could she do about it? She turned to God in prayer.

In answer, she tells us, God gave her the vision of His presence as all-inclusive supply of all things. She wrote the article "All-Sufficiency in All Things" and set out to prove that God's power would supply her. From that time on, no work or ministry of any kind was performed by her for pay. No monthly bills were sent out. No office charges were made. She gave with no thought of return, a free giving.

Yet as her distinguished teacher Emma Curtis Hopkins had written: "There is always at least once when we are called to stand steady to our principles.... Nothing is sure at all in your life until it has been put through the furnace, which is the meeting of the opposite to it, with its noble steadfastness to itself."

For more than two years, Dr. Cady persisted in proving this idea of God as supply, never letting anyone know what she was trying to prove. But alas, it did not work out. More than once, she did not even have money for the bare necessities of life and was faint for want of food. But with supreme fortitude, she kept on, cheerfully teaching all who came to her that God would supply all their needs.

And then, after two years of this, she reached her limit. "Hope deferred makes the heart sick" (Prov. 13:12). Flesh and blood and human self could endure no more. Like many another, both before and since, she cried out to God: "Why? Why this failure? You told me in the vision that if I would give up the old way and trust to You alone, You would prove to me Your sufficiency. Why have You failed to do it?"

What was God's answer? Only a verse of Scripture came into her mind: "Then God said, 'Let there be light'; and there was light" (Gen. 1:3). At first she could not see any relevance in this. But she kept on repeating these words, hoping to see the meaning in them. And as she repeated them, there seemed to be an increasing tendency to stress the word *said*. Suddenly it dawned upon her that never once, in all those two trying years, had she "said" or "spoken the word" for supply.

She saw that she must not just leave the matter of supplying money in God's hands, as she had been doing. She must set the supply principle in motion, into action—activate it and direct it by her spoken words, definite words. She had been expressing a passive, indefinite trust, unbacked by positive and active direction to the supply principle. Apparently this was not enough. Her whole emphasis had been on giving only, not on receiving as well.

Here again, as she had done in freeing her father, she must set God's power in motion, give it direction. In order for God's power to work *for* her, it must work *through* her. At once she spoke the word for supply, and that day the supply problem was ended for all time.

But, in what appears to be an elaboration of this account, she tells us that to establish completely an outward supply of money, she continued to speak the word "vigorously out into the great ocean of substance for something (she) much desired."

During this period she wrote an ordinary business letter to a friend in the country. Much to Dr. Cady's surprise, her friend replied that on receipt of this letter a strange thing happened to her. When she took the letter in her hand, it had the appearance of being covered with the very thing for which Dr. Cady had been speaking the word! When she opened "Miss C.'s letter," the letter took the form of a horn of plenty pouring out in unlimited quantity this same thing. "Have I gone crazy?" the friend wondered.

Not at all, said Dr. Cady. The vibrations of her vigorous thought and spoken word concerning the desired substance or thing had permeated the psychic structure of her letter to the friend, and the friend, having developed some degree of psychic perception, saw the shape that "Miss C." had created by her thought and spoken word!

At this point Dr. Cady comments that the continued speaking of the word soon brought this "shape" or form of supply forth in the visible world, as a solid manifestation of what she desired. How? What happened? Did she receive a legacy? Years ago I remember being told that in some way Dr. Cady became financially independent. What actually happened?

Some light may be thrown on this by a fascinating reference in a book by Richard Ingalese. He mentions Dr. Emilie Cady as being one of a small class of mental workers who could draw supply to themselves without employing physical means. To quote: "Dr. Emily [sic] Cady has performed very remarkable cures (it was said of her that she thought no more of healing a cancer than she did of healing a headache) and has helped the world through her writings as much as any other metaphysician of her time. Dr. Cady had used the law in healing, and her faith was great enough to believe she could make other demonstrations of a more material nature. She ... showed her implicit faith in the law by demanding and receiving a large sum of money, which she needed to reimburse herself for the time and money she had given to suffering humanity. She pictured the amount she wanted and then claimed it for her own, and within a short time after she made her creation, a stranger brought to her what she had demanded. According to her picture and her faith was it given unto her."

Many years later another New York metaphysician, Florence Scovel Shinn, wrote that "God is the Giver and the Gift, and creates His own amazing channels." Whatever the means or the channel, supply did come forth in response to Dr. Cady's demand, while she was looking to God only for it. She stresses this point in *Lessons in Truth*, where, after quoting Psalm 62:5 ("For God alone my soul waits in silence, for my hope is from him."), she asks this question: "Is your hope from Him or is it from books or teachers or friends or meetings or societies?"

Her question is justified and has brought many back on the right track in demonstrating supply. One of the most persistent tendencies we have to deal with is that we do not look to God only in making a demonstration of supply. We tend to "outline" by trying to decide in advance by what means or through what channel our supply will come.

In other words, our anxious human self, which is only praying or treating for supply because it cannot see any ways and means of getting supply, does not leave to God ways and means by which the prayer can be answered, as it should.

On the contrary, we at once appoint ourself as a ways-and-means committee of one, which is not only without ways and means to begin with, but as a rule, cannot even imagine any way in which the supply could come. Instead of having our attention on God as the Source, we have our attention on outward appearances, and it is probable that the prayer will fail.

"What you want is your business. How it comes to you is God's business." Let God choose or create the divinely right channels through which the prayer can be answered.

All this, of course, Emilie Cady knew and knew well. She confided in no one, looked to no one. Joyously animated by

11

God's revelation of the power of her words, she spoke her words into the intangible, universal substance of all good, and the law responded. She proved the law and was supplied.

What did Emilie Cady look like? The only photograph we have of her (the one on her niece's living room wall) reveals that her face had the same dynamic serenity as that of Myrtle Fillmore, born no doubt of a secure and secret faith in God.

She was established in her spiritual convictions. Ella Pomeroy, who knew Emilie Cady personally, wrote of her as being so thoroughly established in her metaphysical philosophy that when views opposed to those she held as Truth were brought up, she merely smiled tolerantly and dismissed them with a gesture.

Judging from her picture, she was robust in body and mind, probably inheriting a strong constitution from her pioneer parents. There was a "no-nonsense quality" about her, Mrs. Pomeroy wrote. She went straight to the point. But this does not mean that she was unsympathetic or brusque. Her dark, rather deepset eyes, as revealed in the photo, were lovingly wise and kind. Her facial expression seems to me to be benevolent, tolerant, and secure; she has a little private smile. And well she might have, after witnessing the frailities and the amazing overcomings of humanity for more than the proverbial threescore-and-ten years.

A spiritual pioneer, yes, as were the Fillmores and other great metaphysicians of that era ... and a spiritual genius as well. How did she formulate her method of "going into the silence," as she explains it in *Lessons in Truth*? How was she able to anticipate the discoveries of modern research into brain waves, which resulted in the current interest in biofeedback?

In her directions for "Finding the Secret Place," she tells us how to wait upon God in the silence, relaxed and open, so that we can actually bypass the comparatively slow workings of the subconscious mind and receive directly from God the actual substance of that which we desire: "While waiting upon God, we should, as much as possible, relax ourselves both mentally and physically. To use a very homely but practical illustration, take much the attitude of the entire being as do the fowl when taking a sunbath in the sand. Yet there is something more than a lax passivity to be maintained through it all. There must be a sort of conscious, active taking of that which God gives freely to us. 'Be still, and know' (Ps. 46:10) that while we wait there, it [meaning the Son, or Christ within] is doing the work."

To me, this suggests much the same principles as those worked out by Dr. Johannes Schultz, professor of neuropsychiatry in West Germany, who speaks of passive concentration and active concentration. Passive concentration, he says, implies a casual attitude. Emilie Cady speaks of an "active passivity" in the silence.

Dr. Schultz says that the trainee must have an indifferent and passive attitude toward the body functions as well as affirming and picturing that the desired result is already achieved. In modern biofeedback, it is found that one cannot will a hand to be warm, but one can affirm passively and picture it in a lazy and indifferent way as being warm. This will result in actually increasing the body temperature in the hand. But strenuous efforts of the will to make the hand warmer only result in failure.

Though some of the results from biofeedback are striking, they cannot be compared to those gained from practicing the silence as instructed by Emilie Cady. To begin with, opportunities for the average person to experiment with biofeedback are still lacking, since the instruments needed are not generally available to the average person.

On the contrary, all one needs to practice the silence is a copy of *Lessons in Truth*, to be read in the privacy of one's own home. If personal instruction is needed, this is available in the hundreds of Unity churches in the United States, Canada, and other countries. According to Ella Pomeroy, whom I previously quoted, something akin to this idea—that healing of the body should be available on a wide scale—might have helped quicken Emilie Cady's early interest in divine healing.

As Mrs. Pomeroy tells it, an evangelist named Simpson held services in a large tent in Brooklyn, and at one point in his service, he called people up from the audience and healed them by the laying on of hands, prayer, and the power of the Holy Spirit. Dr. Cady attended the meetings.

With the practiced eye of a physician, she noted everything. Of course she was pleased and impressed by seeing the sick made well through the power of God. To one of her ardent religious nature, this was good. But to one with her ardent desire to serve humanity, it seemed that there were striking limitations to the method employed by Simpson.

While it was marvelous to see people healed in this way, only a few could be healed by this man, using this method. What was needed was a readily available method of understanding how God's power to heal could be contacted by anybody, not just by those physically able to contact a healer in person. This same need is apparent in our day.

Though there are "charismatic" healers offering their services to those in need today, in some cases their fame and wide publicity draw such numbers to their public services that only a small percentage of those needing healing may be able to receive it. According to reports, many of the sufferers return to their homes disappointed and sorrowful because they were not selected, by whatever means the selecting is done, to receive the ministrations of the healer. It was said that in one audience, estimated to total from fifteen to seventeen thousand, only about a hundred persons were fortunate enough to receive the desired experience.

This is not said in criticism of any charismatic healer, but rather to emphasize what our early Truth pioneers saw a hundred years ago. What is needed is instruction and teaching made available to everybody in some form, telling them how to contact God's healing power for themselves, right where they are. They really do not need any instruments; they do not need to go afar and wait eagerly for hour after hour, perhaps to be bitterly disappointed.

The Master Healer said "Go into all the world and proclaim the good news" (Mk. 16:15). This Emilie Cady did through her writings. They conveyed a remarkable healing quality of absolute Truth. One woman, crippled by an "incurable" bone disease, with death predicted in six months, immersed herself in reading *Lessons in Truth*. She practiced the silence, relaxed in a small area of sunlight available to her, and knew that God was radiating through her as the fullness of what she desired. She was restored to such fullness of health that after having been crippled for twelve years, she was able to skate and dance and entered upon an active professional life for nearly thirty years.

Another young woman who was in a hospital awaiting surgery for a serious ailment read the chapter "Unadulterated Truth" from the book *How I Used Truth*. Suddenly she saw clearly that God was fully present in every part of her and that she was whole. The hospital refused to let her leave without undergoing surgery until the head of her family signed a release. There was never any recurrence of the ailment in the many years that I knew her.

I knew others with acute financial need who practiced Emilie Cady's instructions on prayer and believed that while they waited upon God in active passivity, God was radiating from the center of their being to the circumference and out into the visible world as supply. They received money almost at once. I knew a chiropractor who came into our noonday silence and practiced relaxation and freedom from fear. Her blood pressure had been taken by a colleague just before noon and was very high. After the silence she went back, had it taken again, and it was down thirty points!

In view of the results gained from the study and practice of Dr. H. Emilie Cady's writings, it is little wonder that *Lessons in Truth* has been translated into eleven languages and braille. From all over the world, from the length and breadth of the continent, letters have come, testifying to lives helped and strengthened, of physical ailments, money problems, domestic difficulties, all kinds of inharmonies adjusted, through the study of her inspired book.

All this was a divinely rich harvest from her obedience to the Father. After being repeatedly asked by the Fillmores to write a course of lessons for Unity, she turned to God and received inwardly, like Moses of old, the words. "Now therefore go, and I will be with thy mouth, and teach thee what thou shalt say" (Ex. 4:12 KJV).

Even in the wonderful world of metaphysical Truth, few have made a greater contribution or left a more shining monument to a long life of unselfish service than did Dr. H. Emilie Cady, physician and metaphysician. Long may her work minister to humanity! And long may Unity School of Christianity continue its faithful stewardship of her writings, making them available to God's children everywhere.

—Russell A. Kemp
1975

LESSONS

IN

TRUTH

BOOK ONE

Lessons in Truth was first published in *Unity Magazine* in 1894-95, then published in three paperback volumes in 1896-97. In 1903, the first recorded single volume book was published. There were forty-nine editions printed through 1990.

First Lesson
BONDAGE OR LIBERTY, WHICH?

[In entering upon this course of instruction, each of you should, so far as possible, lay aside, for the time being, all previous theories and beliefs. By so doing, you will be saved the trouble of trying, all the way through the course, to put "new wine into old wineskins" (Lk. 5:37). If there is anything, as we proceed, that you do not understand or agree with, just let it be passively in your mind until you have read the entire book, for many statements that would at first arouse antagonism and discussion will be clear and easily accepted a little further on. After the course is completed, if you wish to return to your old beliefs and ways of living, you are at perfect liberty to do so. But, for the time being, be willing to become as a little child; for, said a Master in spiritual things, "Unless you ... become like children, you will never enter the kingdom of heaven" (Mt. 18:3). If at times there seems to be repetition, please remember that these are lessons, not lectures.][1]

"Finally, be strong in the Lord and in the strength of his power" (Eph. 6:10).

"Whatever is true, whatever is honorable, whatever is just, whatever is pure, whatever is pleasing, whatever is commendable, if there is any excellence and if there is anything worthy of praise, think about these things" (Phil. 4:8).

Every man[2] believes himself to be in bondage to the flesh and

---

1. This paragraph begins the original *Lessons in Truth* too. However, the material that follows was originally found in the twelfth lesson. We have kept it here because we agree it makes for a better beginning.

2. Throughout this book, out of respect for the author and the historical nature of the writing, we have kept her use of the male noun or pronoun when referring to both women and men.

to the things of the flesh. All suffering is the result of this belief. The history of the Children of Israel coming out of their long bondage in Egypt is descriptive of the human soul, or consciousness, growing up out of the animal or sense part of man and into the spiritual part.

"Then the Lord said [speaking to Moses], 'I have observed the misery of my people who are in Egypt; I have heard their cry on account of their taskmasters. Indeed, I know their sufferings, and I have come down to deliver them from the Egyptians, and to bring them up out of that land to a good and broad land, a land flowing with milk and honey' " (Ex. 3:7-8).

These words express exactly the attitude of the Creator toward His highest creation, man.

Today, and all the days, He has been saying to us, His children: "I have surely seen the affliction of you who are in Egypt (darkness of ignorance), and have heard your cry by reason of your taskmasters (sickness, sorrow, and poverty); and I am (not I will, but I am now) come down to deliver you out of all this suffering, and to bring you up unto a good land and a large, unto a land flowing with good things" (Ex. 3:7-8 adapted).

It may, or it may not be here in this phase of life, but sometime, somewhere, every human being must come to himself. Having tired of eating husks, he will "get up and go to my father" (Lk. 15:18).

> "For it is written,
> 'As I live, says the Lord, every knee shall bow
> to me,
> and every tongue shall give praise to God.' "
> —Romans 14:11

This does not mean that God is a stern autocrat who by reason of supreme power compels man to bow to Him. It is, rather, an expression of the order of divine law, the law of all love, all good. Man, who is at first living in the selfish animal part of himself, will grow up through various stages and by various processes to the divine or spiritual understanding wherein he knows that he is one with the Father and wherein he is free from all suffering, because he has conscious dominion over all things. Somewhere on this journey the human consciousness, or intellect, comes to a place where it gladly bows to its spiritual Self and confesses that this spiritual Self, its Christ, is highest and is Lord. Here and forever after, not with sense of bondage, but with joyful freedom, the heart cries out: "The Lord is king" (Ps. 93:1). Everyone must sooner or later come to this point of experience.

You and I, dear reader, have already come to ourselves. Having become conscious of an oppressive bondage, we have arisen and set out on the journey from Egypt to the land of liberty, and now we cannot turn back if we would. Though possibly there will come times to each of us, before we reach the land of milk and honey (the time of full deliverance out of all our sorrows and troubles), when we shall come into a deep wilderness or against a seemingly impassable Red Sea, when our courage will seem to fail. Yet God says to each one of us, as Moses said to the trembling Children of Israel, "Do not be afraid, stand firm, and see the deliverance that the Lord will accomplish for you today" (Ex. 14:13).

Each man must sooner or later learn to stand alone with his God; nothing else avails. Nothing else will ever make you master of your own destiny. There is in your own indwelling Lord all the life and health, all the strength and peace and joy, all the wisdom and support that you can ever need or desire. No one can give to you as can this indwelling Father. He is the spring of all joy and comfort and power.

Hitherto we have believed that we were helped and comforted by others, that we received joy from outside circumstances and surroundings, but it is not so. All joy and strength and good spring up from a fountain within one's own being, and if we only knew this Truth, we should know that, because *God in us* is the fountain out of which springs all our good, nothing that anyone does or says, or fails to do or say, can take away our joy and good.

Someone has said: "Our liberty comes from an understanding of the mind and the thoughts of God toward us." Does God regard man as His servant or as His child? Most of us have believed ourselves not only the slaves of circumstances, but also, at the best, the *servants* of the Most High. Neither belief is true. It is time for us to awake to right thoughts, to know that we are not servants, but children, "and if children, then heirs" (Rom. 8:17). Heirs to what? Why, heirs to all wisdom, so that we need not, through any lack of wisdom, make mistakes; heirs to all love, so that we need know no fear or envy or jealousy; heirs to all strength, all life, all power, all good.

The human intelligence is so accustomed to the sound of words heard from childhood that often they convey to it no real meaning. Do you stop to think, really to comprehend, what it means to be "heirs of God and joint heirs with Christ" (Rom. 8:17)? It means, as Emerson says, that "every man is the inlet, and may become the outlet, of all there is in God." It means that all that God is and has is in reality for us, His only heirs, if we only know how to claim our inheritance.

This claiming of our rightful inheritance, the inheritance that God wants us to have in our daily life, is just what we are learning how to do in these simple talks.

Paul said truly: "Heirs, as long as they are minors, are no better than slaves, though they are the owners of all the property; but they remain under guardians and trustees until the date set by the father. So with us; while we were minors, we were enslaved to the elemental spirits of the world. But when the fullness of time had come, God sent his Son, born of a woman, born under the law, in order to redeem those who were under the law, so that we might receive adoption as children. And because you are children, God has sent the Spirit of his Son into our hearts, crying, 'Abba! Father!' So you are no longer a slave but a child, and if a child then also an heir, through God" (Gal. 4:1-7).

It is through Christ, the indwelling Christ, that we are to receive all that God has and is, as much or as little as we can or dare to claim.

No matter with what object you first started out to seek Truth, it was in reality because it was God's "fullness of time" (Gal. 4:4) for you to arise and begin to claim your inheritance. You were no longer to be satisfied with or under bondage to the elements of the world. Think of it! God's "fullness of time" *now* for you to be free, to have dominion over all things material, to be no longer bond servant, but a son in possession of your inheritance! "You did not choose me but I chose you. And I appointed you to go and bear fruit" (Jn. 15:16).

We have come to a place now where our search for Truth must no longer be for the rewards; it must no longer be our seeking a creed to follow, but it must be our *living a life*. In these simple lessons, we shall take only the first steps out of the Egyptian bondage of selfishness, lust, and sorrow toward the land of liberty, where perfect love and all good reign.

Every right thought that we think, our every unselfish word or action, is bound by immutable laws to be fraught with good results. But in our walk, we must learn to lose sight of results that are the "loaves and the fish" (Mt. 15:36), we must, rather, seek to be the Truth consciously, to be love, to be wisdom, to be life (as we really are unconsciously), and let results take care of themselves.

Every man must take time daily for quiet and meditation. In daily meditation lies the secret of power. No one can grow in either spiritual knowledge or power without it. Practice the presence of God just as you would practice music. No one would ever dream of becoming a master in music except by spending

23

some time daily alone with music. Daily meditation alone with God focuses the divine Presence within us and brings it to our consciousness.

You may be so busy with the doing, the outgoing of love to help others (which is unselfish and Godlike as far as it goes), that you find no time to go apart. But the command, or rather the invitation, is "come away ... by yourselves and rest a while" (Mk. 6:31). And it is the only way in which you will ever gain definite knowledge, true wisdom, newness of experience, steadiness of purpose, or power to meet the unknown, which must come in all daily life. Doing is secondary to being. When we are consciously the Truth, it will radiate from us and accomplish the works without our ever running to and fro. If you have no time for this quiet meditation, make time, take time. Watch carefully, and you will find that there are some things, even in the active unselfish doing, that would better be left undone than that you should neglect regular meditation.

You will find that some time is spent every day in idle conversation with people who "just run in for a few moments" to be entertained. If you can help such people, well; if not, gather yourself together and do not waste a moment idly diffusing and dissipating yourself to gratify their idleness. You have no idea what you lose by it.

When you withdraw from the world for meditation, let it not be to think of yourself or your failures, but invariably to get all your thoughts centered on God and on your relation to the Creator and Upholder of the universe. Let all the little annoying cares and anxieties go for a while, and by effort, if need be, turn your thoughts away from them to some of the simple words of the Nazarene or of the Psalmist. Think of some Truth statement, be it ever so simple.

No person, unless he has practiced it, can know how it quiets all physical nervousness, all fear, all oversensitiveness, all the little raspings of everyday life—just this hour of calm, quiet waiting alone with God. Never let it be an hour of bondage, but always one of restfulness.

Some, having realized the calm and power that come of daily meditation, have made the mistake of drawing themselves from the world, that they may give their entire time to meditation. This is asceticism, which is neither wise nor profitable.

The Nazarene, who is our noblest type of the perfect life, went daily apart from the world only that he[3] might come again into it with renewed spiritual power. So we go apart into the stillness of divine Presence that we may come forth into the world of everyday life with new inspiration and increased courage and power for activity and for overcoming.

We talk to God—that is prayer; God talks to us—that is inspiration. We go apart to get still, that new life, new inspiration, new power of thought, new supply from the Fountainhead may flow in; and then we come forth to shed it on those around us, that they, too, may be lifted up. Inharmony cannot remain in any home where even one member of the family daily practices this hour of the presence of God, so surely does the renewed infilling of the heart by peace and harmony result in the continual outgoing of peace and harmony into the entire surroundings.

Again, in this new way that we have undertaken, this living the life of Spirit instead of the old self, we need to seek always to have more and more of the Christ Spirit of meekness and love incorporated into our daily life. Meekness does not mean servility, but it means a spirit that could stand before a Pilate of false accusation and say nothing. No one else is so grand, so godlike as he who, because he knows the Truth of Being, can stand meekly and unperturbed before the false accusations of the human mind. "Thy gentleness hath made me great" (2 Sam. 22:36 KJV).

We must forgive as we would be forgiven. To forgive does not

---

3. In keeping with Cady's original writings, pronoun references to Jesus are not capitalized. For clarity's sake, we have made an exception when the pronoun refers to the inner Christ, in Jesus or us. Those pronouns are capitalized.

simply mean to arrive at a place of indifference to those who do personal injury to us; it means far more than this. To forgive is to *give for*—to give some actual, definite good in return for evil given. One may say, "I have no one to forgive; I have not a personal enemy in the world." And yet if, under any circumstances, any kind of a "served-him-right" thought springs up within you over anything that any of God's children may do or suffer, you have not yet learned how to forgive.

The very pain that you suffer, the very failure to demonstrate over some matter that touches your own life deeply, may rest upon just this spirit of unforgiveness that you harbor toward the world in general. Put it away with resolution.

Do not be under bondage to false beliefs about your circumstances or environment. God is in everything that happens to you. There are no "second causes." No matter how evil circumstances may appear or how much it may seem that some other personality is at the foundation of your sorrow or trouble, God, good, good alone, is *real* there.

If we have the courage to persist in seeing only God in it all, even "human wrath" (Ps. 76:10) shall be invariably turned to our advantage. Joseph, in speaking of the action of his brethren in selling him into slavery, said, "Even though you intended to do harm to me, God intended it for good" (Gen. 50:20). To them that love God, "all things work together for good for those who love God" (Rom. 8:28), or to them who recognize only God. All things! The very circumstances in your life that seem heartbreaking evils will turn to joy before your very eyes if you will steadfastly refuse to see anything but God in them.

It is perfectly natural for the human mind to seek to escape from its troubles by running away from present environments or by planning some change on the material plane. Such methods of escape are absolutely vain and foolish. "Human help is worthless" (Ps. 60:11).

There is no permanent or real outward way of escape from

miseries or circumstances; all help must come from within.

The words *God is my defense and deliverance* held in the silence until they become part of your very being, will deliver you out of the hands and the arguments of the keenest lawyer in the world.

The real inner consciousness that "the Lord is my shepherd, I shall not want" (Ps. 23:1) will supply all wants more surely and far more liberally than can any human hand.

The ultimate aim of every man should be to come into the consciousness of an indwelling God, and then, in all external matters, to affirm deliverance through and by this Divine One. There should not be a running to and fro, making human efforts to aid the Divine, but a calm, restful, unwavering trust in All-Wisdom and All-Power within one as able to accomplish the thing desired.

Victory must be won in the silence of your own being first, and then you need take no part in the outer demonstration of relief from conditions. The very walls of Jericho that keep you from your desire must fall before you.

The Psalmist said:

> "I lift up my eyes to the hills
>   [or to the Highest One]—
>   from where will my help come?
> My help comes from the Lord,
>   who made heaven and earth....
> The Lord [your indwelling Lord] will keep
>   you from all evil ....
> The Lord will keep your going out and
>   your coming in
> from this time on and forevermore."
>   —Psalm 121:1-2, 7-8

Oh, if we could only realize that this mighty Power to save

and to protect, to deliver and to make alive, lives forever *within us,* and so cease now and forever looking away to others!

There is but one way to obtain this full realization—the way of the Christ. "I am the way, and the truth, and the life" (Jn. 14:6), spoke the Christ through the lips of the Nazarene.

Your holding to the words *Christ is the way,* when you are perplexed and confused and can see no way of escape, will invariably open a way of complete deliverance.

Second Lesson
STATEMENT OF BEING
WHO AND WHAT GOD IS
WHO AND WHAT MAN IS

When Jesus was talking with the Samaritan woman at the well, he said to her, "God is spirit, and those who worship him must worship in spirit and truth." (John 4:24 ASV reads, "God is a Spirit," but the marginal note is, "God is spirit," and some other versions render this passage, "God is Spirit.") To say "a Spirit" would be to imply the existence of more than one spirit. Jesus, in his statement, did not imply this.

Webster in his definition of spirit says: "An animating or vital principle held to give life to physical organisms. A supernatural being or essence; the Holy Spirit."

God, then, is not, as many of us have been taught to believe, a big personage or man residing somewhere in a beautiful region in the sky, called "heaven," where good people go when they die, and see Him clothed in ineffable glory; nor is He a stern, angry judge only awaiting opportunity somewhere to punish bad people who have failed to live a perfect life here.

God is Spirit, or the creative energy that is the cause of all visible things. God as Spirit is the invisible life and intelligence underlying all physical things. There could be no body, or visible part, to anything unless there were first Spirit as creative cause.

God is not a being or person having life, intelligence, love, power. God is that invisible, intangible, but very real, something we call life. God is perfect love and infinite power. God is the total of these, the total of all good, whether manifested or unexpressed.

There is but one God in the universe, but one source of all the different forms of life or intelligence that we see, whether they be men, animals, trees, or rocks.

God is Spirit. We cannot see Spirit with these fleshly eyes; but when Spirit clothes Itself with a body, when Spirit makes Itself visible or manifest through a material form, then we recognize it. You do not see the living, thinking "me" when you look at my body. You see only the form that I am manifesting.

God is love. We cannot see love, nor grasp any comprehension of what love is, except as love is clothed with a form. All the love in the universe is God. The love between husband and wife, between parents and children, is just the least little bit of God, as pushed forth through visible form into manifestation. A mother's love, so infinitely tender, so unfailing, is God's love, only manifested in greater degree by the mother.

God is wisdom and intelligence. All the wisdom and intelligence that we see in the universe is God—is wisdom projected through a visible form. To educate (from *educare*, to lead forth) never means to force into from the outside but always means to draw out from within something already existing there. God as infinite wisdom lies within every human being, only waiting to be led forth into manifestation. This is true education.

Heretofore we have sought knowledge and help from outside sources, not knowing that the source of all knowledge, the very Spirit of Truth, is lying latent within each one of us, waiting to be called on to teach us the truth about all things—most marvelous of teachers, and everywhere present, without money or price!

God is power. Not simply God has power, but God *is* power. In other words, all the power there is to do anything is God. God, the source of our existence every moment, is not simply omnipotent (all-powerful); He is omnipotence (all power). He is not alone omniscient (all-knowing); He is omniscience (all knowledge). He is not only omnipresent, but more—omnipresence. God is not a being having qualities, but He is the good itself. Everything you can think of that is good, when in its absolute perfection, goes to make up that invisible Being we call God.

God, then, is the substance (from *sub*, under, and *stare*, to stand), or the real thing standing under every visible form of life, love, intelligence, or power. Each rock, tree, animal, every visible thing, is a manifestation of the one Spirit—God—differing only in degree of manifestation; and each of the numberless modes of manifestation or individualities, however insignificant, contains the whole.

One drop of water taken from the ocean is just as perfect ocean water as the whole great body. The constituent elements of water are exactly the same, and they are combined in precisely the same ratio or perfect relation to each other, whether we consider one drop, a pailful, a barrelful, or the entire ocean out of which the lesser quantities are taken; each is complete in itself; they differ only in quantity or degree. Each contains the whole, and yet no one would make the mistake of supposing from this statement that each drop is the entire ocean.

So we say that each individual manifestation of God contains the whole; not for a moment meaning that each individual is God in His entirety, so to speak, but that each is God come forth, shall I say? in different quantity or degree.

Man is the last and highest manifestation of divine energy, the fullest and most complete expression (or pressing out) of God. To man, therefore, is given dominion over all other manifestations.

God is not only the creative cause of every visible form of intelligence and life at its commencement, but each moment throughout its existence, He lives within every created thing as the life, the ever-renewing, re-creating, upbuilding cause of it.

He never is and never can be for a moment separated from His creations. Then how can even a sparrow fall to the ground without His knowledge? And "you are of more value than many sparrows" (Mt. 10:31).

God *is*. Man exists (from *ex*, out of, and *sistere*, to stand forth). Man stands forth out of God.

Man is a threefold being, made up of Spirit, soul, and body. Spirit, our innermost, real being, the absolute part of us, the *I* of us, has never changed, though our thoughts and our circumstances may have changed hundreds of times. This part of us is a standing forth of God into visibility. It is the Father in us. At this central part of his being, every person can say, "The Father and I are one" (Jn. 10:30), and speak absolute Truth.

Soul or mortal mind—that which Paul calls "the mind on the flesh" (Rom. 8:6)—is the region of the intellect, where we do conscious thinking. Body is the last or external part of man's being in his descent from God into the material universe.

The great whole of as yet unmanifested Good, or God, from whom we are projections or offspring, in whom "we live and move and have our being" (Acts 17:28) continually, is to me the Father—*our* Father; "and all ye are brethren" (Mt. 23:8 KJV), because all are manifestations of one and the same Spirit. Jesus, recognizing this, said, "Call no one your father on earth, for you have one Father—the one in heaven" (Mt. 23:9). As soon as we recognize our true relationship to all men, we at once slip out of our narrow, personal loves, our "me and mine," into the universal love that takes in all the world, joyfully exclaiming: " 'Who is my mother, and who are my brothers?' And pointing to his disciples, he said, 'Here are my mother and my brothers!' " (Matt. 12:48-49)

Many have thought of God as a personal being. The statement that God is Principle chills them, and in terror, they cry out, "They have taken away my Lord, and I do not know where they have laid him" (Jn. 20:13).

Broader and more learned minds are always cramped by the thought of God as a person, for personality limits to place and time.

God is the name we give to that unchangeable, inexorable principle at the source of all existence. To the individual consciousness, God takes on personality, but as the creative underlying cause of all things, He is principle, impersonal. As expressed in each individual, He becomes personal to that one—a personal, loving, all-giving Father-Mother. All that we can ever need or desire is in the infinite Father-Principle, the great reservoir of unexpressed good. There is no limit to the Source of our being, nor to His willingness to manifest more of Himself through us. The only limit is in our knowledge of how to *draw* from the fountain.

Hitherto we have turned our hearts and efforts toward the external for fulfillment of our desires and for satisfaction, and we have been grievously disappointed. The hunger of everyone for satisfaction is only the cry of the homesick child for its Father-Mother God. It is only the Spirit's desire in us to come forth into our consciousness as more and more perfection, until we shall have become *fully* conscious of our oneness with All-Perfection. Man never has been and never can be satisfied with anything less.

We all have direct access through the Father in us—the central "I" of our being—to the great whole of life, love, wisdom, power, which is God. What we now want to know is how to receive more from the Fountainhead and to make more and more of God (which is but another name for All-Good) manifest in our daily lives.

There is but one Source of Being. This Source is the living fountain of all good, be it life, love, wisdom, power—the Giver of all good gifts. This Source and you are connected, every moment of your existence. You have power to draw on this Source for all of good you are, or ever will be, capable of desiring.

Third Lesson

THINKING

We learned in the second lesson that the real substance within everything we see is God, that all things are one and the same Spirit in different degrees of manifestation, that all the various forms of life are just the same as one life come forth out of the invisible into visible forms, that all the intelligence and all the wisdom in the world are God as wisdom in various degrees of manifestation, that all the love that people feel and express toward others is just a little, so to speak, of God as love come into visibility through the human form.

When we say there is but one Mind in the entire universe, and that this Mind is God, some persons, having followed understandingly the second lesson and recognized God as the one Life, one Spirit, one Power, pushing Himself out into various degrees of manifestation through people and things, will at once say, "Yes, that is all plain."

But someone else will say, "If all the mind there is, is God, then how can I think wrong thoughts or have any but God thoughts?"

The connection between universal Mind and our own individual minds is one of the most difficult things to put into words, but when it once dawns on one, it is easily seen.

There is in reality only one Mind (or Spirit, which is life, intelligence, and so forth) in the universe; and yet there is a sense in which we are individual, or separate, a sense in which we are free wills and not puppets.

Man is made up of Spirit, soul, and body. Spirit is the central unchanging "I" of us, the part that since infancy has never changed, and to all eternity never will change. Soul, or what metaphysical Christians call "mortal mind," is the region of the intellect where we do conscious thinking and are free wills. This part of our being is in constant process of changing.

In our outspringing from God into the material world, Spirit is inner—one with God; soul or mortal mind or intellect is the clothing, as it were, of the Spirit; body is the external clothing of the soul. Yet all are in reality one, the composite man—as steam, water, and ice are one, only in different degrees of condensation. In thinking of ourselves, we must not separate Spirit, soul, and body, but rather hold all as one, if we would be strong and powerful. Man originally lived consciously in the spiritual part of himself. He fell by descending in his consciousness to the external or more material part of himself.

Mortal mind, the term so much used and so distracting to many, is the intellect, which gathers its information from the outside world through the five senses. This mortal mind has no way of knowing truth from falsehood. It is what Paul calls "the mind on the flesh" in contradistinction to spiritual mind, and he flatly says: "The mind on the flesh [believing what the carnal mind says] is death [sorrow, trouble, sickness], but to set the mind on the Spirit [ability to still the carnal mind and let the Spirit speak within us] is life and peace" (Rom. 8:6).

The Spirit within you is Divine Mind, the *real* mind. Without it, the human mind would disappear, just as a shadow disappears when the real thing that casts it is removed. Man then, is Spiritual Mind, mortal mind, and body.

If you find this subject of human mind and universal Mind puzzling to you, do not worry over it. Just drop it for a time, and as you go on with the lessons, you will find that some day an understanding of it will flash suddenly upon you with perfect clearness.

There are today two classes of people, so far as mentality goes, who are seeking deliverance out of sickness, trouble, and unhappiness, by spiritual means. One class requires that every statement made be proved by the most elaborate and logical argument before it can or will be received. The other class is willing at once to "become like children" (Mt. 18:3) and just be taught how to take the first steps toward pure understanding (or knowledge of Truth as God sees it), and then receives the light by direct revelation from the All-Good. Both are seeking and eventually both will reach the same goal, and neither one should be unduly condemned.

If you are one who seeks and expects to get any realizing knowledge of spiritual things through argument or reasoning, no matter how scholarly your attainments or how great you are in worldly wisdom, you are a failure in spiritual understanding. You are attempting an utter impossibility—that of crowding the Infinite into the quart measure of your own intellectual capacity.

"Those who are unspiritual do not receive the gifts of God's Spirit, for they are foolishness to them, and they are unable to understand them because they are spiritually discerned" (1 Cor. 2:14). Eventually you will find that you are only beating around on the outside of the "kingdom of heaven," though in close proximity to it, and you will then become willing to let your intellect take the place of the child, without which no man can enter in.

" 'No eye has seen, nor ear heard, nor the human heart conceived, what God has [not *will*] prepared for those who love him'—these things God has revealed to us through the Spirit.... For what human being knows what is truly human except the human spirit that is within? So also no one comprehends what is truly God's except the Spirit of God" (I Cor. 2:9-11).

For all those who must wade through months and perhaps years of this purely intellectual or mental process, there are today many books to help and many teachers of metaphysics who are doing noble and praiseworthy work in piloting these earnest seekers after Truth and satisfaction. To them we cry: "All speed!"

But we believe with Paul that "God's foolishness is wiser than human" (1 Cor. 1:25) and that each man has direct access to all there is in God. We are writing for the "children" who, without question or discussion, are willing at once to accept and to try a few plain, simple rules, such as Jesus taught the common people, who "heard him gladly" (Mk. 6:20 KJV)—rules by which they can find the Christ (or the Divine) within themselves, that through it, each man for himself may work out his own salvation from all his troubles.

In other words, there is a shortcut to the top of the hill. While there is a good but long roundabout road for those who need it, we prefer the less laborious means of attaining the same end— by seeking directly the Spirit of Truth promised to dwell *in* us and to lead us into all Truth. My advice: If you want to make rapid progress in growth toward spiritual understanding, stop reading many books. They only give you someone's opinion about Truth or a sort of history of the author's experience in seeking Truth. What you want is revelation of Truth in your own soul, and that will never come through the reading of many books.

Seek light from the Spirit of Truth within you. Go alone. Think alone. Seek light alone, and if it does not come at once, do not be discouraged and run off to someone else to get light; for, as we said before, by so doing, you get only the opinion of the intellect, and may be then further away from the Truth you are seeking than ever before; for the mortal mind may make false reports.

The very Spirit of Truth is at your call, within you. "The anointing that you received from him abides in you" (I Jn. 2:27). Seek it. Wait patiently for it to "guide you into all the truth"

(Jn. 16:13) about all things.

"Let the same mind be in you that was in Christ Jesus" (Phil. 2:5). This is the universal Mind, which makes no mistakes. Still the intellect for the time being, and let universal Mind speak to you. When it speaks, though it be but "a still small voice" (1 Kings 19:12 KJV), you will know that what it says is Truth.

How will you know? You will know just as you know that you are alive. All the argument in the world to convince you against Truth that comes to you through direct revelation will fall flat and harmless at your side. And the Truth that you know, not simply believe, you can use to help others. That which comes forth through your spirit will reach the very innermost spirit of him to whom you speak.

What is born from the outside, or intellectual perception, reaches only the intellect of him you would help.

The intellect that is servant to the real Mind, and when servant (but not when master) is good, loves to argue; but when its information is based on the evidence of the senses and not on the true thoughts of the Divine Mind, it is very fallible and full of error.

Intellect argues. Spirit takes the deep things of God and reveals Truth to man. One may be true; the other always is true. Spirit does not give opinions about Truth; it is Truth, and it reveals itself.

Someone has truly said that the merest child who has learned from the depths of his being to say, "Our Father," is infinitely greater than the most intellectual man who has not yet learned it. Paul was a man of gigantic intellect, learned in all the law, a Pharisee of the Pharisees; but after he was spiritually illumined, he wrote, "For God's foolishness is wiser than human wisdom, and God's weakness is stronger than human strength" (I Cor. 1:25).

It does make a great difference in our daily lives what we think about God, about ourselves, about our neighbors.

Heretofore, through ignorance of our real Self and of the results of our thinking, we have let our thoughts flow at random. Our minds have been turned toward the external of our being, our body, and nearly all our information has been gotten through our five senses. We have thought wrong because we have been mis-informed by these senses, and our troubles and sorrows are the results of our wrong thinking.

"But," says someone, "I do not see how my thinking evil or wrong thoughts about God, or about anyone, can make me sick or my husband lose his position."

Well, I will not just now try to explain all the steps by which bad results follow false thinking, but I will just ask you to try thinking true, right thoughts awhile and see what the results will be.

Take the thought "God loves me" and think the words over and over continually for a few days, trying to realize that they are true, and see what the effect will be on your body and circumstances.

First, you get a new exhilaration of mind, with a great desire and a sense of power to please God; then a quicker, better circulation of blood, with sense of a pleasant warmth in the body, followed by better digestion. Later, as Truth flows out through your being into your surroundings, everybody will begin to manifest a new love for you without your knowing why; and finally, circumstances will begin to change and fall into harmony with your desires, instead of being adverse to them.

Everyone knows how strong thoughts of fear or grief have turned hair white in a few hours, how great fear makes the heart beat so rapidly as to seem about to "jump out of the body"; this result not being at all dependent on whether there be any real cause of fear or whether it be a purely imaginary cause. Just so, strong negative thoughts may render the blood acid, causing rheumatism. Bearing mental burdens makes more stooped shoulders than does bearing heavy material loads. Believing that

God regards us as "miserable sinners," that He is continually watching us and our failures with disapproval, brings utter discouragement and a sort of half-paralyzed condition of mind and body, which means failure in all our undertakings.

Is it difficult for you to understand why, if God lives in us all the time, He does not keep our thoughts right instead of permitting us through ignorance to drift into wrong thoughts and so bring trouble on ourselves?

Well, we are not automatons. Your child will never learn to walk alone if you always do his walking. Because you recognize that the only way for him to be strong, self-reliant in all things—in other words, to become a man—is to throw him on himself and let him, through *experience*, come to a knowledge of things for himself; you are not willing to make a mere puppet of him by taking the steps for him, even though you know that he will fall down many times and give himself severe bumps in his ongoing toward perfect physical manhood.

We are in the process of growth into the highest spiritual manhood and womanhood. We get many falls and bumps on the way, but only through these, not necessarily *by* them, can our growth proceed. Father and mother, no matter how strong or deep their love, cannot grow for their children; nor can God, who is Omnipotence, at the center of our being, grow spiritually for us without making of us automatons instead of individuals.

If you keep your thoughts turned toward the external of yourself or of others, you will see only the things that are not real, but temporal, and that pass away. All the faults, failures, or lacks in people or circumstances will seem very real to you, and you will be unhappy and sick.

If you turn your thoughts away from the external toward the spiritual and let them dwell on the good in yourself and in others, all the apparent evil will first drop out of your thoughts and then out of your life. Paul understood this when he wrote to the Philippians: "Finally, beloved, whatever is true, whatever is honorable, whatever is just, whatever is pure, whatever is pleasing, whatever is commendable, if there is any excellence and if there is anything worthy of praise, think about these things" (Phil. 4:8).

We all can learn how to turn the conscious mind toward universal Mind, or Spirit, within us. We can, by practice, learn how to make this everyday, topsy-turvy "mind on the flesh" be still and let the mind that is God (All-Wisdom, All-Love) think in us and out through us.

Imagine, if you will, a great reservoir out of which lead innumerable small rivulets or channels. At its farther end, each channel opens out into a small fountain. This fountain is not only being continually filled and replenished from the reservoir but is itself a radiating center, whence it gives out in all directions that which it receives so that all who come within its radius are refreshed and blessed.

This is our relation to God. Each one of us is a radiating center. Each one, no matter how small or ignorant, is the little fountain at the far end of a channel, the other end of which leads out from all there is in God. This fountain represents our free will or individuality, as separate from the Great Reservoir—God—and yet as one with Him in that we are constantly fed and renewed from Him, and without Him we are nothing.

Each of us, no matter how insignificant he may be in the world, may receive from God unlimited good of whatever kind he desires and radiate it to all about him. But remember, he must radiate if he would receive more. Stagnation is death.

Oh, I want the simplest mind to grasp the idea that the very wisdom of God—the love, the life, and the power of God are ready and waiting with longing impulse to flow out through us in unlimited degree! When it flows in unusual degree through the intellect of a certain person, men exclaim, "What a wonderful mind!" When it flows through the hearts of men, it is the love that melts all bitterness, envy, selfishness, jealousy, before it. When it flows through their bodies as life, no disease can withstand its onward march.

We do not have to beseech God any more than we have to beseech the sun to shine. The sun shines because it is a law of its being to shine, and it cannot help it. No more can God help pouring into us unlimited wisdom, life, power, all good, because to give is a law of His being. Nothing can hinder Him except our own lack of understanding. The sun may shine ever so brightly, but if we have, through willfulness or ignorance, placed ourselves, or have been placed by our progenitors, in the far corner of a damp, dark cellar, we get neither joy nor comfort from its shining; then to us the sun never shines.

So we have heretofore known nothing of how to get ourselves out of the cellar of ignorance, doubt, and despair; to our wrong thinking, God has seemed to withhold the life, wisdom, power, we wanted so much, though we sought Him ever so earnestly.

The sun does not radiate life and warmth today and darkness and chill tomorrow; it cannot, from the nature of its being. Nor does God radiate love at one time, while at other times, anger, wrath, and displeasure flow from His mind toward us.

"Does a spring pour forth from the same opening both fresh and brackish water? Can a fig tree, my brothers and sisters, yield olives, or a grapevine figs?" (Jas. 3:11-12)

God is All-Good—always good, always love. He never changes, no matter what we do or may have done. He is always trying to pour more of Himself through us into visibility so as to make us grander, larger, fuller, freer individuals.

While the child is crying out for its Father-Mother God, the Father-Mother is yearning with infinite tenderness to satisfy the child.

> In the heart of man a cry,
> In the heart of God, supply.

SUMMARY

1. There is but one Mind in the universe.

2. Mortal mind is human mind or intellect. It gathers its information and finds its authority from *without*; Universal Mind sees and speaks from *within*.

3. Intellect is the servant of Spirit. Body is the servant of intellect.

4. Our ways of thinking make our happiness or unhappiness, our success or nonsuccess. We can, by effort, change our ways of thinking.

5. God is at all times, regardless of our so-called sins, trying to pour more good into our lives to make them richer and more successful.

Fourth Lesson
DENIALS

"Then Jesus told his disciples, 'If any want to become my followers, let them deny themselves and take up their cross and follow me.' "

—Matthew 16:24

All systems for spiritualizing the mind include denial.[1] Every religion in all the ages had some sort of denial as one of its foundations.

We all know how the Puritans believed that the more rigidly they denied themselves comfort, the better they pleased God. So far has this idea taken possession of the human mind during some ages that devout souls have even tortured their bodies in various ways, believing that they were thus making themselves more spiritual, or at least were in some way placating an angry God. Even today many interpret the above quoted saying of Jesus as meaning: If any man wants to please God, he must give up about all the enjoyment and comfort he has, all things he likes and wants, and must take up the heavy cross of constantly doing the things that are repugnant to him in his daily life. This is why many young people say, "When I am old, I will be a Christian, but not now, for I want to enjoy life awhile first."

1. In today's usage, the psychological meaning of *denial*, that of refusing to face up to the truth, so predominates that use of this term causes considerable confusion. Whether to accept the reality of something or to deny it is an issue of great delicacy and the reader is encouraged to proceed prayerfully. It seems important to acknowledge the appearance of a circumstance but deny its power over us.

There could, I am sure, be nothing further from the meaning of the Nazarene than the foregoing interpretation. In our ignorance of the nature of God, our Father, and of our relation to Him, we have believed that all our enjoyment came from external sources, usually from gaining possession of something we did not have. The poor see enjoyment only in possessing abundance of money. The rich, who are satiated with life's so-called pleasures until their lives have become like a person with an overloaded stomach, compelled to sit constantly at a well-spread table, are often the most bitter in the complaint that life holds no happiness for them. The sick one believes that, were he well, he would be perfectly happy. The healthy but hardworking person feels the need of some days of rest and recreation, that the monotony of his life may be broken.

So ever the mind has been turned to some external change of condition or circumstance in pursuit of satisfaction and enjoyment. In after years, when men have tried all, getting first this thing and then that which they thought would yield them happiness and have been grievously disappointed; in a kind of desperation, they turn to God and try to find some sort of comfort in believing that sometime, somewhere, they will get what they want and be happy. Thenceforth their lives are patient and submissive, but they are destitute of any real joy.

This same Nazarene, to whom we always return because to us he is the best-known teacher and demonstrator of Truth, spent nearly three years teaching the people—the common everyday people like you and me, who wanted, just as we do, food and rent and clothing, money, friends, and love—to love their enemies and to do good to those who persecuted them, to resist not evil in any way but to give double to anyone who tried to get what belonged to them, to cease from all anxiety regarding the things they needed because "your heavenly Father knows that you need all these things" (Mt. 6:32).

And then in talking one day, he said, "I have said these things to you so that my joy may be in you, and that your joy may be complete" (Jn. 15:11). And he continued, "The Father will give you whatever you ask him in my name" (Jn. 15:16). "Ask and you will receive, so that your joy may be complete.... I do not say to you that I will ask the Father on your behalf; for the Father himself loves you" (Jn. 16:24, 26-27). We have further learned that God is the total of all the good in the universe and that there is in the mind which is God a perpetual desire to pour more of Himself—the substance of all good things—through us into visibility, or into our lives.

Surely all these things do not make it look as though, when Jesus said that the way to be like him and to possess a like power was to *deny* oneself, he meant that we are not to go without the enjoyable comforts of life or in any way deprive or torture ourselves.

In these lessons, we have seen that besides the real innermost Self of each of us—the Self that is the divine Self because it is an expression or pressing out of God into visibility and is always one with the Father—there is a human self, a carnal mind, that reports lies from the external world and is not to be relied upon fully; this is the self of which Jesus spoke when he said, "let them deny themselves" (Mt. 16:24). This intellectual man, carnal mind, or whatever you choose to call him, is envious and jealous and fretful and sick because he is selfish. The human self seeks its own gratification at the expense, if need be, of someone else.

Your divine Self is never sick, never afraid, never selfish. It is the part of you that "does not insist on its own way; it is not irritable or resentful" (1 Cor. 13:5). It is always seeking to give to others, while the human self is always seeking its own. Heretofore we have lived more in the human region. We have believed all that the carnal mind has told us, and the consequence is that we have been overwhelmed with all kinds of privation and suffering.

Some people who, during the last few years, have been making a special study of the mind find it a fact that certain wrong or false beliefs held by us are really the cause of all sorts of trouble—physical, moral, and financial. They have learned that wrong (or, as they call them, *error*) beliefs arise only in the human mind. They have learned and actually proved that we can, by a persistent effort of the will, change our beliefs, and by this means alone, entirely change our troublesome circumstances and bodily conditions.

One of the methods that they have found will work every time in getting rid of troublesome conditions (which are all the result of erroneous thinking and feeling) is to deny them *in toto*: First, to deny that any such things have, or could have, power to make us unhappy; second, to deny that these things do in *reality*[2] exist at all.

The word *deny* has two definitions, according to *Webster.* To deny, in one sense, is "to refuse to grant," as to deny bread to the hungry. To deny, in another sense (and we believe it was in this latter way that Jesus used it) is "to declare untrue," to repudiate as utterly false. To deny oneself, then, is not to withhold comfort or happiness from the external man, much less to inflict torture upon him, but it is to deny the claims of error consciousness, to declare these claims to be untrue.

If you have done any piece of work incorrectly, the very first step toward getting it right is to undo the wrong and begin again from that point. We have believed wrong about God and about ourselves. We have believed that God was angry with us and that we were sinners who ought to be afraid of Him. We have believed that sickness and poverty and other troubles are evil things put here by this same God to torture us in some way into serving Him and loving Him. We have believed that we have pleased God best when we have become so absolutely subdued by our troubles as to be patiently submissive to them all, not

---

2. Reality in the Absolute, not the relative reality we live in daily.

even trying to rise out of them or to overcome them. All this is false, entirely false! And the first step toward freeing ourselves from our troubles is to get rid of our erroneous beliefs about God and about ourselves.

"But," objects one, "if a thing is not true and I have believed a lie about it, I do not see just how my believing wrong about it could affect my bodily health or my circumstances."

A child can be so afraid of an imaginary bugaboo under the bed as to have convulsions. Should you, today, receive a telegraphic message that your husband, wife, or child, who is absent from you, had been suddenly killed, your suffering, mental and physical, and perhaps extending even to your external and financial affairs, would be just as great as though the report really were true, and yet it might be entirely false. Exactly so have these messages of bugaboos behind the doors, bugaboos of divine wrath and of our own weakness, come to us through the senses until we are overcome by our fears of them.

Now, let us arouse ourselves. Denial is the first practical step toward wiping out of our minds the mistaken beliefs of a lifetime—the beliefs that have made such sad havoc in our lives. By denial, we mean declaring not to be true a thing that seems true. Negative appearances are directly opposed to the teachings of Truth. Jesus said, "Do not judge by appearances, but judge with right judgment" (Jn. 7:24).

Suppose you had always been taught that the sun really moved or revolved around the earth, and someone should now try to persuade you that the opposite is the truth: you would see at once that such might be the case, and yet as often as you saw the sun rise, the old impression, made on your mind by the wrong belief of years, would come up and seem almost too real to be disputed. The only way by which you could cleanse your mind of the impression and make the untrue seem unreal would be by repeatedly denying the old beliefs, saying over and over to yourself as often as the subject came up in your mind: "This is not true. The sun does not move; it stands still, and the earth moves." Eventually the sun would only seem to move.

The appearances are that our bodies and our circumstances control our thoughts, but the opposite is true. Our thoughts control our bodies and our circumstances.

If you repeatedly deny a false or unhappy condition, it loses its power to make you unhappy.

What everyone desires is to have only the good manifested in his life and surroundings—to have his life full of love, to have perfect health, to know all things, to have great power and much joy—and this is just exactly what God wants us to have. All love is God in manifestation, as we have learned in a previous lesson. All wisdom is God. All life and health are God. All joy (because all good) and all power are God. All good of whatever kind is God come forth into visibility through people or some other visible form. When we crave more of any good thing, we are in reality craving more of God to come forth into our lives so that we can realize it by the senses. Having more of God does not take out of our lives the good things—it only puts more of them in. In the mind that is God, there is always the desire to give more, for the divine plan is forever to get more good into visibility.

Intellectually we may see the fact of our own God-being, which never changes. What we need is to realize our oneness with the Father at all times. In order to realize it, we deny in ourselves and others the appearances that seem contrary to this—deny them as realities; we declare that they are not true.

There are four common error thoughts to which nearly everyone grants great power. Persons who have grown out of sickness and trouble through prayer have found it good to deny these thoughts in order to cleanse the mind of the direful effects of believing them. They can be denied like this:

First: *There is no evil.*

There is but one power in the universe, and that is God—Good. God is good, and God is omnipresence. Apparent evils are not entities or things of themselves. They are simply apparent absence of the good, just as darkness is an absence of light. But God, or good, is omnipresent, so the apparent absence of good (evil) is unreal. It is only an appearance of evil, just as the moving sun was an appearance. You need not wait to discuss this matter of evil or to understand fully all about why you deny it, but begin to practice the denials in an unprejudiced way and see how marvelously they will, after a while, deliver you from some of the so-called evils of your daily life.

Second: *There is no absence of life, substance, or intelligence anywhere.*

We have seen that the real is the spiritual. "What can be seen is temporary, but what cannot be seen is eternal" (2 Cor. 4:18). By using this denial, you will soon break your bondage to matter and to material conditions. You will know that you are free.

Third: *Pain, sickness, poverty, old age, and death cannot master me, for they are not real.*

Fourth: *There is nothing in all the universe for me to fear, for greater is He that is within me than he that is in the world.*

God says, "I will contend with those who contend with you" (Is. 49:25). He says it to every living child of His, and every person is His child.

Repeat these four denials silently several times a day, not with a strained anxiety to get something out of them, but trying calmly to realize the meaning of the words spoken:

There is no evil (or devil).

There is no absence of life, substance, or intelligence any where.

Pain, sickness, poverty, old age, and death cannot master me, for they are not real.

There is nothing in all the universe for me to fear, for greater is He that is within me than he that is in the world.

Almost hourly little vexations and fears come up in your life. Meet each one with a denial. Calmly and coolly say within yourself, "That's nothing at all. It cannot harm or disturb me or make me unhappy." Do not fight it vigorously but let your denial be the denial of any thought of its superiority over you, as you would deny the power of ants on their little hill to disturb you. If you are angry, stand still and silently deny it. Say that you are not angry, that you are love made manifest and cannot be angry, and the anger will leave you.

If someone shows you ill will, silently deny his power to hurt you or to make you unhappy. Should you find yourself feeling jealous or envious toward anyone, instantly turn the heel of denial on the hydra-headed monsters. Declare that you are not jealous or envious, that you are an expression of perfect love (an expression which is God pressed out into visibility) and cannot feel negation. There is really no reason for jealousy or envy, for all persons are one and the same Spirit. "And there are varieties of activities [or manifestations], but it is the same God who activates all of them in everyone" (1 Cor. 12:6), says Paul. How can you be envious of a part of yourself that seems to you more comely?

Shall the foot be envious of the hand, or the ear of the eye? Are not the seemingly feeble members of the body just as important to the perfection of the whole as the others? Do you seem to be less, or to have less, than some others? Remember that all envy and all jealousy are in the human or mortal mind and that in reality you, however insignificant, are an absolute necessity to God in order to make the perfect whole.

If you find yourself dreading to meet anyone, or afraid to step out and do what you want or ought to do, immediately begin to say, "It is not true; I am not afraid; I am perfect love and can know no fear. No one, nothing in all the universe, can hurt me." You will find after a little that all the fear has disappeared, all trepidation has gone.

Denial brings freedom from bondage, and happiness comes when we can effectually deny the power of anything to touch or to trouble us.

Have you been living in negation for years, denying your ability to succeed, denying your health, denying your Godhood, denying your power to accomplish anything, by feeling yourself a child of the devil or of weakness? If so, this constant negation has paralyzed you and weakened your power.

When, in the next lesson, you learn something about affirmations, the opposite of denials, you will know how to lift yourself out of the realm of failure into that of success.

All your happiness, all your health and power, come from God. They flow in an unbroken stream from the Fountainhead into the very center of your being and radiate from center to circumference. When you acknowledge this constantly and deny that outside things can hinder your happiness or health or power, it helps you to realize health and power and happiness.

No person or thing in the universe, no chain of circumstances, can by any possibility interpose itself between you and all joy—all good. You may think that something stands between you and your heart's desire, and so live with that desire unfulfilled, but it is not true. This "thing" is the bugaboo under the bed that has no reality. Deny it, deny it, and you will find yourself free, and you will realize that this seeming was all false. Then you will see the good flowing into you, and you will see clearly that nothing can stand between you and your own.

Denials may be spoken silently or audibly, but not in a manner to call forth antagonism and discussion.

To some, all this sort of mechanical working will seem a strange way of entering into a more spiritual life. There are those who easily and naturally glide out of the old material life into a deeper spiritual one without any external help, but there are thousands of others who are seeking primarily "the loaves and fish" of bodily health and financial success, but who, without knowing it, really are seeking a higher way of life, who must take these very first steps. For such, the practicing of these mechanical steps in a wholehearted way, without prejudice, is doing the very best thing possible toward attaining purity of heart and life, toward growth in divine knowledge and fullness of joy in all things undertaken.

Fifth Lesson
AFFIRMATIONS

"You will pray to him, and he will hear you,
and you will pay your vows.
You will decide on a matter, and it will be
established for you,
and light will shine on your ways."
—Job 22:27-28

Most people, when they first consciously set out to gain a fuller, higher knowledge of spiritual things, do so because of dissatisfaction—or perhaps unsatisfaction would be the better word—with their present conditions of life. Inherent in the human mind is the thought that somewhere, somehow, it ought to be able to bring to itself that which it desires and which would satisfy. This thought is but the foreshadowing of that which really is.

Our wishes, it is said, do measure just
Our capabilities. Who with his might
Aspires unto the mountain's upper height,
Holds in that aspiration a great trust
To be fulfilled, a warrant that he must
Not disregard, a strength to reach the height
To which his hopes have taken flight.
—Author Unknown

The hunger that we feel is but the prompting of the Divine within us, which longs with an infinite longing to fill us. It is but one side of the law of demand and supply, the other side of which is unchangeably, unfailingly, the promise: "Whatever you ask for in prayer, believe that you have received it, and it will be yours" (Mk. 11:24). The supply is always equal to the demand, but there must first be a demand before supply is of use.

There is, attainable by us, a place where we can see that our doing can cease, because we realize that Spirit is the fulfillment of all of our desires. We simply get still and know that all things whatever we desire are ours already, and this knowing it, or recognizing it, has power to bring the invisible God (or good)—the innermost substance of all things—forth into just the visible form of good that we want.

But in order to attain this place of power, we must take the preliminary steps, faithfully, earnestly, trustingly, though these steps at first glance seem to us as useless and as empty as do the ceremonial forms and religious observances of the ritualistic churchman.

To affirm anything is to assert positively that it is so, even in the face of all contrary evidence. We may not be able to see *how*, by our simply affirming a thing to be true, a thing that to all human reasoning or sight does not seem to be true at all, that we can bring this thing to pass; but we can compel ourselves to cease all futile quibbling and go to work to prove the rule, each one in his own life.

The beautiful Presence all about us and within us is the substance of every good that we can possibly desire—aye, infinitely more than we are capable of desiring, for "no eye has seen, nor ear heard, nor the human heart conceived, what God has prepared for those who love him" (1 Cor. 2:9).

In some way, which it is not easy to put into words—for spiritual laws cannot always be compassed in words, and yet they are none the less infallible, immutable laws that work with precision and certainty—there is power in our word of faith to bring all good things right into our everyday life.

We speak the word, we confidently affirm, but we have nothing to do with the "establishing" of the word, or bringing it to pass. "You will decide on a matter, and it will be established for you" (Job 22:28). So if we decree or affirm unwaveringly, steadfastly, we hold God by His own unalterable laws to do the establishing or fulfilling.

They who have carefully studied spiritual laws find that, besides denying the reality and power of apparent evil, which denying frees them from it, they also can bring any desired good into their lives by persistently affirming it is there already. In the first instructions given to students, the denials and affirmations take a large place. Later on, their own personal experiences and inward guidance lead them up to a higher plane where they no longer need rote repetitions.

The saying over and over of any denial or affirmation is a necessary self-training of a mind that has lived so long in error and false belief that it needs this constant repetition of Truth to unclothe it and to clothe it anew.

As it is with the denials, so with the affirmations. There are four sweeping affirmations of Truth that cover a multitude of lesser ones, and which do marvelous work in bringing good to ourselves and to others.

First: *God is life, love, intelligence, substance, omnipotence, omniscience, omnipresence.*

These ideas you learned in the second lesson—"Statement of Being." As you repeat the affirmation, please remember that every particle of life, love, intelligence, power, or of real substance in the universe is simply a certain degree, or so to speak, a *quantity* of God made manifest or visible through a form. Try to think what it means when you say that God is omnipresent, omnipotent, omniscient.

If God is omnipresence (All-Presence) and All-Good, where is the evil? If He is omnipotence (All-Power), what other power can there be working in the universe?

Since God is omnipotence and omnipresence, put aside forever your traditional teaching of an adverse power, evil (devil), that may at any moment thwart the plans of God and bring you harm.

Do not disturb yourself about the *appearance* of evil all about you, but in the very presence of what seems evil stand true and unwavering in affirming that God, the good, is omnipresence. By so doing, you will see the seeming evil melt away as the darkness before the light or as the dew before the morning sun, and good come to take its place.

Second: *I am a child or manifestation of God, and every moment His life, love, wisdom, power flow into and through me. I am one with God and am governed by His law.*

Remember while repeating this affirmation that nothing—no circumstance, no person or set of persons—can by any possibility interpose between you and the Source of your life, wisdom, or power. It is all "hidden with Christ [the innermost Christ or Spirit of your being] in God" (Col. 3:3). Nothing but your own ignorance of how to receive, or your willfulness, can hinder your having unlimited supply.

No matter how sick or weak or inefficient you *seem* to be, take your eyes and thoughts right off the seeming and turn them within to the central fountain there and say calmly, quietly, but with steadfast assurance: *This appearance of weakness is false; God, manifest as life, wisdom, and power, is now flowing into my entire being and out through me to the external.* You will soon see a marvelous change wrought in yourself by the realization that this spoken word will bring to you.

You do not change God's attitude toward you one iota by either importuning or affirming. You only change your attitude toward Him. By thus affirming, you put yourself in harmony with divine law, which is always working toward your good and never toward your harm or punishment.

Third: *I am Spirit, perfect, holy, harmonious. Nothing can hurt me or make me sick or afraid, for Spirit is God, and God cannot be sick or hurt or afraid. I manifest my real Self through this body now.*

Fourth: *God works in me to will and to do whatever He wishes me to do, and He cannot fail.*

Our affirming His mind working both to will and to do makes us will only the good, and He, the very Father in us, does the works, hence there can be no failure. Whatever we fully commit to the Father to do and affirm is done, we shall see accomplished.

These, then, are the four comprehensive affirmations:

God is life, love, intelligence, substance, omnipotence, omniscience, omnipresence.

I am a child or manifestation of God, and every moment His life, love, wisdom, power flow into and through me. I am one with God and am governed by His law.

I am Spirit, perfect, holy, harmonious. Nothing can hurt me or make me sick or afraid, for Spirit is God, and God cannot be sick or hurt or afraid. I manifest my real Self through this body now.

God works in me to will and to do whatever He wishes me to do, and He cannot fail.

Commit these affirmations to memory so that you can repeat them in the silence of your own mind in any place and at any time. Strangely will they act to deliver you out of the greatest external distresses, places where no human help avails. It is as though the moment you assert emphatically your oneness with

God the Father, there is instantly set into motion all the power of Omnipotent Love to rush to your rescue. And when it has undertaken to work for you, you can cease from external ways and means and boldly claim: *It is done; I have the desires of my heart.*

> "You open your hand,
> satisfying the desire of every living thing."
> —Psalm 145:16

In reality, God is forever in process of movement within us, that He may manifest Himself (All-Good) more fully through us. Our affirming, backed by faith, is the link that connects our conscious human need with His power and supply.

They who have claimed their birthright by thus calmly affirming their oneness with God know how free they can be from human planning and effort, after they have called into operation this marvelous power of affirmation. This power has healed the sick, brought joy in place of mourning, literally opened prison doors and bidden the prisoner go free without the claimants calling for human assistance.

Understand, it is not necessarily the using of just this form of words that has availed in each individual case. It is the denying of apparent evil, and in spite of all contrary evidence, the affirming of good to be all there is, affirming oneness with God's omnipotent power to accomplish, even when there were no visible signs of His being present, that has wrought the deliverance. In one case within my knowledge, just simply claiming *God is your defense and deliverance* for a man who had for five years been an exile from home and country (through a series of deceptions and machinations that for depth and subtlety were unparalleled), opened all the doors wide and restored the man to his family within a month, without any further human effort on the part of himself or his friends, and this, after five years of the most strenuous human efforts of lawyers, had failed utterly to bring the truth to light or to release the prisoner.

Some minds are so constituted that they get better results from repeated use of denials; others, from using denials less and affirmations more.

No definite rules can be laid down as to which will work most effectually in each individual case to eradicate apparent evil and bring the good into manifestation, but some little hint that may be helpful can be given.

Denials have an erasive or dissolving tendency. Affirmations build up and give strength and courage and power. People who remember vividly and are inclined to dwell in their thoughts on the pains, sorrows, and troubles of the past or present need to deny a great deal; for denials cleanse the mind and blot out of memory all seeming evil and unhappiness so that they become as a faraway dream. Again, denials are particularly useful to those who are hard or intolerant, or aggressively sinful; to those who, as a result of success, have become overconfident, thinking the human is sufficient in itself for all things; to the selfish and to any who do not scruple to harm others.

Affirmations should be used by the timid and by those who have a feeling of their own inefficiency, those who stand in fear of other minds, those who "give in" easily, those who are subject to anxiety or doubt, and those who are in positions of responsibility. People who are in any way negative or passive need to use affirmations more; the ones who are self-confident or unforgiving, need denials more.

Deny the appearance of evil; affirm good. Deny weakness; affirm strength. Deny any undesirable condition and affirm the good you desire. This is what Jesus meant when He said, "Whatever you ask for in prayer, believe [or claim and affirm] that you have received it, and it will be yours" (Mk. 11:24). This is what is meant by the promise: "Every place that the sole of your foot will tread upon [or that you stand squarely or firmly upon] I have given to you" (Josh. 1:3).

Practice these denials and affirmations silently in the street, in the car, when you are wakeful during the night, anywhere, everywhere, and they will give you a new, and to you, a strange mastery over external things and over yourself. If there comes a moment when you are in doubt as to what to do, stand still and affirm: *God in me is infinite wisdom; I know just what to do.* "For I will give you words and a wisdom that none of your opponents will be able to withstand or contradict" (Lk. 21:15). Do not get flustered or anxious but depend fully and trustingly on your principle, and you will be surprised at the sudden inspiration that will come to you as the mode of procedure.

So always this principle will work in the solution of all life's problems—I care not what the form of detail is—to free us, God's children, from all undesirable conditions and to bring good into our lives, if we will take up the simple rules and use them faithfully, until they lead us into such realization of our Godhood that we need no longer consciously depend on them.

Sixth Lesson

FAITH

"Truly I tell you, if you say to this mountain, 'Be taken up and thrown into the sea,' and if you do not doubt in your heart, but believe that what you say will come to pass, it will be done for you."

—Mark 11:23

Science was faith once.
—Lowell

The word *faith* is one that has generally been thought to denote a simple form of belief based mostly on ignorance and superstition. It is a word that has drawn forth something akin to scorn from so-called "thinking people"—the people who have believed that intellectual attainment is the highest form of knowledge to be reached. "Blind faith" they have disdainfully chosen to call it—fit only for ministers, women, and children, but not a practical thing on which to establish the everyday business affairs of life.

Some have prided themselves on having outgrown the swaddling clothes of this blind, unreasoning faith, and having grown to the point, as they say, where they have faith only in that which can be seen, or intellectually explained.

The writer of The Epistle to the Hebrews, obviously a most intellectual man and a learned theologian, before writing at length on the nature of faith and the marvelous results attending it, tried to put into a few words a condensed definition of faith: "Faith is the assurance of things hoped for, the conviction of things not seen" (Heb. 11:1).

In other words, faith takes right hold of the substance of the things desired and brings into the world of evidence the things that before were not seen. Further speaking of faith, the writer said, "What is seen was made from things that are not visible" (Heb. 11:3). In some way, then, we understand that whatever we want is in this surrounding invisible substance, and faith is the power that can bring it out into actuality to us.

After having cited innumerable instances of marvelous things brought to pass in the lives of men, not by their work or efforts, but by faith, the Epistle says: "And what more should I say? For time would fail me to tell of Gideon, Barak, Samson, Jephthah, of David and Samuel and the prophets—who through faith conquered kingdoms, administered justice, obtained promises, shut the mouths of lions, quenched raging fire, escaped the edge of the sword, won strength out of weakness, became mighty in war, put foreign armies to flight. Women received their dead by resurrection" (Heb. 11:32-35).

Do you want any more power or any greater thing than is here mentioned—power to conquer kingdoms, to shut the mouths of lions, quench fire, turn to flight whole armies, raise the dead to life again? Even if your desires exceed this, you need not despair or hesitate to claim their fulfillment, for One greater than you, One who knew whereof He spoke, said, "All things can be done for the one who believes" (Mk. 9:23).

Until very recently, whenever anyone has spoken of faith as the one power that can move mountains, we have always felt a sort of hopeless discouragement. While we have believed that God holds all good things in His hand, and is willing to be prevailed upon to dole them out according to our faith, yet how could we, even by straining every nerve of our being toward faith, be sure that we had sufficient to please Him? For does it not say, "Without faith it is impossible to please God" (Heb. 11:6)?

From the moment we began to ask, we began to question our ability to reach God's standard of faith on which hung our fate. We also began to question whether, after all, there is any such power in faith to prevail with the Giver of "every perfect gift" (Jas. 1:17) so as to draw out of Him something that He had never let us have before.

Viewing faith in this light, there is not much wonder that logical minds have looked on it as a sort of will-o'-the-wisp, not a thing from which any real, definite results could ever be obtained—not a thing that the business world could rest upon.

There is a blind faith, to be sure. (Someone has truthfully said that blind faith is better than none at all; for, if held to, it will get its eyes open after a time.) But there is also an understanding faith. Blind faith is an instinctive trust in a power higher than ourselves. Understanding faith is based on immutable principle.

Faith does not depend on physical facts or on the evidence of the senses because it is born of intuition, or the Spirit of Truth ever living at the center of our being. Its action is infinitely higher than that of reason. It is founded on *Truth*; while as you remember from a former lesson, reasoning or intellectual argument is founded on evidence of the senses and is not reliable.

Intuition is the open end, within one's own being, of the invisible channel ever connecting each individual with God. Faith is, as it were, a ray of light shot out from the central sun—God—one end of which ray comes into your being and mine through the open door of intuition. With our consciousness, we perceive the ray of light, and though intellect cannot grasp it or give the why or wherefore thereof, yet we instinctively feel that the other end of the ray opens out into all there is of God (Good). This is "blind faith." It is based on Truth, but a Truth of which everyone is not at the time conscious. Even this kind of faith will, if persisted in, bring results.

What is understanding faith? There are some things that God has so indissolubly joined together that it is impossible for even Him to put them asunder. They are bound together by fixed, immutable laws; if we have one of them, we must have the other.

This is illustrated by the laws of geometry. For instance, the sum of the angles of a triangle is equal to two right angles. No matter how large or small the triangle, no matter whether it is made on the mountaintop or leagues under the sea, if we are asked the sum of its angles, we can unhesitatingly answer, without waiting an instant to count or reckon this particular triangle, that it is just two right angles. This is absolutely certain. It is certain even before the triangle is drawn by visible lines; we can know it beforehand because it is based on unchangeable laws, on the truth or reality of the thing. It was true just as much before anyone recognized it as it is today. Our knowing it or not knowing it does not change the truth. Only in proportion as we come to know it as an eternally true fact, can we be benefitted by it.

It is also a simple fact that one plus one equals two; it is an eternal truth. You cannot put one and one together without two resulting. You may believe it or not; that does not alter the truth. But unless you do put the one and one together, you do not produce the two, for each is eternally dependent on the other.

The mental and spiritual world or realms are governed by laws that are just as real and unfailing as the laws that govern the natural world. Certain conditions of mind are so connected with certain results that the two are inseparable. If we have the one, we must have the other, as surely as the night follows the day—not because we believe some wise person's testimony that such is the case, not even because the voice of intuition tells us that it is so, but because the whole matter is based on laws that can neither fail nor be broken.

When we know something of these laws, we can know positively beforehand just what results will follow certain mental states.

God, the one creative cause of all things, is Spirit, invisible as we have learned. God is the sum total of all good. There is no good that you can desire in your life that, at its center, is not God. God is the substance of all things—the real thing within every visible form of good.

God, the invisible substance out of which all visible things are formed, is all around us waiting to come forth into manifestation.

This good substance all about us is unlimited and is itself the supply of every demand that can be made, of every need that exists in the visible or natural world.

One of the unerring Truths in the Universe (by "Universe," I mean the spiritual and natural worlds combined) is that there is already provided a lavish abundance for every human want. In other words, the supply of every good always awaits the demand. Another Truth is that the demand must be made before the supply can come forth to fill it. To recognize these two statements of Truth and to affirm them are the whole secret of understanding faith—faith based on principle.

Let us square this by the definition of faith, given earlier in the lesson: "Faith is the assurance of things hoped for, the conviction of things not seen." Faith takes hold of the substance of the thing hoped for and brings into evidence, or visibility, the things not seen.

What are usually called the promises of God are certain eternal, unchangeable Truths that are true whether they are found in the Bible or in the almanac. They are unvarying statements of Truth that cannot be altered. A promise, according to *Webster*, is a something sent beforehand to indicate that something unseen is at hand. It is a declaration that gives the person to whom it is made the right to expect and claim the performance of the act.

The Nazarene recognized the unchangeable Truth that, in the unseen, the supply of every want awaits demand. When he said, "Ask and you will receive" (Jn. 16:24), he was simply stating an unalterable Truth. He knew that the instant we ask or desire (for asking is desire expressed), we touch a secret spring which starts on its way toward us the good we want. He knew that there need not be any coaxing or pleading about it, that our asking is simply our complying with an unfailing law that is bound to work; there is no escape from it. Asking and receiving are the two ends of the same thing. We cannot have one without the other.

Asking springs from desire to possess some good. What is desire? Desire in the heart is always God tapping at the door of your consciousness with His infinite supply—a supply that is forever useless unless there be demand for it. "Before they call I will answer" (Is. 65:24). Before you are ever conscious of any lack, of any desire for more happiness, or for fullness of joy, the great Father-Mother heart has desired them for you. It is He in you desiring them that you feel, and think it is only yourself (separate from Him) desiring them. With God, the desire to give and giving are one and the same thing. Someone has said, "Desire for anything is the thing itself in incipiency"; that is, the thing you desire is not only for you but has already been started toward you out of the heart of God; it is the first approach of the thing itself striking you that makes you desire it or even think of it at all.

The only way God has of letting us know of His infinite supply and His desire to make it ours is for Him to push gently on the divine spark living within each one of us. He wants you to be a strong, self-sufficient man or woman, to have more power and dominion over all before you; so He quietly and silently pushes a little more of Himself, His desire, into the center of your being. He enlarges, so to speak, your real Self, and at once you become conscious of new desire to be bigger, grander, stronger. If He had not pushed at the center of your being first, you would never have thought of new desires but would have remained perfectly content as you were.

You think that you want better health, more love, a brighter, more cheerful home all of your very own; in short, you want less evil (or no evil) and more good in your life. This is only God pushing at the inner door of your being, as if He were saying, "My child, let Me in; I want to give you all good, that you may be more comfortable and happy." "My servants shall eat ... my servants shall drink ... my servants shall rejoice ... my servants shall sing for gladness of heart .... They shall build houses and inhabit them" (Is. 65:13-14, 21).

Remember this: Desire in the heart for anything is God's sure promise sent beforehand to indicate that it is yours already in the limitless realm of supply, and whatever you want you can have for the taking.

Taking is simply recognizing the law of supply and demand (even if you cannot see a sign of the supply any more than Elijah did when he had affirmed for rain, and not a cloud even so big as a man's hand was for a long time to be seen). Affirm your possession of the good that you desire; have faith in it, because you are working with divine law and cannot fail; do not be argued off your basic principle by anyone; and sooner will the heavens fall than that you fail to get that which you desire.

"Whatever you ask for in prayer, believe that you have received it, and it will be yours" (Mk. 11:24).

Knowing the law of abundant supply and the Truth that supply always precedes the demand, demand simply being the call that brings the supply into sight; knowing that all desire in the heart for any good is really God's desire in us and for us, how shall we obtain the fulfillment of our every desire, and that right speedily?

"Take delight in the Lord,
    and he will give you the desires of your heart."
                                                —Psalm 37:4

Take right hold of God with an unwavering faith. Begin and continue to rejoice and thank Him that you have (not *will* have) the desires of your heart, never losing sight of the fact that the desire is the thing itself in incipiency. If the good were not already yours in the invisible realm of supply, you could not, by any possibility, desire it.

Someone asks: "Suppose I desire my neighbor's wife or his property, is that desire born of God? And can I see it fulfilled by affirming that it is mine?"

You do not and cannot, by any possibility, desire that which *belongs* to another. You do not desire your neighbor's wife. You desire the love that seems to you to be represented by your neighbor's wife. You desire something to fill your heart's craving for love. Affirm that there is for you a rightful and an overflowing supply, and claim its manifestation. It will surely come, and your so-called desire to possess your neighbor's wife will suddenly disappear.

So you do not in reality desire anything that belongs to your neighbor. You want the equivalent of that for which his possessions stand. You want your own. There is today an unlimited supply of All-Good provided in the unseen for every human being. No man need have less that another may have more. Your very own awaits you. Your understanding faith or trust is the power that will bring it to you.

Emerson said that the man who knows the law "is sure that his welfare is dear to the heart of being .... He believes that he cannot escape from his good."

Knowing divine law and obeying it, we can forever rest from all anxiety, all fear, for "you open your hand, satisfying the desire of every living thing" (Ps. 145:16).

Seventh Lesson

DEFINITION OF TERMS: CHEMICALIZATION, PERSONALITY, AND INDIVIDUALITY

One of the greatest beauties of the Sermon on the Mount is the childlike simplicity of its language. Every child, every grown person, be he ever so uneducated, if he can read at all can understand it. Not a word in it requires the use of a dictionary; not a sentence in it that does not tell the way so plainly that "no traveler, not even fools, shall go astray" (Is. 35:8). And yet the Nazarene was the fullest, most complete manifestation of the one Mind that has ever lived; that is to say, more of the wisdom that is God came forth through him into visibility than through anyone else who has ever lived. The more any person manifests the true wisdom, which is God, the more simple are his ways of thinking and acting, the more simple are the words through which he expresses his ideas. The greater the truth to be expressed, the more simply can it (and should it) be clothed.

Emerson said, "Converse with a mind that is grandly simple, and all literature [high sounding sentences to convey ideas] looks like wordcatching."

In the metaphysical literature of today, a good many terms are used that are very confusing to those who have not taken a consecutive course of lessons on the subject. It seems to me wise to give here a clear, simple explanation of three words frequently used, so that even the most unlearned may read understand-

71

ingly.

One term often used and not always clearly understood is *chemicalization.*[1]

Did you ever put soda into sour milk, cider, or other acid fluid and witness the agitation or excited action that takes place? One of the substances neutralizes the other, and something better results from the action.

This is a good illustration of what takes place sometimes in the minds and bodies of people. Suppose a man has lived in wrong thought and molded his body by wrong thought for years, until, as you might say, he has become solidified in that wrong belief. You introduce the Truth to him by strong denials and affirmations as has been taught. The very newness of it (and because it is Truth) creates in the first few days: new hope, new joy, and health. After a little time a sort of mental ferment or agitation takes place. One is apt to feel very nervous and seared way down in the depths of himself. If he has ever been sick, he will begin to feel the old diseases; if he has been morally bad, the old desires and habits will take possession of him with new force; if he has been holding denials and affirmations about business affairs until they have looked hopeful, all at once they collapse and seem darker and more hopeless than ever. All the new beliefs that lifted him into a new world for a few days seem failures, and he seems on the very verge of breaking up generally.

What has happened? Why, simply this. There has been a clash between the old condition—which was based on falsehood, fear, and wrong ways of thinking—and the new thought or Truth entering into you. The old mortal is kicking vigorously

---

1 All editions of *Lessons in Truth* since 1942, with the exception of the 1967, 1971, and 1972 editions, did not include this material on *chemicalization* It had been thought of as too negative and confusing. We are returning it with all its nineteenth-century flavor because many people experience this phenomenon (by whatever name it is called) and would benefit by reading about it. In the original manuscript, Dr. Cady also included a section on *thought transference*, which we have chosen to leave out because it required considerable rewriting and was not a crucial concept.

against the Truth. You have a feeling of discouragement or of fear, a feeling such as one would have if caught at something disreputable. Do not be frightened. That which you feel is, on the spiritual plane, a similar excitement and agitation to that which was seen in the chemical action between the alkali and acid on the material plane. And *something higher and better always results.*

This agitation does not always take place with everyone but is most apt to occur with those who have been most fixed and (as it were) solidified in the old beliefs. Such people break up with more resistance. Those who are not very settled in their convictions are more malleable mentally and physically, are not so apt to chemicalize. Vigorous use of denials are also more apt to produce chemicalization than is the use of affirmations. There is always less resistance by the mind when it is gently led into the Truth than when its errors are directly and vigorously combated. Should you find yourself in this state of internal aggravation, you need only affirm: *There is nothing to fear, absolutely nothing to fear. Perfect Love reigns and all is good. Peace be still, and so on,* and very soon the brighter conditions will appear, and you will find yourself on a much higher plane than you have ever been before.

Do not be afraid of this word (or the condition) *chemicalization*—as many have been—for truly, there *is* nothing to fear in it.

The words *personality* and *individuality* present distinct meanings to the trained mind, but by the untrained mind, they are often used interchangeably and apart from their real meanings.[2]

Personality applies to the human part of you—the person, the external. It belongs to the region governed by the intellect. Your

2. Today *individuality* and *personality* continue to be used interchangeably in common usage. As with the term *denial*, it is difficult to glean one meaning from a word when it already has another, virtually opposite, meaning in place. Perhaps it may be advisable to use *God Self* instead of *individuality*.

personality may be agreeable or disagreeable to others. When you say that you dislike anyone, you mean that you dislike his personality—that exterior something that presents itself from the outside. It is the outer changeable man, in contradistinction to the inner or real man.

Individuality is the term used to denote the *real* man. The more God comes into visibility through a person, the more individualized he becomes. By this, I do not mean that one's individuality is greater when one is more religious. Remember, God is wisdom, intelligence, love, power. The more pronounced the manner in which any one of these qualities—or all of them—comes forth into visibility through a man, the greater his individuality.

Emerson was a man of large individuality, but retiring personality. He was grandly simple. He was of a shrinking, retiring nature (or personality). But just in proportion as the human side of him was willing to retire and be thought little of, did the immortal, the God in him, shine forth in greater degree.

John the Baptist represents the illumined intellect, the highest development of human consciousness. We may think of him as standing for personality, whereas Jesus typifies the divine Self or individuality. John, recognizing the superiority of Jesus, said, "He must increase, but I must decrease" (Jn. 3:30).

One's individuality is that part of one that never changes its identity. It is the God Self. One's personality may become like that of others with whom one associates. Individuality never changes.

Do not confound the terms. One may have an aggressive, pronounced personality, or external man, which will, for a time, fight its way through obstacles and gain its point. But a pronounced individuality never battles; it is never puffed up; it is never governed by likes and dislikes and never causes them in others; it is God come forth in greater degree through a man, and all mere personality instinctively bends the knee before it in recognition of its superiority.

We cultivate individuality by listening to the "still small voice" (1 Kings 19:12 KJV) down deep within us, and boldly following it, even if it does make us different from others, as it surely will. We cultivate personality, in which live pride, fear of criticism, and all manner of selfishness, by listening to the voices outside ourselves and by being governed by selfish motives, instead of by the highest within us. Seek always to cultivate, or to bring into visibility, individuality, not personality. In proportion as one increases, the other must decrease.

Whenever we fear a man, or shrink before him, it is because his personality, being the stronger, overcomes ours. Many timid persons go through life always feeling that they are inefficient, that others are wiser or better than they. They dread to meet a positive, self-possessed person, and when in the presence of such a one, they are laid low, just as a field of tall wheat is after a fierce windstorm has swept across it. They feel as though they would like to get out of sight forever.

All this, dear timid ones, is not because your fellow really is wiser or better than you, but because his personality—the external man—is stronger than yours. You never have a similar feeling in the presence of strong individuality. Individuality in another not only produces in you an admiration for its superiority, but it also gives you, when you are in its presence, a strange new sense of your own inherent possibilities, a sense that is full of exhilaration and comfort and encouragement to you. This is because a pronounced individuality simply means more of God comes forth into visibility through a person, and by some mind process, it has power to call forth more of God through you.

If you want to know how to avoid being overcome and thrown off your feet by the strong personality of others, I will tell you: Always remember that personality is of the human and individuality is of God. Silently affirm your own individuality, your oneness with God and your superiority to personality. Can God fear any person?

If you are naturally inclined to be timid or shrinking, practice of the following will help you overcome it. As you walk down the street and see anyone coming toward you, even a stranger to you, silently affirm such words as: *I am a part of God in visibility; I am one with the Father; this person has no power over me, for I am superior to all personality.* Cultivate this habit of thinking and affirming whenever you approach any person, and you will soon find that no personality, however strong and aggressive, has the power to throw you out of the most perfect poise. You will be Self-possessed because you are God-possessed.

Some years ago I found myself under a sense of bondage to a strong, aggressive personality with whom, externally, I had been quite intimately associated for several months. I seemed to see things through another's eyes, and while I was more than half conscious of this, I could not seem to throw it off. This personality was able, with a very few words, to make me feel as if all that I said or did was a mistake and that I was a most miserable failure. I was always utterly discouraged after being in this presence and felt that I had no ability to accomplish anything.

After vainly trying for weeks to free myself, one day I was walking along the street with a most intense desire and determination to be free. Many times before, I had affirmed that this personality could not affect or overcome me, but with no effect. This day I struck out further and declared (silently of course): *There is no such personality in the universe as this one,* affirming it again and again many times. After a few moments I began to feel wondrously lifted and as if chains were dropping off. Then the voice within me urged me on a step farther to say: *There is no personality in the universe; there is nothing but God.* After a short time spent in vigorously using these words, I seemed to break every fetter. From that day to this, without further effort, I have been as free from any influence of that personality as though it had never existed.

If at any time the lesser affirmation of Truth fails to free you from the influence of other minds, try this more sweeping one: *There is no personality in the universe; there is nothing but God,* and you are bound to be made free.

The more you learn to act from the "still small voice" within you, the stronger and more pronounced will be individuality in you.

If you are inclined to wilt before strong personalities, always remember that God has need of you, through whom, in some special manner, to manifest Himself—some manner for which He cannot use any other organ—what need have you to quail before any person, no matter how important?

However humble your place in life, however unknown to the world you may be, however small your capabilities may seem at present to you, you are just as much a necessity to God in His efforts to get Himself into visibility as is the most brilliant intellect, the most thoroughly cultured person in the world. Remember this always, and act from the highest within you.

Eighth Lesson
SPIRITUAL UNDERSTANDING

"Happy are those who find wisdom,
    and those who get understanding,
for her income is better than silver,
    and her revenue better than gold.
She is more precious than jewels,
    and nothing you desire can compare with her.
Long life is in her right hand;
    in her left hand are riches and honor.
Her ways are ways of pleasantness,
    and all her paths are peace.
She is a tree of life to those who lay hold of her;
    those who hold her fast are called happy....
And whatever else you get, get insight."
               —Proverbs 3:13-18, 4:7

What is this understanding on the getting of which depends so much? Is it intellectual lore, obtained from delving deep into books of other men's making? Is it knowledge obtained from studying rocks (geology) or stars (astronomy) or even the human body (physiology)? Nay, verily, for when did such knowledge ever ensure life and health and peace, ways of pleasantness, with riches and honor?

Understanding is a spiritual birth, a revelation of God within the heart of man. Jesus touched the root of the matter when, after having asked the apostles a question that was answered variously, according to the intellectual perception of the men, he asked another question to which Peter gave a reply not based on external reasoning, but on intuition. He said to Peter, "Blessed are you, Simon Son of Jonah! For flesh and blood has not revealed this to you, but my Father in heaven" (Mt. 16:17).

You may have an intellectual perception of Truth. You may easily grasp with the mind the statement that God is the giver of all good gifts—life, health, love—just as people have for centuries grasped it. Or you may go further, and intellectually see that God is not only the giver, but the gift itself; that He is life, health, love, in us. But unless Truth is "revealed ... to you" by "my Father in heaven," it is of no practical benefit to you or to anyone else.

This revelation of Truth to the consciousness of a person is spiritual understanding.

You may say to yourself or another may say silently to you, over and over again, that you are well and wise and happy. On the mental plane, a certain "cure" is effected, and for a time you will feel well and wise and happy. This is simply a form of hypnotism, or mind cure. But until, down in the depths of your being, you are *conscious* of your oneness with the Father, until you know within yourself that the spring of all wisdom and health and joy is within your own being, ready at any moment to leap forth at the call of your need, you will not have spiritual understanding.

All the teachings of Jesus were for the purpose of leading men into this consciousness of their oneness with the Father. He had to begin at the external man—because people then as now were living mostly in external things—and teach him to love his enemies, to do good to others, and so forth. These were external steps for them to take—a sort of lopping off of the ends of the branches; but they were steps that led on up to the place of desire and attainment where finally the Master said, "I still have many things to say to you, but you cannot bear them now" (Jn. 16:12).

He told them of the Comforter that was in them, and which would teach them all things, revealing the "depths of God" (1 Cor. 2:10) to them, showing them things to come. In other words, he told them how they might find the kingdom of heaven *within* themselves—the kingdom of love, of power, of life.

The coming of the Comforter to their hearts and lives, giving them power over every form of sin, sickness, sorrow, and over even death itself, is exactly what we mean by understanding or realization. The power that this consciousness of the indwelling Father gives is for us today as much as it was for those to whom the Nazarene spoke. Aye, more; for did he not say, "The one who believes in me will also do the works that I do and, in fact, will do greater works than these" (Jn. 14:12)?

All the foregoing lessons have been stepping-stones leading up to the point where man may realize the ever-abiding inner presence of the Most High, God. "Do you not know that your body is a temple of the Holy Spirit within you?" (1 Cor. 6:19)

I cannot reveal God to you. You cannot reveal God to another. If I have learned, I may tell you, and you may tell another how to seek and find God, each within himself. But the new birth into the consciousness of our spiritual faculties and possibilities is indeed like the wind that "blows where it chooses, and you hear the sound of it, but you do not know where it comes from or where it goes. So it is with everyone who is born of the Spirit" (Jn. 3:8). The new birth takes place in the silence, in the invisible.

Intellectual lore can be bought and sold; understanding, or realization, cannot. A man, Simon by name, once attempted to buy the power that spiritual understanding gives from another who possessed it. "But Peter said to him, 'May your silver perish with you, because you thought you could obtain God's gift with money! You have no part or share in this, for your heart is not right before God' " (Acts 8:20-21).

Nor will crying and beseeching bring spiritual understanding. Hundreds of people have tried this method and have not received that for which they earnestly but ignorantly sought. They have not received, because they did not know how to take that which God freely offered. Others have sought with selfish motives this spiritual understanding, or consciousness of the indwelling Father, because of the power it would give them. "You ask and do not receive, because you ask wrongly, in order to spend what you get on your pleasures [or to serve selfish ends]" (Jas. 4:3).

Understanding, or realization of the presence of God within us, is as Jesus said, "the gift of God" (Jn. 4:10). It comes to any and all who learn how to seek it aright. Emerson said, "This energy [consciousness of God in the soul] does not descend into individual life on any other condition than entire possession. It comes to the lowly and simple; it comes to whomsoever will put off what is foreign and proud; it comes as insight; it comes as serenity and grandeur. When we see those whom it inhabits, we are apprised of new degrees of greatness. From that inspiration [consciousness] the man comes back with a changed tone. He does not talk with men with an eye to their opinion. He tries them.... But the soul that ascends to worship the great God is plain and true; has no rose color, no fine friends ... no adventures; does not want admiration; dwells in the hour that now is."

"When you search for me, you will find me; if you seek me with all your heart" (Jer. 29:13). In that day when, more than riches and honor and power and selfish glory, you shall desire spiritual understanding, in that day will come to you the revelation of God in you, and you will be conscious of the indwelling Father, who is life and strength and power and peace.

One may so desire a partial revelation of God within himself, a revelation along one line—as, for instance, that of health—as to seek it with all his heart. And if he has learned how to take the desired gift, by uncompromising affirmation that it is his already, he will get understanding, or realization, of God as his perfect health. So as with any other desired gift of God, this is a step in the right direction. It is learning how to take God by faith for whatever one desires. But in the onward growth, the time will come to every man when he will hear the divine voice within him saying, "Come up higher," and he will pass beyond any merely selfish desires that are just for his own comfort's sake. He will desire good that he may have the more to give out, knowing that as good (God) flows through him to others, it will make him "every whit whole" (Jn. 7:23 KJV).

In the beginning of Solomon's reign as king over Israel, the divine Presence appeared to him in a dream at night, saying, "Ask what I should give you" (1 Kings 3:5). And Solomon said, "Give your servant therefore an understanding mind" (1 Kings 3:9)

"It pleased the Lord that Solomon had asked this. God said to him, 'Because you have asked this, and have not asked for yourself long life or riches, or for the life of your enemies, but have asked for yourself understanding to discern what is right, I now do according to your word. Indeed I give you a wise and discerning mind; no one like you has been before you and no one like you shall arise after you. I give you also what you have not asked, both riches and honor all your life; no other king shall compare with you' " (1 Kings 3:10-13).

Thus in losing sight of all worldly goods and chattels, all merely selfish ends, and desiring above all things an understanding heart (or a spiritual consciousness of God within him as wisdom, life, power), Solomon received all the goods or good things included, so that there was none among the kings like unto him in worldly possessions. "Strive first for the kingdom of God [consciousness] and his righteousness, and all these things will be given to you" (Mt. 6:33). "For those who want to save their life [or the things of his life] will lose it, and those who lose their life for my sake [or he that is willing to forget the goods of this life for the truth's sake, choosing before all things the finding of God in his own soul] will find it" (Mt. 16:25).

When you first consciously desire spiritual understanding, you do not attain it at once. You have been living in the external of your being and have believed yourself cut off from God. Your first step after coming to yourself like the prodigal son is to say as he did, "I will get up and go to my father" (Lk. 15:18) to turn your thoughts away from the external seeming toward the central and real; to know intellectually that you are not cut off from God, and that He forever desires to manifest Himself within you as your present deliverance from all suffering and sin. Just as Jesus taught, we begin our journey toward understanding by cutting off the branches of our selfishness. We try to love instead of to hate. Instead of avenging ourselves, we begin to forgive, even if it costs us great mental effort. We begin to deny envy, jealousy, anger, sickness, and all imperfection, and to affirm love, peace, and health.

Begin with the words of Truth that you have learned and which perhaps you have as yet only comprehended with the intellect. You must be willing to take the very first light you receive and use it faithfully, earnestly, to help both yourself and others. Sometimes you will be almost overcome by questions and doubts arising in your own mind when you are looking in vain for results. But you must with effort pass the place of doubt; and some day, in the fullness of God's time, while you are using the words of Truth, they will suddenly be illumined and become to you the Living Word within you—"the true light, which enlightens everyone, was coming into the world" (Jn. 1:9). You will no longer dwell in darkness, for the light will be within your own heart, and the word will be made flesh to you; that is, you will be conscious of a new and diviner life in your body, and a new and diviner love for all people, a new and diviner power to accomplish.

This is spiritual understanding. This is a flash of the Most High within your consciousness. "Everything old has passed away; see, everything has become new!" (2 Cor. 5:17) This will be the time when you will not talk with men with an eye to their opinion. This is when you will suddenly become plain and true, when you will cease to desire admiration, when all words of congratulation from others on your success will fill you with an inexpressible sense of humility, when all mere compliments will be to you as "a noisy gong or a clanging cymbal" (1 Cor. 13:1). Truly, from that inspiration, a man comes back with a changed tone!

With spiritual understanding comes new light on the Scriptures. The very Spirit of Truth, which has come to abide with you forever in your consciousness, takes the deep things of God and reveals them to you. You will no longer run to and fro, seeking teachers or healers and rely solely on them for guidance. You know that the living light, the living word within you, will "guide you into all the truth" (Jn. 16:13).

What we need to do is to seek the revelation of the living Christ within our own being, each for himself, knowing that only this divinity come forth can make us powerful and happy.

Every person in his heart desires, though he may not yet quite know it, this new birth into a higher life, into spiritual consciousness. Everyone wants more power, more good, more joy. And though, to the unawakened mind, it may seem that it is more money as money, or more goods that he wants, it is, nevertheless, more of good (God) that he craves, for all good is God.

Many today are conscious that the inner hunger cannot be satisfied with worldly goods and are with all earnestness seeking spiritual understanding, or consciousness, of an immanent God. They have been seeking long, with a great desire of unselfishness and a feeling that when they have truly found God, they will begin to do for others. Faithful service for others hastens the day-dawning for us. The gifts of God are not given in reward for

Complete Works of H. Emilie Cady

faithful service, as a fond mother gives cake to her child for being good; nevertheless they are a reward, inasmuch as service is one of the steps that lead up to the place where all the fullness of God awaits men. And while spiritual understanding is in reality a "gift of God," it comes to us more or less quickly in proportion as we use the light that we already have.

I believe that too much introspection, too much of what people usually call "spiritual seeking," is detrimental rather than helpful to the end desired—spiritual growth. Spiritual seeking is a sort of spiritual selfishness, paradoxical as this may seem. From the beginning to the end, Jesus taught the giving of what one possesses to him who has none.

"Is not this the fast that I choose:" said the Spirit of God through the prophet Isaiah, "to loose the bonds of injustice, to undo the thongs of the yoke, to let the oppressed go free ...? Is it not to share your bread with the hungry, and bring the homeless poor into your house; when you see the naked, to cover them ...? Then your light shall break forth like the dawn, and your healing shall spring up quickly .... Then you shall call, and the Lord will answer ... Here I am....

"If you offer your food to the hungry and satisfy the needs of the afflicted, then your light shall rise in the darkness and your gloom be like the noonday. The Lord will guide you continually, and satisfy your needs in parched places, and make your bones strong; and you shall be like a watered garden, like a spring of water whose waters never fail" (Is. 58:6-11).

Stagnation is death. A pool cannot be kept clean and sweet and renewed unless there is an outlet as well as an inlet. It is our business to keep the outlet open and God's business to keep the stream flowing in and through us. Unless you use for the service of others what God has already given to you, you will find it a long, weary road to spiritual understanding.

We cry out and strain every nerve to obtain full understanding, just as sometimes we have heard earnest people, but people wholly ignorant of divine laws, beseech God for the full baptism of "the Holy Spirit" (Lk. 3:16) as in the day of Pentecost. Jesus said, "I still have many things to say to you, but you cannot bear them now" (Jn. 16:12). We grow by using for others the light and knowledge we have. We expand, as we go on step-by-step in spiritual insight, until in the fullness of time—which means when we have grown spiritually to the place where God sees that we are able to bear the many things—we receive the desire of our hearts, understanding.

Seek your own Lord. Take the light as it is revealed to you, and use it for others, and prove for yourself whether there be Truth in this prophecy of Isaiah, that "then your light shall rise in the darkness and your gloom be like the noonday" (Is. 58:10) and "then your light shall break forth like the dawn, and your healing shall spring up quickly" (Is. 58:8).

Ninth Lesson
THE SECRET PLACE OF THE MOST HIGH

There is nothing the human heart so longs for, so cries out after, as to know God, "whom to know aright is life eternal."

With a restlessness that is pitiful to see, people are ever shifting from one thing to another, always hoping to find rest and satisfaction in some anticipated accomplishment or possession. Men fancy that they want houses and lands, great learning or power. They pursue these things and gain them only to find themselves still restless, still unsatisfied.

At the great heart of humanity there is a deep and awful homesickness that never has been and never can be satisfied with anything less than a clear, vivid consciousness of the indwelling presence of God, our Father. In all ages, earnest men and women who have recognized this inner hunger as the heart's cry after God, have left seeking after things and have sought, by devoted worship and by service to others, to enter into this consciousness, but few have succeeded in reaching the promised place where their "joy" is "complete" (Jn. 16:24). Others have hoped and feared alternately; they have tried, with the best knowledge they possessed, to "work out" their "own salvation" (Phil. 2:12), not yet having learned that there must be an *in*working as well as an *out*working. "By grace [or free gift] you have been saved through faith, and this is not your own doing [nor of any human working]; it is the gift of God—not the results of works, so that no one may boast" (Eph. 2:8-9).

To him who "dwelleth in the secret place of the most High,"

there is promised immunity from "the snare of the fowler" and "the deadly pestilence," from "the terror by night" and "the arrow that flieth by day" (Ps 91:1, 3, 5 KJV); and even immunity from *fear* of these things. Oh, the awfully paralyzing effect of fear and evil! It makes us helpless as babes. It makes us ants, whereas we might be giants were we only free from it. It is at the root of all our failures, of nearly all sickness, poverty, and distress. But we have the promise of deliverance from even the fear and evil when we are in the "secret place." "Thou shalt not be afraid for the terror by night" (Ps. 91:5 KJV), and so forth.

> "For he will hide me in his shelter
> in the day of trouble;
> he will conceal me under the cover of his tent."
> —Psalm 27:5

> "In the shelter of your presence you hide them
> from human plots;
> you hold them safe under your shelter
> from contentious tongues."
> —Psalm 31:20

The secret place! Why called a *secret* place? What is it? Where may we find it? How abide in it?

It is a secret place because it is a place of meeting between the Christ at the center of your being and your consciousness—a hidden place into which no outside person can either induct you or enter himself. We must drop the idea that this place of realization of our divinity can be given to us by any human being. No one can come into it from the outside. Hundreds of earnest persons are seeking, night and day, to get this inner revealing. They run from teacher to teacher, many of them making the most frantic efforts to meet the financial obligations thus incurred.

You may study with human teachers and from man-made books until doomsday; you may get all the theological lore of the ages; you may understand intellectually all the statements of Truth, and be able to prate healing formulas as glibly as oil flows, but until there is a definite inner revealing of the reality of an indwelling Christ through whom and by whom come life, health, peace, power, *all* things—aye, who *is* all things—you have not yet found "the friendship of the Lord" (Ps. 25:14).

In order to gain this knowledge—this consciousness of God within themselves—many are willing (and wisely so, for this is greater than all other knowledge) to spend all they possess. Even Paul, after twenty-five years of service and of most marvelous preaching, said: "I regard everything as loss because of the surpassing value of knowing Christ Jesus my Lord.... I regard them as rubbish, in order that I may gain Christ [or the consciousness of his divine Self]" (Phil. 3:8).

Beloved, that which you so earnestly desire will never be found by your seeking it through the mental side alone, any more than it has heretofore been found through the emotional side alone. Intuition and intellect are meant to travel together, intuition always holding the reins to guide intellect. "Come now, and let us reason together, saith the Lord" (Is. 1:18 KJV). If you have been thus far on the way cultivating and enlarging only the mental side of Truth, as probably is the case, you need, in order to come into the fullness of understanding, to let the mental, the reasoning side rest awhile. "Become like children" (Mt. 18:3), and learning how to be still, listen to that which the Father will say to you through the intuitional part of your being. The light that you so crave will come out of the deep silence and become manifest to you from within yourself, if you will but keep still and look for it from that source.

And conscious knowledge of an indwelling God, which we so crave, is that of which Paul wrote to the Colossians, as "the mystery that has been hidden throughout the ages and generations but has now been revealed to his saints.... Christ in you, the hope of glory" (Col. 1:26-27). "The secret place of the most High" (Ps. 91:1 KJV), where each one of us may dwell and be safe from all harm or fear of evil, is the point of mystical union between man and Spirit (or God in us), wherein we no longer believe, but know, that God in Christ abides always at the center of our being as our perfect health, deliverance, prosperity, power, ready to come forth into manifestation at any moment we claim it. We know it. We *know* it. We feel our oneness with the Father, and we manifest this oneness.

To possess the secret of anything gives one power over it. This personal, conscious knowledge of the Father in us is the secret that is the key to all power. What we want is the revelation to us of this marvelous "secret." What will give it to us—who can give it to us except Him, the "Spirit of truth who comes from the Father" (Jn. 15:26)? Surely none other. That which God would say to you and do through you is a great secret that no man on the face of the earth knows, or ever will know, except yourself as it is revealed to you by the Spirit that is in you. The secret that He tells me is not revealed to you, nor yours to me; but each man must, after all is said and done, deal directly with the Father through the Son within himself.

Secrets are not told upon the housetop; nor is it possible to pass this, the greatest of secrets, from one to another. God, the creator of our being, must Himself whisper it to each man living in the very innermost of himself. "To everyone who conquers [or is consciously in process of overcoming] I will give some of the hidden manna, and I will give a white stone [or a mind like a clean white tablet], and on the white stone is written a new name that no one knows except the one who receives it" (Rev. 2:17). It is so secret that it cannot even be put into human language or repeated by human lips.

What you want today and what I want is that the words that we have learned to say as Truth be made alive to us. We want a revelation of God in us as life, to be made to our own personal consciousness as health. We no longer care to have somebody just tell us the words from the outside. We want a revelation of God as love within us, so that our whole being will be filled and thrilled with love—a love that will not have to be pumped up by a determined effort because we know that it is right to love and wrong not to love, but a love that will flow with the spontaneity and fullness of an artesian well, because it is so full at the bottom that it *must* flow out.

What we want today is a revelation to our consciousness of God within us as omnipotent power so that we can, by a word—or a look—"accomplish that which I purpose, and succeed in the thing for which I sent it" (Is. 55:11). We want the manifestation to us of the Father in us so that we can know Him personally. We want to be conscious of God working in us "both to will and to work" (Phil. 2:13) so that we may "work out" our "salvation" (Phil. 2:12). We have been learning how to do the outworking but have now come to a point where we must learn more of how to place ourselves in an attitude where we can each be conscious of the divine inner working.

Mary talked with the risen Jesus, supposing that he was the gardener, until suddenly, as he spoke her name, there flashed into her consciousness a ray of pure intelligence, and in an instant the revelation of his identity was made to her.

According to the same sacred history, Thomas Didymus had walked daily for three years with the most wonderful teacher of spiritual things that has ever lived. He had watched this teacher's life and had been partaker of his very presence, physical and mental. He had had just what you and I have thus far received of mental training and external teaching. But there came a time when there was an inner revealing that made him exclaim, "My Lord and my God!" (Jn. 20:28) The secret name, which no other man could know for him, had that moment been given to him. There had come, in the twinkling of an eye, the manifestation to his consciousness of the Father in him as his Lord and his God. No longer simply our Father and our Lord, but my Lord and my God—my divine Self revealed to me personally.

Is not this that which you are craving?

Each man must come to a time when he no longer seeks external helps, when he knows that the inner revelation of "my Lord and my God" to his consciousness can come to him only through an indwelling power that has been there all the time, waiting with infinite longing and patience to reveal the Father to the child.

This revelation will never come through the intellect of man to the consciousness, but must ever come through the intuitional to the intellect as a manifestation of Spirit to man. "Those who are unspiritual do not receive [or impart] the gifts of God's Spirit, for they are foolishness to them, and they are unable to understand them because they are spiritually discerned" (1 Cor. 2:14), and they must be spiritually imparted.

In our eagerness, we have waited upon every source that we could reach for the light that we want. Because we have not known how to wait upon Spirit within us for the desired revelation, we have run to and fro. Let no one misunderstand me in what I say about withdrawing himself from teachers. Teachers are good and are necessary, up to a certain point. "How are they to call on one in whom they have not believed? And how are they to believe in one of whom they have never heard? And how are they to hear without someone to proclaim him?" (Rom. 10:14)

Books and lectures are good, teachers are good, but you must learn for yourself that Christ, the Son of God, lives in you, that He within you is your light and life and all. When you have once grasped this beyond a doubt with the intellect, you cease looking to teachers to bring you spiritual insight. That Christ lives in you, Spirit itself must reveal to you. Teachers talk about the light, but the light itself must flash into the darkness before you can see the light.

Had the Master remained with the disciples, I doubt whether they would ever have gotten beyond hanging on his words and following in the footsteps of his personality.

Jesus knew that his treatments for spiritual illumination, given to his disciples from his recognition of Truth, would act in them as a seed thought, but he also knew that each man must for himself wait upon God for the inner illumination which is lasting and real. God alone can whisper the secret to each one separately.

The enduement of power was not to come to them by the spoken word through another personality, not even through that of Jesus, with his great spiritual power and discernment. It was to come from "on high" (Is. 32:15) to each individual consciousness. It was the "promise of the Father, which ... ye have heard of me" (Acts 1:4 KJV). He had merely told them about it but had no power to give it to them.

So to each of us this spiritual illumination that we are crying out after, this enduement of power for which we are willing to sell all that we have, must come from "on high," that is, to the consciousness from the Spirit within our being. This is the secret that the Father longs with an infinite yearning to reveal to each individual. It is because of the Father's desire within us to show us the secret that we desire the revelation. It is the purpose for which we came into the world—that we might grow step-by-step, as we are doing, to the place where we could bear to have the secret of His inner abiding revealed to us.

Do not be confused by seeming contradictions in the lessons. I have said heretofore that too much introspection is not good. I repeat it, for there are those who, in earnest desire to know God, are always seeking light for themselves but neglect to use that which they already have to help others.

There must be an equal conscious receiving from the Father and giving out to the world, a perfect equilibrium between the inflowing and the outgiving, to keep perfect harmony. We must each learn how to wait renewedly upon God for the infilling and then go and give out to every creature that which we have received, as Spirit leads us to give, either in preaching, teaching, or silently living the Truth. That which fills us will radiate from us without effort right in the place in life where we stand.

In nearly all teaching of Truth from the purely mental side, there is much said about the working out of our salvation by the holding of right thoughts, by denials and affirmations. This is all good. But there is another side that we need to know a little more about. We must learn how to be still and let Spirit, the I AM, work in us, that we may indeed be made "a new creation" (Gal. 6:15), that we may have the mind of Christ in all things.

When you have learned how to abandon yourself to infinite Spirit and have seasons of doing this daily, you will be surprised at the marvelous change that will be wrought in you without any conscious effort of your own.

It will search far below your conscious mind and root out things in your nature of which you have scarcely been conscious, simply because they have lain latent there, waiting for something to bring them out. It will work into your consciousness light and life and love and all good, perfectly filling all your lack while you just quietly wait and receive. Of the practical steps in this direction, we will speak in another lesson.

Paul, who had learned this way of faith, this way of being still and letting the I AM work itself into his conscious mind as the fullness of all his needs, was neither afraid nor ashamed to say:

"For this reason I bow my knees before the Father, from whom every family in heaven and on earth takes its name. I pray that, according to the riches of his glory, he may grant that you may be strengthened in your inner being with power through his Spirit, and that Christ may dwell in your hearts through faith, as you are being rooted and grounded in love. I pray that you may have the power to comprehend, with all the saints, what is the breadth and length and height and depth, and to know the love of Christ that surpasses knowledge, so that you may be filled with all the fullness of God" (Eph. 3:14-19).

And then he gives an ascription: "To him who by the power at work within us is able to accomplish abundantly far more than all we can ask or imagine" (Eph. 3:20).

Tenth Lesson
FINDING THE SECRET PLACE

How to seek the secret place—where to find it—how to abide in it—these are questions that today, more than at any other time in the history of the world, are engaging the hearts of men. More than anything else it is what I want. It is what you want.

All the steps that we are taking by speaking words of Truth and striving to manifest the light that we have already received are carrying us on swiftly to the time when we shall have consciously the perfect mind of Christ, with all the love and beauty and health and power which that implies.

We need not be anxious or in a hurry for the full manifestation. Let us not at any time lose sight of the fact that our desire, great as it is, is only God's desire in us. "No one can come to me, unless drawn by the Father who sent me" (Jn. 6:44). The Father in us desires to reveal to us the secret of His presence, else we had not known any hunger for the secret or for Truth.

"You did not choose me but I chose you. And I appointed you to go and bear fruit" (Jn. 15:16).

Whoever you are that read these words, wherever you stand in the world, be it on the platform preaching the gospel or in the humblest little home seeking Truth, that you may make it manifest in a sweeter, stronger, less selfish life, know once and forever that you are not seeking God, but God is seeking you. Your longing for greater manifestation is the eternal energy that holds the worlds in their orbits, *outpushing* through you to get into fuller manifestation. You need not worry. You need not be anxious. You need not strive—only *let* it. Learn how to let it.

After all our beating about the bush, seeking here and there for our heart's desire, we must come right to Him who is the fulfillment of every desire, who waits to manifest more of Himself to us and through us. If you wanted my love or anything that I am (not that I *have*), you would not go to Tom Jones or to Mary Smith to get it. Either of these persons might tell you that I could and would give myself, but you would have to come directly to me and receive of me that which only I am, because I am it.

In some way, after all our seeking for the light and Truth, we must learn to wait, each one for himself, upon God for this inner revelation of Truth and our oneness with Him.

The light that we want is not some thing that God has to give; it is God Himself. God does not give us life or love as a thing. God is life and light and love. More of Himself in our consciousness, then, is what we all want, no matter what other name we may give it.

My enduement of power must come from "on high," from a higher region within myself than my present conscious mind; so must yours. It must be a descent of the Holy (whole, entire, complete) Spirit at the center of your being into your conscious mind. The illumination we want can never come in any other way, nor can the power to make good manifest.

We hear a great deal about "sitting in the silence." To many, it does not mean very much, for they have not yet learned how to "wait ... upon God" (Ps. 62:5 KJV), or to hear any voice except external ones. Noise belongs to the outside world, not to God. God works in the stillness, and we can so wait upon the Father of our being as to be conscious of the still, inner working—conscious of the fulfillment of our desires. "Those who seek the Lord lack no good thing" (Ps. 34:10). "Those who wait for the Lord shall renew their strength" (Is. 40:31).

In one of Edward Everett Hale's stories, he speaks of a little girl who, amidst her play with the butterflies and birds in a country place, used to run into a nearby chapel frequently to pray, and after praying, always remained perfectly still a few minutes. "Waiting," she said, "to see if God wanted to say anything" to her. Children are often nearest the kingdom.

When beginning the practice of sitting in the silence, do not feel that you must go and sit with some other person. The presence of another personality is apt to distract the mind. Learn first how to commune alone with the Creator of the universe, who is all-companionship. When you are able to withdraw from the outside and be alone with Him, then sitting with others may be profitable to you and to them.

There are those who are quite able to still their minds from all outside thoughts, but who, as soon as they get still, find themselves floating out on the astral or psychic plane where spirits of those departed, appear to them, wanting recognition and communication. Right here is a tremendous temptation. The experience is a new one and is more or less fascinating, but if you want the *highest* that is for you, this should not be for a moment yielded to. If, when you begin to get still you find this taking place, get up resolutely and shake it off. Declare it is not what you want; you want the highest spiritual illumination and will not take any other or be intruded upon. If necessary, in order to free yourself, postpone your sitting until another time, when perhaps you will have no trouble.

The psychic plane is all good upon its own level. But it is not what you are seeking. You want your own Spirit brought forth, in all its glorious fullness and Godlikeness, into manifestation. And if you stop on a lower plane to dabble with things there, it will only retard the day of your own realization and manifestation. Put it down at once and it will soon cease to trouble you.[1]

1. The preceding two paragraphs had been deleted from recent editions. We have returned them for their superb commentary on the importance of "psychic" phenomena. Beginners on the path should be assured that the experience Cady refers to here is not a common experience and it is not to be feared.

"Sitting in the silence" is not merely a sort of lazy drifting. It is a passive, but a definite, waiting upon God. When you want to do this, take a time when you are not likely to be disturbed, and when you can, for a little while, lay off all care. Begin your silence by lifting up your heart in prayer to the Father of your being. Do not be afraid that, if you begin to pray, you will be too "orthodox." You are not going to supplicate God, who has already given you "whatever you ask for" (Mk. 11:24). You have already learned that before you call He has sent that which you desire; otherwise, you would not desire it.

You know better than to plead with or to beseech God with an unbelieving prayer. But spending the first few moments of your silence in speaking directly to the Father centers your mind on the Eternal. Many who earnestly try to get still and wait upon God have found that the moment they sit down and close their eyes, their thoughts, instead of being concentrated, are filled with every sort of vain imagination. The most trivial things, from the fixing of a shoestring to the gossipy conversation of a week ago, chase one another in rapid succession through their minds, and at the end of an hour, the persons have gained nothing. This is to them discouraging.

This is but a natural result of trying not to think at all. Nature abhors a vacuum, and if you make (or try to make) your mind a vacuum, the thought images of others that fill the atmosphere about you will rush in to fill it, leaving you as far away from the consciousness of the divine Presence as ever. You can prevent this by beginning your silence with prayer.

It is always easier for the mind to say realizingly, *"Thy will is being done in me now,"* after having prayed, "Let Thy will be done in me." It is always easier to say with realization, *"God flows through me as life and peace and power,"* after having prayed, "Let Thy life flow through me anew while I wait." Of course prayer does not change God's attitude toward us, but it is easier for the human mind to take several successive steps with firmness and assurance than for it to take one big, bold leap to a point of eminence and hold itself steady there. While you are thus concentrating your thoughts on God, in definite conversation with the author of your being, no outside thought images can possibly rush in to torment or distract you. Your mind, instead of being open toward the external, is closed to it, and open only to God, the source of all the good you desire.

Of course there is to be no set form of words used. But sometimes using words similar to the first few verses of the 103rd Psalm, in the beginning of the silent communion, makes it a matter of face-to-face speaking: "You forgive all my iniquities [or mistakes]; You heal all my diseases; You redeem my life from destruction; and crown me with loving-kindness, now, now, while I wait upon You." Sometimes we may enter into the inner chamber with the words of a familiar hymn:

> Thou art the life within me,
> O Christ, Thou King of Kings
> Thou art Thyself the answer
> To all my questionings.

Repeat the words many times, not anxiously or with strained effort, not reaching out and up and away to an outside God; but let the petition be the quiet, earnest uplifting of the heart to a higher something right within itself, even to "the Father ... in me" (Jn. 14:11). Let it be made with the quietness and assurance of a child speaking to his loving father.

Some persons carry in their faces a strained, white look that comes from an abnormal "sitting in the silence," as they term it. It is hard for them to know that God is right here within them, and while in the silence they fall into the way of reaching away out and up after Him. Such are earnest men truly feeling after God if haply they may find Him, when all the time He is near them, even in their very hearts. Do not reach out thus. This is as though a seed were planted in the earth, and just because it recognized a vivifying, life-giving principle in the sun's rays, it did nothing but strain and stretch itself upward and outward to get more of the sun. You can see at a glance that by so doing it would get no solid roots in the earth where God intended them to be. The seed needs to send roots downward while it keeps its face turned toward the sun and lets itself be drawn upward by the sun.

Some of us, in our desire to grow and having recognized the necessity of waiting upon God in the stillness for the vivifying and renewing of life, make the mistake of climbing up and away from our bodies. Such abnormal outstretching and upreaching is neither wise nor profitable. After a little of it, one begins to get cold feet and congested head. While one is thus reaching out, the body is left alone, and it becomes correspondingly weak and negative. This is all wrong. We are not to reach out away from the body even after the Son of righteousness. We are, rather, to be still and let the Son shine on us right where we are. The sun draws the shoot up as fast as it can bear it and be strong. We do not need to grow ourselves, only to let the Son "grow" us.

But we are consciously to let it, not merely to take the attitude of negatively letting it by not opposing it, but to put ourselves consciously where the Son can shine on us and then "be still, and know" (Ps. 46:10) that while we wait there, it is doing the work. While waiting upon God, we should, as much as possible, relax ourselves both mentally and physically. To use a very homely but practical illustration, take much the attitude of the entire being as do the fowl when taking a sunbath in the sand. Yet there is something more than a lax passivity to be maintained through it all. There must be a sort of conscious, active taking of that which God gives freely to us.

Let me see if I can make it plain. First, withdraw yourself bodily and mentally from the outside world. "Go into your room and shut the door [the closet of your being, the very innermost part of yourself]" (Mt. 6:6), by turning your thoughts within. Just say: *You abide within me; You are alive there now; You have all power; You are now the answer to all I desire; You do now radiate Yourself from the center of my being to the circumference, and out into the visible world as the fullness of my desire.* Then be still, absolutely still. Relax every part of your being, and believe that it is being done. The divine substance does flow in at the center and out into the visible world every moment you wait; for it is an immutable law that "everyone who asks receives" (Mt. 7:8). And substance will come forth as the fulfillment of your desire if you expect it to. "According to your faith let it be done to you" (Mt. 9:29).

If you find your mind wandering, bring it right back by saying again: *It is being done; You are working in me; I am receiving that which I desire,* and so forth. Do not look for signs and wonders; but just be still and know that the very thing you want is flowing in and will come forth into manifestation either at once or a little further on.

Go even beyond this and speak words of thanksgiving to this innermost Presence, that it has heard and answered, that it does now come forth into visibility. There is something about the mental act of thanksgiving that seems to carry the human mind far beyond the region of doubt into the clear atmosphere of faith and trust, where "all things are possible" (Mt. 19:26). Even if at first you are not conscious of having received anything from God, do not worry or cease from your thanksgiving. Do not return to the asking, but continue giving thanks that while you waited you did receive and that what you received is now manifest; and believe me, you will soon rejoice and give thanks, not rigidly from a sense of duty, but because of the sure manifest fulfillment of your desire.

Do not let waiting in the silence become a bondage to you. If you find yourself getting into a strained attitude of mind, or "heady," get up and go about some external work for a time. Or, if you find that your mind will wander, do not insist on concentrating; for the moment you get into a rigid mental attitude, you shut off all inflow of the Divine into your consciousness. There must be a sort of relaxed passivity and yet an active taking it by faith. Shall I call it *active passivity*?

Of course, as we go in spiritual understanding and desire, we very soon come to the place where we want more than anything else that the desires of infinite wisdom and love be fulfilled in us. "My thoughts are not your thoughts, nor are your ways my ways, says the Lord. For as the heavens are higher than the earth, so are my ways higher than your ways and my thoughts than your thoughts" (Is. 55:8-9).

Our desires are God's desires, but in a limited degree. We soon throw aside our limitations, our circumscribed desires (as soon, at least, as we see that more of God means more of good and joy and happiness), and with all our hearts, we cry out in the silent sitting: *Fulfill Thy highest thought in me now!* We make ourselves as clay in the potter's hands, willing to be molded anew, to be "transformed into the same image" (2 Cor. 3:18), to be made after the mind of the indwelling Christ.

We repeat from time to time, while waiting, words something like these: *You are now renewing me according to Your highest thought for me; You are radiating Your very Self throughout my entire being, making me like Yourself—for there is nothing else but You, Father, I thank You, I thank You.* Be still, be still while He works. "Not by might, nor by power, but by my spirit, says the Lord of hosts" (Zech. 4:6).

While you thus wait and let Him, He will work marvelous changes in you. You will have a strange new consciousness of serenity and quiet, a feeling that something has been done, that some new power to overcome has come to you. You will be able to say, "The Father and I are one" (Jn. 10:30) with a new meaning, a new sense of reality and awe that will make you feel very still. Oh! how one conscious touch of the Oversoul makes all life seem different! All the hard things become easy; the troublesome things no longer have power to worry; the rasping people and things of the world lose all power to annoy. Why? Because, for the time, we see things from the Christ side of ourselves; we see as He sees. We do not have to deny evil; we know in that moment that it is nothing at all. We no longer rigidly affirm the good from sense of duty, but with delight and spontaneity, because we cannot help it. It is revealed to us as good. Faith has become reality.

Do not be discouraged if you do not at once get conscious results in this silent sitting. Every moment that you wait, Spirit is working to make you a new creation in Christ—a creation possessing consciously His very own qualities and powers. There may be a working for days before you see any change, but it will surely come. You will soon get so that you can go into the silence, into conscious communion with your Lord, at a moment's notice, at any time, in any place.

There is no conflict or inconsistency between this waiting upon God to be made perfect and the way of "speaking the word" out toward the external to make perfection visible. Waiting upon and consciously receiving from the Source only make the outspeaking (the holding of right thoughts and words) easy, instead of laborious. Try it and see.

Clear revelation—the word made alive as Truth to the consciousness—must come to every man who continues to wait upon God. But remember, there are two conditions imposed. You are to wait upon God, not simply to run in and out, but to abide, to dwell "in the secret place of the most High" (Ps. 91:1 KJV).

Of course I do not mean that you are to give all the time to sitting alone in meditation and silence, but that your mind shall be continually in an attitude of waiting upon God, not an attitude of clamoring for things, but of listening for the Father's voice and expecting a manifestation of the Father to your consciousness.

Jesus, our Master in spiritual knowledge and power, had many hours of lone communion with the Father, and his greatest works were done after these. So may we, so must we, commune alone with the Father if we would manifest the Christ. But Jesus did not spend all his time in receiving. He poured forth into everyday use, among the children of men in the ordinary vocations of life, that which he received of the Father. His knowledge of spiritual things was used constantly to uplift and to help other persons. We must do likewise, for newness of life and of revelation flows in the faster as we give out that which we have to help others. "Go, preach .... Heal the sick ... freely ye have received, freely give" (Mt. 10:7-8 KJV), he said. Go manifest the Christ within you, which you have received of the Father. God works in us to will and to do, but we must work out our own salvation.

The second indispensable condition to finding the secret place and abiding in it is "my hope is from him":

> "For God alone my soul waits in silence,
>   for my hope is from him."
>   —Psalm 62:5

"Truly in vain is salvation hoped for from the hills, and from the multitude of mountains: truly in the Lord our God is the salvation of Israel" (Jer. 3:23 KJV). It is good that a man should both hope and quietly wait for the salvation of the Lord.

Is your hope from Him, or is it from books or teachers or friends or meetings or societies?

"The king of Israel, the Lord, is in your midst" (Zeph. 3:15). Think of it—in the midst of you—at the center of your being this moment while you read these words. Say it, say it, think it, dwell on it, whoever you are, wherever you are! In the midst of you! Then what need for all this running around? What need for all this strained outreaching after Him?

"The Lord, your God, is in your midst [not just God in the midst of others, but in the midst of you, standing right where you are], a warrior who gives victory; he will rejoice over you with gladness, he will renew you in his love; he will exult over you with loud singing" (Zeph. 3:17). You are His love. It is you that He will rejoice in with singing if you will turn away from people to Him within you. His singing and joy will so fill you that your life will be a great thanksgiving.

The Lord is the Lord within our own being. The Lord is the Christ of our own being.

There is one Spirit, one Father of all, in us all, but who manifests uniquely in each of us. Your Lord is He who will deliver you out of all your troubles. Your Lord has no other business but to manifest Himself to you and through you, and so make you mighty with His own mightiness made visible, whole with His health, perfect by showing forth the Christ perfection.

Standing in the place of intellect or conscious mind, we thus look to Spirit. Spirit flows in and illumines intellect making it see its oneness with Spirit; and then we—conscious mind—stand at the center, and, looking from within outward say, "The Father and I are one."

Let all your hope be from your Lord. Let your communion be with Him. Wait upon the inner abiding Christ often, just as you would wait upon any visible teacher. When you are sick "wait thou only upon God" (Ps. 62:5 KJV) as the Most High, rather than upon healers. When you lack wisdom in small or large matters, "wait thou only upon God," and see what marvelous wisdom for action will be given you. When desiring to speak the word that will deliver another from the bondage of sickness or sin or sorrow, "wait thou only upon God" and exactly the right word will be given you, and power will go with it, for it will be alive with the power of Spirit.

Eleventh Lesson
SPIRITUAL GIFTS

It is very natural for the human heart first to set out in search of Truth because of the "loaves and the fish" (Mt. 15:36).

Perhaps it is not too much to say that the majority of people first turn to God because of some weakness, some failure, some almost unbearable want in their lives. After having vainly tried in all other ways to overcome or to satisfy the want, they turn in desperation to God.

There is in the heart of even the most depraved human being, though he would not for worlds have others know it, an instinctive feeling that somewhere there is a power that is able to give him just what he wants; that if he could only reach that which to his conception is God, he could prevail on Him to grant the things desired. This feeling is itself God-given. It is the divine Self, though only a spark at the center of the man's being, suggesting to him the true remedy for all his ills.

Especially have people been led to seek Truth for the reward, for "the works themselves" (Jn. 14:11), during the last few years, since they have come to know that God is not only able, but willing, to deliver them from all the burdens of their everyday life. Everyone wants to be free, free, free as the birds of the air—free from sickness, free from suffering, free from bondage, free from poverty, free from all forms of evil—and he has a right to be; it is a God-given desire and a God-given right.

Thus far nearly all teaching has limited the manifestation of infinite love to one form—that of healing. Sickness, seemingly incurable disease, and suffering reigned on every side, and every sufferer wanted to be free. We had not yet known that there was willingness as there was power—aye, more, that there was intense desire—on the part of our Father to give us something more than sweet, patient submission to suffering.

When first the Truth was taught that the divine Presence ever lives in man as perfect life and can be drawn on by our recognition and faith to come forth into full and abounding health, it attracted widespread attention, and justly so. Both teachers and students centered their gaze on this one outcome of a spiritual life, losing sight of any larger, fuller, or more complete manifestation of the indwelling Father. Teachers told all of their pupils most emphatically that this knowledge of Truth would enable them to heal, and they devoted all of their teaching to explanation of the principles and to giving formulas and other instructions for healing the body. This has brought both disappointment and discouragement to many. Failing to heal, they have, for the time, abandoned the entire principle. Time has shown that there are larger and broader views of the Truth about spiritual gifts.

Healing of the body is beautiful and good. Power to heal *is* a divine gift, and as such you are fully justified in seeking it. But God wants to give you infinitely more.

Why should you and I restrict the limitless One to the bestowal of a particular gift, unless, indeed, we be so fairly consumed with an inborn desire for it that we are sure that it is God's highest desire for us? In that case, we shall not have to try to heal. Healing will flow from us wherever we are. Even in a crowd of people, without any effort of our own, the one who *needs* healing will receive it from us; that one will "touch" (Mt. 9:21) us, as did the one woman in all the multitude jostling and crowding against Jesus. Only one *touched* him.

The power to heal the body has heretofore been, as I have already said, set up as a test of one's spiritual understanding.

At first, all who come into some knowledge of the Truth do heal more or less; but there comes a time to many when, in their onward growth, they fail to heal.

This has brought great disappointment not unmixed with considerable humiliation. But, my dear friends, do not let such an experience discourage you. It only means that *God is leading you upward into higher things.* Every denial of evil and affirmation of good you have made has served to push you upward. Do not fear or get nervous because you seem to "fail." Failure is often success written with a capital S.

The time has probably come in your spiritual growth when you are no longer to cling to just the one spiritual gift. God's thoughts for you are not as your thoughts for yourself. "For as the heavens are higher than the earth, so are my ways higher than your ways and my thoughts than your thoughts" (Is. 55:9).

Healing is truly a "branch" of "the vine" (Jn. 15:4), but it is not the only branch. There are many branches, all of which are necessary to the perfect vine, which is seeking through you and me to bear much fruit. What God wants is that we shall grow into such conscious oneness with Him, such realization that He who is the substance of all good really abides in us, that "ask for whatever you wish, and it will be done for you" (Jn. 15:7).

If you are faithfully and earnestly living what Truth you know and still find that your power to heal is not so great as it was at first, recognize it as All-Good. Be assured, no matter what anyone else says to you or thinks, that the seeming failure does not mean loss of power. It means that you are to let go of the lesser in order that you may grasp the whole in which the lesser is included. Do not fear for a moment to let go of just this one little branch of divine power; choose rather to have the highest thoughts of Infinite Mind, let them be what they may, fulfilled through you. We need to take our eyes off the ends of the branches, the results, and keep them centered in the vine.

Some are excellent physical healers but it is astonishing how little their other spiritual gifts are developed. At least, it would be astonishing if we did not know that healing is probably their special gift. Divine life flows through them in great abundance because, to them, physical life and health are the highest desire and attainment. Hence they become channels for divine Presence to flow through in that one direction alone. They are chosen vessels for that purpose.

You are a vessel for some purpose. If, when the time comes, you let go cheerfully, without humiliation or shame or sense of failure, your tense, rigid mortal grasp on some particular form of manifestation, such as healing, and "strive for the greater gifts" (1 Cor. 12:31), whatever they may be in your individual case, you will do "works" in the one specific direction that will be simply marvelous in the eyes of men. These works will be done without effort on your part, because they will be God, omnipotent, omniscient, manifesting Himself through you in His own chosen direction.

Paul said: "Now concerning spiritual gifts, brothers and sisters, I do not want you to be uninformed.... There are varieties of gifts, but the same Spirit .... To one is given through the Spirit the utterance of wisdom, and to another the utterance of knowledge according to the same Spirit ... faith ... gifts of healing ... the working of miracles ... prophecy ... discernment of spirits ... various kinds of tongues, to another the interpretation of tongues" (1 Cor. 12:1, 4, 8-10).

Spirit is always and forever the same, one God, one Spirit, but in different forms of manifestation. The gift of healing is no more, no greater, than the gift of prophecy; the gift of prophecy is no greater than faith, for faith (when it is really God's faith manifested through us), even as a grain of mustard seed, shall be able to remove mountains. The working of miracles is no greater than the power to discern spirits (or the thoughts and intents of other men's hearts, which are open always to Spirit). And "greatest of these is love" (1 Cor. 13:13); for "love never ends" (1 Cor. 13:8) to melt down all forms of sin, sorrow, sickness, and trouble. "Love never ends."

"All these are activated by one and the same Spirit, who allots to each one individually just as the Spirit chooses. For just as the body is one and has many members, and all the members of the body, though many, are one body, so it is with Christ.... If the whole body were an eye [or gift of healing], where would the hearing be? If the whole body were hearing, where would the sense of smell be?... The eye cannot say to the hand, 'I have no need of you,' nor again the head to the feet, 'I have no need of you.' But as it is, God arranged the members in the body, each one of them, as he chose" (1 Cor. 12:11-12, 17, 21, 18).

Thus Paul enumerates some of the free "gifts" of the Spirit to those who will not limit the manifestations of the Holy One, but yield themselves to Spirit's desire within them. Why should we so fear to abandon ourselves to the workings of infinite love and wisdom? Why be so afraid to let Him have His own way with us and through us?

Has not the gift of healing, the only gift we have thus far sought, been a good and blessed one, not only to ourselves, but to all with whom we come in contact?

Then why should we fear to wait upon God with a perfect willingness that the Holy Spirit manifest itself through us as it will, knowing that, whatever the manifestation, it will be good—all good to us and to those around us!

Oh, for more men who have the courage to abandon themselves utterly to Infinite Will—men who dare let go every human being for guidance, and seeking the Christ within themselves, let the manifestation be what He wills!

Such courage might possibly mean, and probably would mean at first, a seeming failure, a going down from some apparent success that had been in the past. But the going down would only mean a mighty coming up, a most glorious resurrection of God into visibility through you in His own chosen way, right here and now. The failure, for the time, would only mean a grand, glorious success a little later on.

Do not fear failure, but call failure good, for it really is. Did not Jesus stand as an utter failure, to all appearances, when he stood dumb before Pilate, all his cherished principles come to naught, unable (yes, I say it, *unable* or else not tempted in all points as we are) to deliver himself, or to "demonstrate" over the agonizing circumstances of his position?[1]

But had he not "failed" right at that point, there never would have been the infinitely grander demonstration of the Resurrection a little later on. "Unless a grain of wheat falls into the earth and dies, it remains just a single grain; but if it dies, it bears much fruit" (Jn. 12:24). If you have clung to one spiritual gift because you were taught that, and you begin to fail, believe me, it is only the seeming death, the seeming disappearance, of one gift, in order that out of it may spring many new gifts— brighter, higher, fuller ones, because they are the ones that God has chosen for you.

Your greatest work will be done in your own God-appointed channel. If you will let Spirit possess you wholly, if you will to have the highest will done in you and through you continually, you will be quickly moved by it out of your present limitations, which a half success always indicates, into a manifestation as much fuller and more perfect and beautiful as is the new grain than the old seed, which had to fall into the ground and die.

Old ways must die. Failure is only the death of the old that there may be the hundredfold following. If there comes to you a time when you do not demonstrate over sickness, as you did at first, do not think that you need lean on others entirely. It is beautiful and good for another to "heal" you bodily by calling forth universal life through you, but right here there is something higher and better for you.

---

1. *Unable* in the sense of being unable to go against God's will. Our personal demonstrations must always be in harmony with and not in resistance to the will of God

Spirit, the Holy Spirit, which is God in movement, wants to teach you something, to open a bigger, brighter way to you. This apparent failure is His call to you to arrest your attention and turn you to Him.

> "Agree with God, and be at peace;
> in this way good will come to you."
> —Job 22:21

Turn to the divine Presence within yourself. Seek Him. Be still before Him. Wait upon God quietly, earnestly, but constantly and trustingly, for days—aye weeks, if need be! Let Him work in you, and sooner or later you will spring up into a resurrected life of newness and power that you never before dreamed of.

When these transition periods come, in which God would lead us higher, should we get frightened or discouraged, we only miss the lesson that He would teach and so postpone the day of receiving our own fullest, highest gift. In our ignorance and fear, we are thus hanging on to the old grain of wheat that we can see, not daring to let it go into the ground (of failure) and die (or fail), lest there be no resurrection, no newness of life, nothing bigger and grander to come out of it.

Oh, do not let us longer fear our God, who is all good, and who longs only to make us each one a giant instead of an ant!

What we all need to do above everything else is to cultivate the acquaintance or consciousness of Spirit within ourselves. We must take our attention off results and seek to live the life. Results will be "given to" (Mt. 6:33) us in greater measure when we turn our thoughts less to the "works" and more to embodying the indwelling Christ in our entire being. We have come to a time when there must be less talking about Truth, less treating and being treated merely for the purpose of being delivered from some evil result of wrong living; there must be more living of Truth and teaching others to do so. There must be more incorporating of Truth in our very flesh and bone.

How are you to do this?

"I am the way, and the truth, and the life" (Jn. 14:6), says the Christ at the center of your being.

"I am the vine, you are the branches. Those who abide [consciously] in me and I in them [in His consciousness], bear much fruit, because apart from me [or severed from me in your consciousness] you can do nothing.... If you abide in me, and my words abide in you, ask for whatever you wish, and it will be done for you" (Jn. 15:5, 7).

I do assure you, as do all teachers, that you can bring good things of whatever kind you desire into your life by holding to them as yours in the invisible until they become manifest. But, beloved, do you not see that your highest, your first—aye, your continual—thought should be to seek the abiding in Him, to seek the knowing as a living reality, not as a finespun theory that He abides in you? After that, ask what you will, be it power to heal, to cast out demons, or even the "greater works" (Jn. 14:12), and "it will be done for you" (Jn. 15:7).

There is one Spirit—"One God and Father of all, who is above all and through all and in all. But each of us was given grace [or free gift] according to the measure of Christ's gift" (Eph. 4:6-7)—in us.

"For this reason I remind you to rekindle the gift of God that is within you" (2 Tim. 1:6).

Do not be afraid, "for God did not give us a spirit of cowardice, but rather a spirit of power and of love and of self-discipline" (2 Tim. 1:7).

It is all one and the same Spirit. To be the greatest success, you do not want my gift, nor do I want yours; each wants his own, such as will fit his size and shape, his capacity and desires, such as not the human mind of us, but the highest in us, shall choose. Seek to be filled with Spirit, to have the reality of things incarnated in larger degree in your consciousness. Spirit will reveal to your understanding your own specific gift, or the manner of God's desired manifestation through you.

Let us not desert our own work, our own God within us, to gaze or pattern after our neighbor. Let us not seek to make his gift ours; let us not criticize his failure to manifest any specific gift. Whenever he "fails," give thanks to God that He is leading him into a higher place, where there can be a fuller and more complete manifestation of the divine Presence through him.

And "I ... beg you to lead a life worthy of the calling to which you have been called, with all humility and gentleness, with patience, bearing with one another in love, making every effort to maintain the unity of the Spirit in the bond of peace" (Eph. 4:1-3).

Twelfth Lesson
UNITY OF THE SPIRIT

If we did not know it as a living reality that behind all the multitude and variety of human endeavors to bring about the millennium there stands forever the master Mind, which sees the end from the beginning, the master Artist who, through human vessels as His hands, is putting on the picture here a touch of one color and there a touch of another according to the vessel used, we might sometimes be discouraged.

Were it not at times so utterly ridiculous, it would always be pitiful to see the human mind of man trying to limit God to personal comprehension as though the finite ever could completely encompass or comprehend the Infinite. However much any one of us may know of God, there will always be unexplored fields in the realms of expression, and it is evidence of our narrow vision to say: "This is all there is of God."

Suppose that a dozen persons are standing on the dark side of a wall in which are various sized openings. Viewing the scene outside through the opening assigned to him, one sees all there is within a certain radius. He says, "I see the whole world; in it are trees and fields." Another, through a larger opening, has a more extended view; he says, "I see trees and fields and houses; I see the whole world." The next one, looking through a still larger opening, exclaims: "Oh! You are all wrong! I alone see the whole world; I see trees and fields and houses and rivers and animals."

The fact is, each one looking at the same world sees according to the size of the aperture through which he is looking, and he limits the world to just his own circumscribed view of it. You would say at once that such limitation was only a mark of each man's ignorance and narrowness. Everyone would pity the man who thus displayed—aye, fairly vaunted—his ignorance.

From time immemorial, there have been schisms and divisions among religious sects and denominations. And now with the newer light that we have, even the light of the knowledge of one God immanent in all men, many still cling to external differences, so postponing, instead of hastening, the day of the millennium; at least they postpone it for themselves.

I want, if possible, to help break down the seeming "dividing wall" (Eph. 2:14), even as Christ, the living Christ, does in reality break down or destroy all misunderstanding. I want to help you to see that there is no real wall of difference between all the various sects of the new theology, except such as appear to you because of your circumscribed view. I want you to see, if you do not already, that every time you try to limit God's manifestation of Himself in any person or through any person, in order to make that manifestation conform to what you see as Truth, you are only crying loudly: "Ho! Everyone, come and view my narrowness and my ignorance!"

I want to stimulate you to lose sight of all differences, all side issues and lesser things, and seek but for one thing—that is the consciousness of the presence of an indwelling God in you and your life. And believe me, just as there is less separation between the spokes of a wheel the nearer they get to the hub, so you will find that the nearer you both come to the perfect Center, which is the Father, the less difference will there be between you and your brother.

The faith healer, he who professes to believe only in what he terms "divine healing" (as though there could be any other healing than divine), differs from the so-called spiritual scientist only in believing that he must ask, seek, knock, importune, before he can receive; while he of the Truth teaching knows that he has already received God's free gift of life and health and all things and that by speaking the word of Truth the gifts are made manifest. Both get like results (God made visible) through faith in the invisible. The mind of the one is lifted to a place of faith by asking or praying; the mind of the other is lifted to a place of faith by speaking words of Truth.

Is there any real difference?

The mental scientist usually scorns to be classed with either of the other two sects. He loudly declares that "all is mind" and that all the God he knows or cares anything about is the invincible, unconquerable *I* within him, which nothing can daunt or overcome.

He talks about conscious mind and subconscious mind, and he fancies that he has something entirely different from and infinitely higher than either of the other sects. He boldly proclaims, "I have Truth; the others are in error, too orthodox," and thus he calls the world's attention to the small size of the aperture through which he is looking at the stupendous whole.

Beloved, as surely as you and I live, it is all one and the same Truth. There may be a distinction, but it is without difference.

The happy person who will from his heart exclaim, "Praise the Lord!" no matter what occurs to him, and who thereby finds that "all things work together for good for those who love God " (Rom. 8:28), is in reality saying the "all is good" of the metaphysician. Each one does simply "in all your ways acknowledge him [or God, Good]" (Prov. 3:6), which is indeed a magical wand, bringing sure deliverance out of any trouble to all who faithfully use it.

The teachings of Spirit are intrinsically the same, because Spirit is one. I heard an uneducated woman speak in a most orthodox prayer meeting some time ago. She knew no more of religious science than a babe knows of Latin. Her face, however, was radiant with the light of the Christ manifest through her. She told how, five or six years before, she had been earnestly seeking to know more of God (seeking in prayer, as she knew nothing about seeking spiritual light from people), and one day, in all earnestness, she asked that some special word of His will might be given directly to her as a sort of private message. These words flashed into her mind: "If therefore thine eye be single, thy whole body shall be full of light.... No man can serve two masters" (Mt. 6:22, 24 KJV).

She had read these words many times, but that day they were illumined by Spirit; and she saw that to have an eye "single" meant seeing but one power in her life; while she saw two powers (God and devil, good and evil) she was serving two masters. From that day to this, though she had passed through all sorts of troublous circumstances—trials of poverty, illness in family, intemperate husband—she found always the most marvelous, full, and complete deliverance out of them all by resolutely adhering to the "single" eye—seeing God only. She would not look even for a moment at the seeming evil to combat it or rid herself of it, because, as she said, "Lookin' at God with one eye and this evil with the other is bein' double-eyed, and God told me to keep my eye single."

This woman, who had never heard of any science or metaphysical teaching or laws of mind was combating and actually overcoming the tribulations of this world by positively refusing to have anything but a single eye. She had been taught in a single day by infinite Spirit the whole secret of how to banish evil and have only good and joy in her. Isn't it all very simple?

At the center, all is one and the same God forevermore. I believe that the veriest heathen that ever lived, he who worships the golden calf as his highest conception of god, worships God. His mind has not yet expanded to a state where he can grasp any idea of God apart from a visible form, something that he can see with human eyes and handle with fleshly hands. But at heart, he is seeking something higher than his present conscious self to be his deliverance out of evil.

Are you and I, with all our boasted knowledge, doing anything more or different?

The Spirit at the center of even the heathen, who is God's child, is thus seeking, though blindly, its Father-God. Shall anyone dare to say that it will not find that which it seeks—its Father? Shall we not rather say it will find, because of that immutable law that "everyone who searches finds" (Mt. 7:8)?

You have now come to know that, at the center of your being, God (omnipotent power) ever lives. From the nature of your relationship to Him, and by His own immutable laws, you may become conscious of His presence and eternally abide in Him and He in you.

The moment that any man really comes to recognize that which is absolute Truth—namely, that one Spirit, even the Father, being made manifest in the Son, ever lives at the center of all human beings—he will know that he can cease forever from any undue anxiety about bringing others into the same external fold that he is in. If your friend or your son or your husband or your brother does not see Truth as you see it, do not try by repeated external arguments to convert him.

"And I, when I am lifted up from the earth, will draw all people to myself" (Jn. 12:32). That which is needed is not that you (the human, which is so fond of talk and argument) try to lift up your brother. The Holy Spirit, or Christ within him, declares: "And I, when I am lifted up ... will draw all people." You can silently lift up this *I* within the man's own being, and it will draw the man up unto—what? Your teaching? No, unto Christ, the Divine in him.

Keep your own light lifted by living the victorious life of Spirit. And then, remembering that your dear one, as well as yourself, is an incarnation of the Father, keep him silently committed to the care of his own divine Spirit. You do not know what God wants to do in him; you never can know.

If you fully recognize that the God that dwells in you dwells in all men, you know that each one's own Lord, the Christ within each one, will make no mistake. The greatest help that you can give to any man is to tell him silently, whenever you think of him: *The Holy Spirit lives within you; He cares for you, is working in you that which He would have you do, and is manifesting Himself through you.* Then let him alone. Be at perfect rest about him, and the result will be infinitely better than you could have asked.

Keep ever in mind that each living person in all God's universe is a radiating center of the same perfect One, some radiating more and some less, according to the awakened consciousness of the individual. If you have become conscious of this radiation in yourself, keep your thought centered right there, and the Spirit of the living God will radiate from you in all directions with mighty power, doing without noise or words a great work in lifting others up. If you want to help others who are not yet awakened to this knowledge, center your thoughts on this same idea of them—that they are radiating centers of the All-Perfect. Keep your eye "single" for them, as did the uneducated woman for herself, and Spirit will teach them more in a day than you could in years.

Throughout the ages, man has leaned to the idea of separateness instead of oneness. He has believed himself separate from God and separate from other men. And even in these latter days when we talk so much about oneness, most teachers of metaphysics manage again to separate God's children from Him by saying that while the child may suffer, the Father knows no suffering, nor does He take cognizance of the child's suffering; that we, His children, forever a part of Him, are torn and lacerated, while He, knowing nothing of this, goes on as serenely and indifferently as the full moon sails through the heavens on a winter night.

It is little wonder that many, to whom the first practical lessons in the gospel of the Christ came as liberation and power, should in time of failure and heartache have turned back to the old limited belief of the fatherhood of God.

There is no real reason why we, having come to recognize God as infinite substance, should be by this recognition deprived of the familiar fatherly companionship that in all ages has been so dear to the human heart. There is no necessity for us to separate God as substance and God as tender Father; no reason why we should not, and every reason why we should, have both in one; they are one—God principle outside of us as unchangeable law, God within us as tender, loving Father-Mother, who has compassion for our every sorrow.

There is no reason why, because in our earlier years some of us were forced into the narrow puritanical limits that stood for a religious belief, we should now so exaggerate our freedom as to fancy that we are entirely self-sufficient and shall never again need the sweet, uplifting communion between Father and child. The created, who ever lives, moves, and has his being in his Creator, needs the conscious presence of that Creator, and cannot be entirely happy in knowing God only as cold, unsympathetic principle. Why cannot both conceptions find lodgment in the minds and hearts? Both are true, and both are necessary parts of a whole. The two were made to go together, and in the highest, cannot be separated.

God as the underlying substance of all things, God as principle, is unchanging and does remain forever uncognizant of and unmoved by the changing things of time and sense. It is true that God as principle does not feel pain, is not moved by the cries of children of men for help. It is a grand, stupendous thought that this power is unchanging law, just as unchanging in its control of our affairs as it is in the government of the starry heavens. One is fairly conscious of his entire being expanding into grandeur as he dwells on the thought.

But this is not all, any more than the emotional side is all. True, there is law, but there is gospel also. Gospel does not make law of no effect; it fulfills law. God is principle, but God is individual also. Principle becomes individualized the moment it comes to dwell in external manifestation in a human body.

Principle does not change because of pity or sympathy, even "as a father has compassion for his children" (Ps. 103:13). The Father in us always moves into helpfulness when called on and trusted. It is as though infinite wisdom and power, which outside are Creator, Upholder, and Principle, become transformed into infinite love, which is Father-Mother, with all the warmth and tender helpfulness that this word implies, when they become focalized, so to speak, within a human body.

I do not at all understand it, but in some way, this indwelling One does move to lift the consciousness of His children up and to place it parallel with God, Principle, Law, so that no longer two are crossed, but the two—aye, the three—the human consciousness, the indwelling individual Father, and the Holy Spirit—are made one. In every life, with our present limited understanding, there come times when the bravest heart goes down, for the moment, under the apparent burdens of life; times when the strongest intellect bends like "a reed shaken by the wind" (Mt. 11:7), when the most self-sufficient mind feels a helplessness that wrings from it a cry for help from "the rock that is higher than I" (Ps. 61:2).

Every metaphysician either has reached, or must in the future reach, this place—the place where God as cold principle alone will not suffice any more than in the past God as personality alone could wholly satisfy. There will come moments when the human heart is so suddenly struck as to paralyze it, and for the moment it is impossible, even with strained effort, to think right thoughts.

At such times there will come but little comfort from the thought: This suffering comes as the result of my wrong thinking; but God, my Father, takes no cognizance of it: I must work it out unaided and alone. Just here we must have, and we do have, the motherhood of God, which is not cold principle any more than your love for your child is cold. I would not make God as principle less, but God as individual more.

The whole business of your Lord (the Father in you) is to care for you, to love you with an everlasting love, to note your slightest cry, and to rescue you.

Then you ask, "Why doesn't He do it?" Because you do not recognize His indwelling and His power, and by resolutely affirming that He does now manifest Himself as your all-sufficiency, call Him forth into visibility.

God (Father-Mother) is a present help in time of need; but there must be a recognition of His presence, a turning away from human efforts, and an acknowledgment of *God only* (a single eye) before He becomes manifest.

HOW I
USED
TRUTH

BOOK TWO

How I Used Truth was first published in 1916 under the title of *Miscellaneous Writings*; it was first published as *How I Used Truth* in 1939. There were seventeen editions printed through 1985; in 1986 a revised edition was published. There have been three printings of it through 1991, twenty editions in all.

FOREWORD

Because of repeated requests of many friends who have been helped by reading my various booklets and magazine articles, it seemed best to publish them all under one cover, to offer a convenient way for readers always to have help at hand. The articles that make up this volume have been written from time to time as a result of practical daily experience. In none of them is there anything occult or mysterious, neither has there been any attempt at literature. Each chapter is plain and simple.

In revising the articles, there have been a few nonessential changes, yet the Principle and its application remain the same. Truth is that *which is so*, and it can never change. Every true statement here is as true and as workable today as it was when these articles were written. We ask no one to believe that which is here written simply because it is presented as Truth. "Prove all things" for yourself; it is possible to prove every statement in this book. Every statement given was proved before it was written. No person can solve another's problem. Each must work out his own salvation. Here are some effectual rules, suggestions, and helps; results that one obtains from them will depend on how faithfully and persistently one uses the helps given.

I am grateful for the many words of appreciation that have come to me from time to time. These words are encouraging to one who is trying to solve her own life's problems, as you are trying to solve yours, by the teachings of the Master.

Lessons In Truth, because of its effective helpfulness, has been published in many languages and in braille for the blind. Let us hope that this book, now sent forth with the same objective—that of being a practical living help in daily life—may meet the same fate.

—H. Emilie Cady
January 1, 1916

Chapter 1
WHY?

The following is a letter written by H. Emilie Cady to Lowell Fillmore. In this letter, Dr. Cady says many helpful and inspiring things that we believe will be welcomed by those who read *How I Used Truth,* originally titled *Miscellaneous Writings.*

Dear Mr. Fillmore:

When I sent you, a few weeks ago, a copy of the little pamphlet *All-Sufficiency In All Things*, which you said had been surreptitiously printed by an anonymous publisher, you wondered why I felt so keenly about the fact the article had been broken up, put under different headings, and so forth. Let me tell you why.

Almost every one of the simply written articles in *Miscellaneous Writings [How I Used Truth]* was born out of the travail of my soul after I had been weeks, months, sometimes years trying by affirmations, by claiming the promises of Jesus Christ, using all the knowledge of Truth I possessed to deliver myself or others from some distressing bondage which defied all human help.

One of these cases was that of my own father, who, though perfectly innocent, had been kept in exile for five years, put there by the wicked machinations of another man. No process of law that I had invoked, no human help, not even the prayers that I had offered had seemed to avail for his deliverance. One day while sitting alone in my room, my hands busy with other things, my heart cried out, "O God, stretch forth Thy hand and deliver!" Instantly the answer came: "I have no hands but human hands. Your hand is my hand; stretch it forth spiritually and give whatsoever you will to whomsoever you will, and I will establish it."

Unquestioningly I obeyed. From that moment, without any further external help or striving, the way of his release was opened ahead of us more rapidly almost than we could step into it. Within a few days my dear father came home a free man, justified, exonerated, both publicly and privately, beyond anything we could have asked or thought.

The case was written up by all the papers in the country in which my father resided as well as in the *New York Sun*. His innocence was clearly established. Once again he sat happily under the trees of his own dooryard and received congratulations. Delegation after delegation came from miles around; friends who had known him from childhood came to assure him that his long life of uprightness had, in their minds, never been questioned. He was seventy-five years of age and, being an honest man, had felt the disgrace deeply. These staunch friends had been unable to help until God moved. The faith of many was renewed by his exoneration. I then wrote "God's Hand."

Another case was that of a dear young friend who had been placed in my care. He was just entering on a life of drinking and dissipation. There were weeks of awful anxiety, as I saw him drinking day by day, before I reached the place where I could "loose him, and let him go." When I did reach that place and stood there steadfastly (in spite of appearances), it required only a few hours to see him so fully healed that although forty years have passed, he has yet to touch a drop of liquor or indulge in any form of dissipation since that time. The lesson "Loose Him and Let Him Go" was then written.

Another was the dreadful question of money supply. I had a

good profession with plenty of patients paying their bills monthly. But there were also other people coming to me daily for help, people whose visible means of support were gone. These cases of lack, as they presented themselves to me, were like cases of gnawing cancer or painful rheumatism. Therefore, there must be a way out through Truth, and I must find it. As always, instead of rushing to others for help in these tight places, I stayed at home within my own soul and asked God to show me the way. He did. He gave me the clear vision of Himself as All-Sufficiency In All Things, and then He said: "Now prove it, so that you can be of real help to the hundreds who do not have a profession or business on which to depend." From that day on, no ministry or work of any kind was ever done by me for "pay." No monthly bills were sent, no office charges made. I saw plainly that I must be working as God works, without expectation or thought of return. Free gift.

For more than two years I worked at this problem, never letting a human being know what I was trying to prove, for had He not said to me, "Prove me now herewith ... if I will not open you the windows of heaven, and pour you out a blessing, that there shall not be room enough to receive it" (Mal. 3:10 KJV)?

More than once in the ongoing the body was faint for want of food, and yet, so sure was I of what God had shown me that day after day I taught cheerfully and confidently to those who came to my office the Truth of God as the substance of all supply— and there were many in those days. At the end of two years of apparent failure, I suddenly felt that I could not endure the privation any longer. Again, in near desperation from deferred hope of success, I went direct to God and cried out: "Why, why this failure? You told me in the vision that if I would give up the old way and trust to You alone, You would prove to me Your sufficiency. Why have You failed to do it?"

His answer came flashing back in these words: "God said, Let there be light: and there was light" (Gen. 1:3 KJV). It was all the answer He gave. At the moment I did not understand. I kept repeating it again and again, the words *God said* becoming more and more emphasized, until at last they were followed by the words "Without him [the Word] was not anything made that was made" (Jn. 1:3 KJV). That was all I needed. I saw plainly that while I had, for two years, hopefully and happily gone on enduring hardships, believing that God would supply, I had not once spoken the word: *It is done: God is now manifested as my supply.*

Believe me, that day I spoke the word of my deliverance. Suffice it to say that the supply problem was ended that day for all time and has never entered my life or mind since. This is the why of the article "The Spoken Word."

I should like to give one more "why" of *Miscellaneous Writings.*

After days of excruciating pain from a badly sprained ankle, the ankle became enormously swollen, and it was impossible for me to attend to my professional work as an active medical practitioner. Ordinary affirmations of Truth were entirely ineffectual, and I soon struck out for the very highest statement of Truth that I could formulate. It was this: *There is only God; all else is a lie.* I vehemently affirmed it and steadfastly stuck to it. In twenty-four hours all pain and swelling—in fact, the entire "lie"—had disappeared. Out of this experience I wrote "Unadulterated Truth."

You can see, dear Mr. Fillmore, that these children born, as I said before, out of the very travail of my soul, are precious to me, and how I felt I would rather never see them again than to see them changed in any way. I thank the Fillmores that they have kept them just as they were written, for they are God's own burning words to anyone suffering under like conditions, however simple they may seem to one not needing them.

Yours in His name,
H. Emilie Cady—1930

Chapter 2
FINDING THE CHRIST IN OURSELVES

Throughout all his teaching, Jesus tried to show those who listened to him how he was related to the Father and to teach them that they were related to the same Father in exactly the same way. Over and over he tried in different ways to explain to them that God lived within them, that He was "God not of the dead, but of the living" (Mt. 22:32). And never once did he assume to do anything of himself, always saying, "I do nothing on my own" (Jn. 8:28). "The Father who dwells in me does his works" (Jn. 14:10). But it was very hard then for people to understand, just as it is very hard for us to understand today.

There were, in the person of Jesus, two distinct regions. There was the fleshly, mortal part that was Jesus, the son of man; then there was the central, living, real part that was Spirit, the Son of God—that was the Christ, the Anointed. So each one of us has two regions of being—one the fleshly, mortal part, which feels its weakness and insufficiency in all things, saying, "I can't." Then at the very center of our being, there is a something that, in our highest moments, knows itself more than conqueror over all things; it always says, "I can, and I will." It is the Christ child, the Son of God, and Anointed in us. "And call no one your father on earth," said Jesus, "for you have one Father—the one in heaven" (Mt. 23:9).

He who created us did not make us and set us apart from

Himself, as a workman makes a table or a chair and puts it away as something completed and only to be returned to the maker when it needs repairing. Not at all. God not only created us in the beginning, but He is the very fountain of life abiding within us. From this fountain constantly springs new life to re-create our mortal bodies. He is the ever-abiding Intelligence that fills and renews our minds. His creatures would not exist a moment were He to be, or could He be, separated from them. "We are the temple of the living God; as God said, 'I will live in them and walk among them' " (2 Cor. 6:16).

Let us suppose that a beautiful fountain is supplied from some hidden but inexhaustible source. At its center, it is full of strong, vigorous life, bubbling up continually with great activity, but at the outer edge, the water is so nearly motionless as to have become impure and covered with scum. This exactly represents man. He is composed of a substance infinitely more subtle, more real than water. "We too are his offspring" (Acts 17:28). Man is the offspring—or the springing forth into visibility—of God the Father. At the center, he is pure Spirit, made in the image and likeness of the Father, substance of the Father, one with the Father, fed and renewed continually from the inexhaustible good, which is the Father. "In him we live and move and have our being" (Acts 17:28). At the outer edge, where stagnation has taken place (which is man's body), there is not much that looks Godlike in any way. We get our eyes fixed on the circumference, or external of our being. We lose consciousness of the indwelling, ever-active, unchanging God at the center, and we see ourselves sick, weak, and in every way miserable. It is not until we learn to live at the center and to know that we have power to radiate from that center this unceasing, abundant life, that we are well and strong.

Jesus kept his eyes away from the external altogether and kept his thoughts at the central part of his being, which was the

Christ. "Do not judge by appearances," he said, that is, according to the external, "but judge with right judgment" (Jn. 7:24) according to the real Truth, or judge from Spirit. In Jesus, the Christ, or the central spark that was God, the same that lives in each of us today, was drawn forth to show itself perfectly, over and above the body, or fleshly man. He did all his mighty works, not because he was given some greater or different power from that which God has given us—not because he was in some different way a *Son* of God and we only *children* of God—but because this same divine spark, which the Father has implanted in every child, had been fanned into a bright flame by his prenatal influences, early surroundings, and by his own later efforts in holding himself in constant, conscious communion with the Father, the Source of all love, life, and power.

To be tested does not mean to have things come to you which, however much they may affect others, do not affect you, because of some superiority in you. It means to be *tried,* to suffer, and to have to make an effort to resist. The book of Hebrews speaks of Jesus as "one who in every respect has been tested as we are" (Heb. 4:15). And Jesus himself confessed to having been tested when he said to his disciples, "You are those who have stood by me in my trials" (Lk. 22:28). The humanity of the Nazarene "was tested [or tried] by what he suffered" (Heb. 2:18), just as much as you and I suffer today because of temptations and trials and in exactly the same way.

We know that during his public ministry, Jesus spent hours each day alone with God. None of us knows what he went through in the years of his early manhood—just as you and I are doing today—in overcoming the mortal, his fleshly desires, his doubts and fears, until he came into the perfect recognition of this indwelling Presence, this "Father in me," to whom he ascribed the credit for his wonderful works. He had to learn as we are having to learn; he had to hold fast as we are having

141

today to hold fast; he had to try over and over to overcome, as we are doing, or else he was not "in every respect" tested as we are.

We all must recognize that it was the Christ within that made Jesus what he was, and our power now to help ourselves and to help others lies in our comprehending the Truth—for it is a Truth, whether we realize it or not—that this same Christ that lived in Jesus lives within us. It is the part of himself that God has put within us, which ever lives there with an inexpressible love and desire to spring to the circumference of our being, or to our consciousness, as our sufficiency in all things. "The Lord, your God, is in your midst, a warrior who gives victory; he will rejoice over you with gladness, he will renew you in his love; he will exult over you with loud singing" (Zeph. 3:17). Christ within us is the "beloved Son," the same as it was in Jesus. It is the "I in them and you in me, that they may become completely one" (Jn. 17:23) of which Jesus spoke.

In all this explanation, we would detract nothing from Jesus. He is still our Savior, in that he went through unutterable suffering, through the perfect crucifixion of self, that he might lead us to God; that he might show us the way out of our sin, sickness, and trouble; that he might manifest the Father to us and teach us how this same Father loves us and lives in us. We love Jesus and must ever love him with a love that is greater than all others, and to prove our love, we would follow his teachings and his life closely. In no way can we do this perfectly, except by trying to get at the real meaning of all that he said and letting the Father work through us as he did through him, our perfect Elder Brother and Savior.

Jesus sometimes spoke from the mortal part of himself, but he lived so almost wholly in the Christ part of himself, so consciously in the center of his being, where the very essence of the Father was bubbling up in ceaseless activity, that he usually spoke from that part.

When he said, "Come to me ... and I will give you rest" (Mt. 11:28), he could not have meant to invite humankind to come unto his personal, mortal self, for he knew of the millions of men and women who could never reach him. He was then speaking from the Christ Self of him, meaning not "Come to me, Jesus," but "Come to the Christ"; nor did he mean, "Come to the Christ living in me," for comparatively few could ever do that. But he said, "The words that I say to you I do not speak on my own; but the Father who dwells in me does his works" (Jn. 14:10). Then it was the Father saying not "Come to Jesus," but "Come to me"; that is, "Come up out of the mortal part of you where all is sickness and sorrow and trouble, into the Christ part where I dwell, and I will give you rest. Come up into the realization that you are one with the Father, that you are surrounded and filled with divine love, that there is nothing in the universe that is real but the good, and that all good is yours, and it will give you rest."

"No one comes to the Father except through me" (Jn. 14:6) does not mean that God is a stern father whom we must coax and conciliate by going to Him through Jesus, His kinder, more easily entreated Son. Did not Jesus say, "Whoever has seen me has seen the Father" (Jn. 14:9) or in other words, "As I am in love and gentleness and accessibility, so is the Father"? These words mean that no one can come to the Father except through the Christ part of himself. You cannot come around through some other person or by any outside way. Another may teach you how to come and assure you of all that is yours if you do come, but you must retire within your own soul, find the Christ there, and look to the Father through the Son, for whatever you want.

Jesus was always trying to get the minds of the people away from his personality and to fix them on the Father in him as the source of his power. And when toward the last they were clinging to his mortal self, because their eyes had not yet been opened to understand about the Christ within their own souls, he said, "It is to your advantage that I go away, for if I do not go away, the Advocate will not come to you" (Jn. 16:7). If he remained where they could keep looking to his personality, they would never know that the same Spirit of Truth and Power lived within them.

There is a great difference between a Christian life and a Christ life. To live a Christian life is to follow the teachings of Jesus, with the thought that God and Christ are wholly outside us, to be called on but not always to answer. To live a Christ life is to follow Jesus' teachings in the knowledge that God's indwelling presence, which is always life, love, and power within us, is now ready and waiting to flow forth abundantly, lavishly into our consciousness and through us to others, the moment we open ourselves to it and trustfully expect it. One is a following after Christ, which is beautiful and good so far as it goes, but is always imperfect; the other is a letting Christ, the perfect Son of God, be manifested through us. One is an expecting to be saved sometime from sin, sickness, and trouble; the other is a knowing that we are, in reality, saved now from all these errors by the indwelling Christ, and by faith affirming it until the evidence is manifested in our bodies.

Simply believing that Jesus died on the Cross to appease God's wrath never saved and can never save anyone from present sin, sickness, or want, and was not what Jesus taught. "The demons believe—and shudder" (Jas. 2:19), we are told, but they are not saved thereby. There must be something more than this, a living touch of some kind, a sort of intersphering of our own souls with the divine Source of all good and giving. We are to have faith in the Christ, believe that the Christ lives in us and is God's Son in us; that this indwelling One has power to save and make us whole; even more, that He has made us whole already.

For did not the Master say, "Whatever you ask for in prayer with faith, you will receive" (Mt. 21:22)?

If, then, you are manifesting sickness, you are to ignore the seeming—which is the external, or circumference of the pool where the water is stagnant and the scum has risen—and, speaking from the center of your being, say: "This body is the temple of the living God; the Lord is now in His holy temple; Christ in me is my life; Christ is my health; Christ is my strength; Christ is perfect. Therefore, I am now perfect, because He dwells in me as perfect life, health, strength." Say these words with all earnestness, trying to realize what you are saying, and almost immediately the perennial Fountain of Life at the center of your being will begin to bubble up and continue with rapidly increasing activity, until new life will radiate through pain, sickness, sores, all diseases, to the surface, and your body will show forth the perfect life of Christ.

Suppose it is money that you need. Take the thought: *Christ is my abundant supply (not supplier). He is here within me now, and greatly desires to manifest Himself as my supply. His desires are fulfilled now.* Do not let your thoughts run off into how He is going to do it, but just hold steadily to the thought of the supply here and now, taking your eyes off all other sources, and He will surely honor your faith by manifesting Himself as your supply a hundredfold more abundantly than you have asked or thought. So also with "whatever you ask for in prayer." But remember the earnest words of James, the apostle: "The one who doubts is like a wave of the sea, driven and tossed by the wind; for the doubter, being double-minded and unstable in every way, must not expect to receive anything from the Lord" (Jas. 1:6-8).

Nowhere in the New Testament is the thought conveyed that Jesus Christ came that there might be, after death, a remission of the *penalty* for sin. That belief is a pure fiction of our ignorant, carnal minds. In many places in the Bible, reference is made to "forgiveness of sins." According to Luke, Jesus said that repentance and forgiveness of sins should be preached in His name unto all the nations.

The word *sins*, in the original text, does not mean crime-deserving punishment. It means any mistake or failure that brings suffering. Jesus came that there might be forgiveness or cessation of sins, of wrongs, of mistakes, which were inevitably followed by suffering. He came to bring "good news of great joy for all the people" (Lk. 2:10). News of what? News of salvation. When? Where? Not salvation from punishment after death, but salvation from mistakes and failures here and now. He came to show us that God, our Creator and Father, longs to be to us, through the Christ, the abundance of all things that we need or desire. But our part is to choose to have Him and then follow His admonition to "hold fast to what you have until I come" (Rev. 2:25)—not till He comes after death, but until He manifests Himself. For instance, in looking to Him for health, when by an act of your will you stop looking to any material source (and this is not always easy to do) and declare the Christ in you to be the only life of the body and always perfect life, you need only to hold steadfastly, without wavering, to the thought, in order to become well.

When once you have put matter into the hands of the indwelling, ever-present Christ, in whom there is at all times an irrepressible desire to spring to our rescue and to do all things for us, do not dare to take it back into your mortal hands again to work out for yourself, for by so doing you simply put off the time of His bringing it to pass. All you have to do in the matter is to hold to the thought: *It is done. It is manifest now.* This divine Presence is our sufficiency in all things and will materialize itself as such in whatever we need or desire if we but trustfully expect it.

This matter of trusting the Christ within to do all things for us—realizing that we are one with Christ and that to Christ is given all power—is not something that comes to any of us spontaneously. It comes by persistent effort. We begin by determining that we will trust Him as our deliverance, as our health, our riches, our wisdom, our all, and we keep on by a labored effort, until we form a spiritual habit. No habit bursts full-grown into our lives, but comes from a succession of little acts. When you see anyone doing the works of Christ, healing the sick, loosing the bound, and so forth, by the word of Truth spoken in faith, you may be sure that this faith did not come to him from some outside source all at once. If you knew the facts, you would probably know of days and nights when with clenched fists and set teeth the person held fast to the Christ within, trusting where they could not trace, until he found himself possessing the very "faith of Jesus."

If we want the Father within, which is the Christ, to manifest as all things through us, we must learn to keep the mortal of us still, to still all its doubts and fears and false beliefs and to hold rigidly to the Christ only. In His name, we may speak the words of healing, of peace, and of deliverance to others, but as Jesus said of himself, so we must also say of ourselves: "I do nothing on my own" (Jn. 8:28) and "the Father who dwells in me does his works" (Jn. 14:10). He is the ever-present power to overcome all errors, sickness, weakness, ignorance, or whatever they may be. We claim this Power, or bring it into our consciousness where it is of practical use, by declaring over and over that it is ours already. Saying and trying to realize, "Christ is my wisdom, therefore I know Truth," will in a short time make us understand spiritual things better than months of study will do. Our saying: *Christ is my strength, I cannot be weak or frail,* will make us strong enough to meet any emergency with calm assurance.

Remember, we do not begin by feeling these things at first, but by earnestly and faithfully saying them, and acting as though they were true—and this is the faith that brings the Power into manifestation.

The Christ lives in us always. God, the creative energy, sent His Son first, even before the body was formed, and He ever abides within: "the firstborn of all creation" (Col. 1:15). But it is with us as it was with the ship on the tempestuous sea after the storm arose: Jesus being in the vessel did not keep it from rocking or the angry waves from beating against it, for he was asleep. It was only after he was awakened and brought out to manifest His power that the sea became still and the danger was over.

The Christ in us has been there all the time, but we have not known it, and so our little ships have been tossed about by sickness and poverty and distrust until we have seemed almost lost. I, the true spiritual Self of me, am one with the Christ. You, the true spiritual Self of you, are one with the Christ. The true Self of every person is the child of God, made in His image. "Beloved, we are God's children now; what we will be has not yet been revealed. What we do know is this: when he is revealed, we will be like him, for we will see him as he is" (1 Jn. 3:2). Now, already, we are sons. When He shall appear—not when, sometime after the transition called death, He, some great, glorious Being, shall burst into view, but when we have learned to still the mortal of us and let the Father manifest at our surface, through the indwelling Christ—then we shall be like Him, for He only will be visible through us.

"See what love the Father has given us, that we should be called children of God; and that is what we are" (1 Jn. 3:1). We are not simply reflections or images of God, but expressions (from *ex*, out of, and *premere*, to press or force), hence a forcing out of God, the All-Good, the All-Perfect. We are projections of the invisible Presence into visibility. God made us one with the Father, even as Jesus was, and just in proportion as we recognize this fact and claim our birthright, the Father in us will be manifested to the world.

Most of us innately avoid saying, "Your will be done" (Mt. 6:10). Because of false teaching and from associations, we have believed that this prayer, if answered, would take away from us all that gives us joy or happiness. Surely nothing could be further from the truth. Oh, how we have tried to crowd the broad love of God into the narrow limits of human mind! The grandest, most generous, loving father that ever lived is but the least bit of God's fatherhood manifested through the flesh. God's will for us means more love, more purity, more power, more joy in our lives every day.

No study of spiritual or material things, no effort, though it be superhuman on our part, could ever be as effectual in making grand, Godlike creatures, showing forth the same limitless soul that Jesus showed, as just praying continually the one prayer, "Thy will be done in me"; for the Father's will is to manifest His perfect Being through us. "Among the creatures one is better than another, according as the Eternal Good manifests itself and works more in one than in another. Now that creature in which Eternal Good most manifests itself, shines forth, works, is most known and loved, is the best, and that wherein the Eternal Good least manifests itself is the least good of all creatures."[1]

"For in him all the fullness of God was pleased to dwell" (Col. 1:19) fullness of love, fullness of life, fullness of joy, of power, of All-Good. "You have come to fullness in him" (Col. 2:10). Christ is in us, one with us, so we may boldly and with confidence say, "In Christ all things are mine." Declaring it will make it manifest.

Above all things learn to keep to the Christ within yourself, not that within someone else. Let the Father manifest through you in His own way, though His manifestation differs from that

---

1. *Theologia Germanica*, Pantheon Books, Inc., New York, 1949, p. 122.

in His other children. Heretofore even the most spiritually enlightened of us have been mere ants, because we have, by the action of our conscious thought, limited the divine manifestation to make it conform to the manifestation through someone else. God will make of us spiritual giants if we will but take away all limits and give Him opportunity.

"Although it be good and profitable that we should ask and learn and know what good and holy men have wrought and suffered, and likewise how God has willed and wrought in and through them, yet were it a thousand times better that we should in ourselves learn and perceive and understand, who we are, how and what our own life is, what God is in us and works in us, what He will have from us."[2]

All the blessings promised in the twenty-eighth chapter of Deuteronomy are to those who "hearken diligently unto my commandments (Deut. 11:13 KJV). This means those who seek the inner voice in their own souls and learn to listen to and obey what it says to them individually, regardless of what it says to any other person, no matter how far he or she may be advanced in spiritual understanding. This voice will not lead you exactly as it leads any other, but, in the infinite variety, there will be perfect harmony, for there is but "one God and Father of all, who is above all and through all and in all" (Eph. 4:6).

Ralph Waldo Emerson says, "Every soul is not only the inlet but may become the outlet of all there is in God." We can only be this by keeping ourselves consciously in open communication with God without the intervention of any other person between God and us. "The anointing that you received from him abides in you, and so you do not need anyone to teach you" (1 Jn. 2:27). "But the Advocate, the Holy Spirit, whom the Father will send in my name, will teach you everything" (Jn. 14:26).

---

2. *Theologia Germanica*, p. 127.

"When the Spirit of truth comes, he will guide you into all the truth; for he will not speak on his own, but will speak whatever he hears, and he will declare to you the things that are to come" (Jn. 16:13).

It needs but the one other little word *now*, firmly and persistently held in the mind, to bring into manifestation through us the highest ideal that we are capable of forming; far higher, for does it not say, "As the heavens are higher than the earth, so are my ways higher than your ways and my thoughts than your thoughts" (Is. 55:9)? This manifestation through us will be the fulfillment of God's ideal, instead of our limited, mortal ideal, when we learn to let Spirit lead and to hold our conscious minds to the *now*.

You want to manifest the perfect Christ. Affirm with all your heart and soul and strength that you do so manifest now, that you manifest health and strength and love and Truth and power. Let go the notion of being or doing anything in the future. God knows no time but the eternal now. You can never know any other time, for there is no other. You cannot live an hour or ten minutes in the future. You cannot live it until you reach it, and then it becomes the now. Saying or believing salvation and deliverance are to be, will forever, and through all the eternal ages, keep them just a little ahead of you, always to be reached but never quite realized.

"Now is the acceptable time; see, now is the day of salvation!" (2 Cor. 6:2) said Paul. He said nothing about our being saved from our distresses after death, but always taught present salvation. God's work is finished in us now. All the fullness abides in the indwelling Christ now. Whatever we persistently declare is done now, is manifested now, we shall see fulfilled.

Chapter 3
NEITHER DO I CONDEMN THEE

Few of us have any idea of the destructive potency of condemnatory words or thoughts. Even among Truth students who know the power of the spoken word—and because they know it, so much greater is that power—there is a widespread tendency to condemn the churches and all orthodox Christians, to criticize and speak despairingly of students of different schools (as though there could be only one school of Christ), and even to discuss among themselves the failings of individuals who, in ways differing from their own, earnestly seek the Christ.

Let us stop and see what we are doing. Why should we condemn the churches? Did not Jesus teach in the synagogues? He did not withdraw from the church and speak contemptuously of it. No, He remained in it, trying to show people wherein they were making mistakes, trying to lead them up to a higher view of God as their Father, and to stimulate them to live more truly righteous lives. If Jesus found hypocrisy in the churches, he did not content himself with saying, "I am holier than thou," but remained with them and taught them a more excellent way—that the *inside* of the platter must be made clean.

Is the servant greater than his Lord? Shall not we, whom the Father has called into such marvelous light, rather help those sitting in darkness, even in the churches, than utter one word of condemnation against them? A loyal son or daughter does not condemn his or her father or mother because in their day and generation, with the limitations of their day, they did not grow to his or her present standard. We do not condemn the tallow candle or the stagecoach because we have grown into a knowledge of electricity and steam power. We only see that out of the old grew the new, and that the old was necessary to the new.

God, in His eternal purposes, is carrying every living soul on toward a higher knowledge of the Truth, a more perfect evolvement of Himself through the soul. If some are being pushed on into the light of Truth and consequent liberty more rapidly than others, shall they turn and rend those who are walking more slowly but just as surely toward the perfect light? No; but let them, praising God for the marvelous revelation of Himself within their own souls, lift up rather than condemn any who are struggling toward the light. Let them become workers together with God, doers of the law, not judges.

Let no one who has been born into a knowledge of God dare to speak or even *think* disparagingly of or to anyone who is seemingly behind him in spiritual growth, lest by so doing he be found working *against* God, who is infinite wisdom as well as love.

Jesus said to the disciples, after they had come into the consciousness of their oneness with the Father by receiving the Holy Spirit: "If you forgive the sins of any, they are forgiven them; if you retain the sins of any, they are retained" (Jn. 20:23). With what mighty meaning these words are fraught in this new light that God has given us! See how our speaking, even our very *thinking*, of the sins or mistakes of others tends to fasten those mistakes on them as realities.

Strong thoughts of condemnation about anyone by any person will give him the physical sensation of having been hit in the pit of the stomach with a stone. If he does not immediately throw off the feeling—as he can easily do by looking to the Father and saying over and over until it becomes reality, "God, approve of me"—it will destroy his consciousness of perfect life, and he will fall into a belief of weakness and discouragement more quickly than from any other cause.

We read that the eyes of God are too pure to behold iniquity. A pure person sees no licentiousness in another. A pure person sees no falsity in another. Perfect love responds not to envy or fear or jealousy in another. It "thinks no evil." Jesus said, "The ruler of this world is coming. He has no power over me" (Jn. 14:30). So, unless there is something within us that responds to sin in others, we shall not see it in them. "By your words you will be justified, and by your words you will be condemned" (Mt. 12:37). The moment we begin to criticize or condemn another, we prove ourselves guilty of the same fault to which we are giving cognizance.

All condemnation springs from looking at personality. Personality (Latin, *persona*, a mask) is the outward appearance, not the real Self. That anyone utters a word of condemnation of another is the surest proof that he is yet living largely in the external of his being, the personality; that he has not yet risen beyond the plane of those to whom the pure Nazarene said, "Let anyone among you who is without sin be the first to throw a stone" (Jn. 8:7). Just in proportion as we return to God, as we withdraw from the external to the within of ourselves, keeping our thoughts centered on Him who is perfect, shall we lose sight of personality, of divisions and differences, and become conscious of our oneness with one another and our oneness with God.

We are one always and forever, whether or not we realize it. Knowing this, you will see a new meaning in the words: "Do not judge, so that you may not be judged. For with the judgment you make you will be judged" (Mt. 7:1-2).

"Indeed, God did not send the Son into the world to condemn

155

the world, but in order that the world might be saved through him" (Jn. 3:17). Yet when Philip said to Jesus, "Lord, show us the Father, and we will be satisfied" (Jn. 14:8), Jesus replied, "Whoever has seen me has seen the Father" (Jn. 14:9). Then, if God does not condemn, shall we, dare we, even in the smallest things? To each of us the Master says, "What is that to thee? Follow me."

Not while we are looking at the imperfect either in ourselves or in our brother, but while we "seeing the glory of the Lord ... are being transformed into the same image from one degree of glory to another; for this comes from the Lord, the Spirit" (2 Cor. 3:18).

Chapter 4
IN HIS NAME

Has it ever occurred to you that you almost daily take God's name in vain? Unless you are very watchful, very careful, you do so.

When God called Moses to lead the Children of Israel out of Egypt, "Moses said to God, 'If I come to the Israelites and say to them, "The God of your ancestors has sent me to you," and they ask me, "What is his name?" what shall I say to them?' God said to Moses, 'I am who I am.' He said further, 'Thus you shall say to the Israelites, "I am has sent me to you." ' ... 'This is my name forever, and this my title for all generations' " (Ex. 3:13-15).

"I AM" is God's name. Every time you say, "I am sick," "I am weak," "I am discouraged," you are speaking God's name in vain.

I AM cannot be sick; I AM cannot be weary or faint or power-less, for I AM is all-life, all-power, All-Good.

"I AM," spoken with a downward tendency, is always false, always "in vain." A commandment says, "You shall not take the name of the Lord your God in vain; for the Lord will not hold him guiltless who takes his name in vain" (Ex. 20:7 RSV). And Jesus said, "By your words you will be justified, and by your words you will be condemned" (Mt. 12:37).

If you speak the "I AM" falsely, you will get the result of false speaking. If you say, "I am sick," you will get sickness; if you say, "I am poor," you will get poverty; for the law is "you reap whatever you sow" (Gal. 6:7). "I AM," spoken upward, toward the good, the true, is sure to outpicture in visible good, in success, in happiness.

Does all this sound foolish to you? Do you doubt that such power goes with the speaking of God's name? If so, just go alone, close your eyes, and in the depth of your own soul say over and over the name "I AM." Soon you will find your whole being filled with a sense of power that you never had before— power to overcome, power to accomplish, power to do all things.

I am because Thou art. I am what Thou art. I am one with Thee, O Thou infinite I AM! I am good. I am holy. I am well. I am, because Thou art.

"The name of the Lord is a strong tower; the righteous run into it and are safe" (Prov. 18:10). They who think rightly about the power of the I AM spoken upward, simply have to run into it, as into a strong tower or fortress, and they are safe.

Did you ever go into a meeting where the "testimonies" given were the "I AM" spoken upward—"I am happy to be here," "I am glad I am a Christian," "I am hoping and trusting in God," and so forth? Attend such a gathering, and almost before you know it, you will find yourself lifted above your troubles and anxieties. You leave such a meeting with a feeling of joy and lightness, and a consciousness that you have the power to overcome all troubles and worries; you go, singing and confident, toward the very thing that an hour before seemed about to consume you.

Dear friends, you who at times feel discouraged, you who are continually irritated by the petty worries and anxieties of life, try for one week saying "I AM" upward, toward the good, and see what the result will be. Instead of saying, "I am afraid it will rain," say "I hope it will not rain"; instead of "I am sorry," say "I would have been glad had it been so and so"; instead of saying, "I am weak and cannot accomplish," say, "*I am*, because Thou art; I can accomplish, because *I am*." You will be astonished at the result.

The Christ, speaking through Jesus, said to the Jews who were boasting of being descendants of Abraham: "Very truly, I tell you, before Abraham was, I am" (Jn. 8:58). And Paul, writing to Timothy, said, "Let everyone who calls on the name of the Lord turn away from wickedness" (2 Tim. 2:19). Let everyone who speaks the "I AM" keep it separated from iniquity, or from false speaking. Let it be spoken always upward, never downward. Jesus also said, "If you ask anything of the Father in my name, he will give it to you" (Jn. 16:23). That is, in the name I AM. Whenever you desire—not supplicate, but desire, speaking the "I AM" upward—He will give what you ask. Every time you say, "I am happy," you ask in His name for happiness. Every time you say, "I am unhappy," you ask in His name for unhappiness. "Until now," he said to the disciples, "you have not asked for anything in my name. Ask and you will receive, so that your joy may be complete" (Jn. 16:24). Is not this the trouble? Previously, what have we been asking in His name? Have we been asking for health or for sickness, for happiness or for unhappiness, for riches or for poverty, by the manner of our speaking the name I AM?

Have we spoken it upward, toward the good, or downward toward the not good? That which we have been receiving will tell the story. Jesus said that if they asked rightly in His name, their "joy may be made complete." Is your joy full? If not, then give heed to your asking.

The disciples healed "in the name of Jesus Christ" (Acts 2:38). In the name of Jesus Christ is the name of the I AM.

Suppose that a messenger is sent out from the executive mansion in Washington to do certain things in the name of the

President of the United States. These three little words *in his name* invest the messenger with the full power of the President, so far as the performing of that service is concerned.

In writing to the Colossians, Paul said: "And whatever you do, in word or deed, do everything in the name of the Lord Jesus, giving thanks to God the Father through him" (Col. 3:17). Whatever we do heartily and sincerely in the name of Christ or the I AM carries with it the power of the I AM to accomplish—a power from a higher source, as the presidential messenger receives his power from a higher source. All power is given to Christ. Doing all things "in His name" puts aside our mortal personality and lets the Christ do the work. When Moses, with a sense of his personal insufficiency for so great a work, shrank from it, saying, "O my Lord, I have never been eloquent ... I am slow of speech and slow of tongue" (Ex. 4:10), Jehovah said to him, "Who gives speech to mortals?... Is it not I, the Lord? Now go, and I will be with your mouth and teach you what you are to speak" (Ex. 4:11-12).

In Edward Everett Hale's novel, *In His Name*, a story in a setting of seven hundred years ago, it is no fairy tale that invests the words *in His name* with such magic power. This little password carried safely, through the most dangerous places, all who went on errands of good. Locked doors were readily opened at the sound of the words. Soldier, sentry, officer of the guard, all gave way respectfully and instantly before it. Men were willing to leave their homes at a moment's notice and plunge into the greatest hardships "in His name."

Ministering today in His name, I say to you, troubled one, anxious one, weary one: Be strong! Be of good courage! Be hopeful! The world—the mortal—is overcome already. The Christ, the I AM, speaking through Jesus, has spoken, saying: "I have conquered the world!" (Jn. 16:33)

"To everyone who conquers [that is, to him who recognizes

that already the world is overcome by the I AM, that there is nothing in all the universe but the I AM] I will give some of the hidden manna, and I will give a white stone, and on the white stone is written a new name that no one knows except the one who receives it" (Rev. 2:17).

"If you conquer, I will make you a pillar in the temple of my God; you will never go out of it. I will write on you the name of my God" (Rev. 3:12) even the name I AM.

Chapter 5
LOOSE HIM AND LET HIM GO

One of the natural tendencies of the mortal mind is toward proselyting.

The moment we believe something to be true, we begin to try to convert others to our belief. In our eagerness, we forget that Truth is kaleidoscopic in its forms. We learn to say, with some degree of realization, "God works in me to will and to work for His good pleasure," but we quite forget that the same God is working equally in our brother "to will and to work."

Among the wise sayings of the ancient philosopher, Epictetus, we find these words: "Does any one bathe hastily?? Do not say that he does it ill, but hastily. Does any one drink much wine? Do not say that he does ill, but that he drinks a great deal. For unless you perfectly understand his motives, how should you know if he acts ill? Thus you will not risk yielding to any appearances but such as you fully comprehend."

Every person has an inherent right to freedom of choice, a right to live his life in his own way. One of the surest signs that a person is no longer in bondage himself is his willingness to give others their freedom, to allow others the privilege of seeking and finding God as they will.

Our great basic statement is "All is good, because all is God." In other words, God is the only intelligence, the only life at the center of every form of existing life. We say that we believe the highest manifestation of God is in humankind, that God ever abides at the center of all people and is always in the process of manifesting more and more of Himself, pure intelligence, perfect love, through our consciousness until we come to be consciously one with the Father in all things.

Do you believe this statement? If you believe it, where is there any cause for anxiety that you feel about your loved ones who are not, as you say, "in the Truth"?

If we truly believe that "all is good," we should not be troubled about those who apparently are going wrong. They may be going wrong according to our limited conception of right and wrong. But my brother, my sister, you are not your brother's keeper. He that will redeem, indeed, He that has already redeemed your brother or sister lives within him or her. The Christ, who ever loves at the center of every soul, "will neither slumber nor sleep" (Ps. 121:4). God works in others to bring them to themselves just as much as He is working in you and in me. We have absolutely nothing to fear about the eventual success of this worker. God never fails.

You have perhaps come to the flowering of the fruiting season in your growth out of the darkness of sense belief into the light of spiritual understanding. It is blessed and beautiful to be where you are, and it is hard to human belief to see those whom you love just barely showing their heads above the earth of sin and mistake, further away from your conception of the good than ever before.

But here is the place for us to cling faithfully and trustingly to our basic statement. Paul said, "For in hope we were saved. Now hope that is seen is not hope" (Rom. 8:24). Faith is not sight. Is our basic statement, "All is good," founded on Principle or on evidence of the senses? If on Principle, then it is immutable, unchangeable. And God is just as surely abiding at the center of your loved husband or son, working in him, when he is going down, as when he is coming up.

God is just as much the life of the seed when it is being planted in the dark earth, where, to the human sense, it is dead and all is lost, as He is the life of the new leaf which a few days later bursts into sight. In fact, it is because God is there at the center, working in the stillness, unseen, and not at all because of the fussy, noisy outside work that you and I do, that the seed comes forth into newness of life.

"Unless a grain of wheat falls into the earth and dies, it remains just a single grain; but if it dies, it bears much fruit" (Jn. 12:24).

Thus it would seem that the dying, the failure, the going down of the old is a necessary step in all true salvation. Every person must go down until he strikes his own level, his own self, before there can be any real growth. We may seem to hold another up for a while, but eventually he or she must walk alone. The time of walking alone with his or her own indwelling Christ, his or her own true Self, will depend largely on our letting go of him or her. No one will seek anything higher than he is today, until the need of something higher is felt. Your dear ones must have the liberty to live out their own lives, and you must let them, or else you are the one who puts off the day of their salvation.

"But," says someone whose heart is aching over the error ways of a loved one, "should you not help anyone? Should you not run after him, and urge him continually to turn into the right way?"

Yes and no. I gladly, joyfully help anyone when he or she wants help, but I could not urge others to leave their own light and walk by my light. Nor would I, like an overly fond mother, pick up another and try to carry that person in my arms by continually "treating" him.

A mother may—and sometimes does, mentally and morally, if not physically—through her false conception of love, carry her child until he is twenty years old, lest he, not knowing how to walk, fall and bump his nose a few times. But if she does this until he is grown, what will he do? He will turn and rend her, because she has stolen from him his inherent right to become strong and self-reliant. She has interposed herself between him and the power within him that was waiting, from birth, to be his strength and sufficiency in all things. She should have placed him on his own feet, made him know that there was something in him that could stand, encouraged and steadied him, and so helped him to be self-reliant and independent.

Hundreds of anxious fathers and mothers, sisters and wives say, "Ah, but I love this one so I cannot stand still and see him rushing on to inevitable suffering."

Yes, you love this person. But it takes an infinitely greater, more Godlike love to stand still and see your child burn his hand a little, that he may gain self-knowledge, than it does to be a slave to him, ever on the alert to prevent the possibility of his learning through a little suffering. Are you equal to this larger love? Having come to a knowledge of the mighty truth that "God is all and in all," have you the moral courage to "be still, and know"; to take off all restrictions and rules from others, and to let the God within them grow them as He will; and, trusting Him to do it in the *right* way, keep yourself from all anxiety in the matter?

When Jesus preached of a glorious freedom from suffering, through a kingdom within, He often interspersed His preaching with the words: "Let anyone with ears to hear listen!" (Mk. 4:9) In other words, the Gospel message of deliverance is for all who are ready for it. Let him who has come to where he *wants* it, take it. No one has a right to coerce another to accept his ideal. Every person has a right to keep his own ideal until he desires to change it.

God is leading your friend by a way you do not and cannot know. It is a safe and sure way; it is the shortest and only way. It is the Christ way, the within way. "I am the door," says the Christ within every soul. "If any man enter in, [that is, by way of the Christ in himself], he shall be saved" (Jn. 10:9 KJV).

Now you are trying to have your friend enter through your door. Your friend must enter through his own Christ, his own desire, and you must leave him alone to the workings of that indwelling One if you want him to manifest good.

"But," you say, "is there nothing I can do when I see my friend going down?"

Yes, there is something you can do, and a very effectual something too.

"The sword of the Spirit ... is the word of God" (Eph. 6:17). You can, whenever you think of your friend, speak the word of freedom to him or her. You can always and in all ways "loose him, and let him go," not forgetting that the letting go is as important as the loosing. Tell him mentally that Christ lives within him and makes him free, forever free; that he manifests the Holy One wherever he goes and at all times, for there is nothing else to manifest. Then see that you do not recognize any other manifestation than the good in him.

It is written: "If you forgive the sins of any, they are forgiven them; if you retain the sins of any, they are retained" (Jn. 20:23). Will you invariably speak the word of remission or loosing to your erring ones? Or will you bind them closer, tighter in the bondage that is breaking your own heart, by speaking the word of retention to them continually?

If you really want your friends to be free, loose them and let them go. For it is the promise of the Father, that "whatever you bind on earth will be bound in heaven" (Mt. 16:19).

Chapter 6
ALL-SUFFICIENCY IN ALL THINGS

There is that within every human being which is capable of bringing forth into the everyday, material world every good thing any person may desire.

Here and there are pious souls who, despite their consciously abiding in the secret place of the Most High and being taught by the Spirit of Truth, dimly recognize this. They say only, "The Holy Spirit abiding within us is able to do all things for us." Here and there are metaphysicians, in whom the intuitive faculty is largely developed, who do apprehend it as demonstrable Truth yet carefully avoid all pious words, lest they be considered in the old rut of religious belief. They say, "The outer or visible man has no need that the inner or invisible man cannot supply."

Let us not haggle over terms. There need be no schism. Each means the same thing. The only difference is in words. Each one is getting at the same Truth in his own way, and eventually the two will clasp hands in unity and see eye to eye.

The Spirit of the living God within us, fed ever from the Fountainhead, is not only the Giver of all good gifts, the supplier of all supply, but *is the gift itself.* We must come right up to this point. The Giver and the Gift are one.

God Himself is the fulfillment—or the substance which fills full—of every desire.

Truly we are coming to know of "God in His world"; of God,

the immanent creative Cause of all things, ever dwelling in us, ready and willing at any moment to re-create or renew our bodies and minds, or to manifest Himself through us as anything needed by us.

The certainty of this manifestation depends on the ability to recognize and accept Truth.

One recognizes God within as indwelling purity and holiness. To this one, God is sanctification, and in proportion to the recognition and the trust with which this divine Presence is regarded as immanent holiness, does it spring forth into the outer, everyday life of a person as holiness, so that even they who run may perceive something more than human in him.

Another recognizes and accepts the God within himself as the life of his body, and instantly this divine life, always perfect, strong, and vigorous, and always desiring with the mighty desire of omnipotent love to manifest itself through someone or something as perfection, begins to flow through his body from center to circumference until his entire body is charged with a fullness of life that is felt even by others who come in contact with him. This is divine healing, and the time required for the process of complete healing depends, not on any changeableness of God— for God knows no time but the eternal now—but entirely on the ability of the person to recognize and trust the power that works in him.

The one who recognizes the indwelling God as his holiness, but cannot mentally grasp any more Truth, lives a holy, beautiful life, but perhaps lives it through years of bodily disease and sickness. Another who recognizes the same immanent God as his health and is made both holy and physically well by the recognition and acceptance, stops there and wonders when he is well and living a life entirely unselfish and Godlike, why he should always be poor, lacking even the bare necessities of life.

Can you not see that this same indwelling God who is your

holiness and your health is also your sustenance and support? Is God not our All-Sufficiency in all things? Is it not the natural impulse of the divine Being to flow forth through us into all things—"whatever you ask for in prayer" (Mt. 21:22)? Is there any limit, except as our poor human mind has set? Does He not say, "Every place that the sole of your foot will tread upon I have given to you" (Josh. 1:3)? What does this mean? Is it not saying, "Whatever you dare to claim, that will I be to you"?

This divine energy is the substance (from *sub*, under, and *stare*, to stand), the real thing that stands under or within the visible or unreal of all things—food and clothing as well as life and health.

How do we get holiness? Not by outside works of purifying ourselves, but by turning to the Holy Spirit within and letting it flow forth into our human nature until we become permeated with the Divine. How is perfect health through divine or spiritual healing obtained? Is it by looking to or trusting external efforts or appliances? Surely not; but rather by ceasing entirely to look to the without, and turning our thoughts and our faith to the Father in us.

How, then, are we to get our abundant supply—aye, even more than we can ask or think (for God gives not according to our need, but "according to his riches" [Phil. 4:19] we are told)?

"Acquaint now thyself with him, and be at peace: thereby good shall come unto thee.... If thou return to the Almighty, thou shalt be built up .... The Almighty shall be thy defence, and thou shalt have plenty of silver" (Job 22:21, 23, 25, KJV). Cease to look to outside sources and turn within. Be still and know that God—the indwelling God—is our supply.

It is not enough to believe simply that God is our supplier—the One who shall by His omnipotent power influence the mind of someone possessing an abundance to divide with us. This is limitation. God being our health means far more than God being our healer. God as our supply is infinitely more than God as our supplier. God is the Giver and the Gift.

When Elisha multiplied the widow's oil, he did not, recognizing God simply as the supplier, ask, and then for answer receive a few barrels of oil from someone overly wealthy in that commodity, someone in whose heart the Spirit of God was working. That would have been a good but a very limited way, for had the demand continued, in time not only the village but the whole country around would have been destitute of oil.

Elisha understood the divine law of working and put himself into harmony with it; then God Himself, the substance of all things, became manifest as the unlimited supply—a supply which could easily have flowed until this time had there been need and vessels enough.

Jesus' increase of the loaves and fishes did not come up from the village in response to some silent word spoken by him to a person having a quantity. He never recognized that he had any right to seek the surplus possessions of another, even though he was going to use them to benefit others. In order to feed the multitude, he did not reach out after that which belonged to anyone, or even that which was already in manifestation. The extra supply was a new and increased manifestation of divine Substance as bread and fish. So with the oil of Elisha, who was a man "just like you" (Acts 14:15). In both these cases, nothing came from without to supply the need, but the supply proceeded *from within outward.*

This divine Substance—call it God, Creative Energy, or whatever you will—is ever abiding within us and stands ready today to manifest itself in whatever form you and I need or wish to manifest, just as it did in Elisha's time. It is the same yesterday, today, and forever. Our desire is the cup that shapes the form of its coming, and our trust—the highest form of faith—sets the time and the degree.

Abundant supply by the manifestation of the Father in us, from within outward, is as much a legitimate outcome of the Christ life or spiritual understanding as is bodily healing.

The Word—or Spirit—is made flesh (or clothed with materiality) in both cases, and both are equally in God's order. The law of "work-to-earn" is only a schoolmaster beating us with many stripes, breaking us into many pieces when we fall across it in our failures, just to bring us to Christ. "But now that faith is come, we are no longer under a tutor." Then Christ—the Divine in us—becomes the fulfillment of the law.

"Do not work for the food that perishes" (Jn. 6:27), said the Nazarene. Cease to work with the one object, namely, for a living or for supply. Be forever free from the law of poverty and want, as you are from the law of sin and disease—through faith in Christ; that is, by taking the indwelling Christ, or Spirit, or Invisible Man as your abundant supply, and looking up to no other source, hold to it until it manifests itself as such. Recognize it. Reckon it. Be still and know it. Do not struggle and work and worry while you know it, but just be still. In Psalm 46:10, it says, "Be still, and know that I am"—what? Part of God? No. "Know that I am God!"—all of God, all of good. I am life. I am health. I am love. I am supply. I am the *substance* of all that human souls and bodies can need or want.

The law says: "By the sweat of your face you shall eat bread" (Gen. 3:19). The gospel brings "good news of great joy for all the people" (Lk. 2:10). The law says work out your salvation from sin, sickness, and poverty. The Gospel teaches that Christ, the Father in you, is your salvation. Have faith in Him. The law says work all you can, and God will do the rest. The law is *a* way; Gospel, or Christ, is *the* way: "Choose this day whom you will serve" (Josh. 24:15).

"But," says someone, "will not such teaching that our abundance is not at all dependent on the labor of our hands or head foster selfishness and indolence? Is it not a teaching dangerous to the masses?"

Jesus never thought the gospel dangerous for the masses. It has not proved dangerous to teach that health is a free gift of God—a gift that we need not labor for, but just recognize and accept.

Does anyone attempt to hide away from others, like a talent hidden deep in the earth, the newborn health that is God-manifest in response to recognition and faith? If he does, he soon finds that his health has disappeared, for selfishness and the consciousness of an indwelling God cannot both abide in the same heart.

Let not anyone for a moment suppose that he can use gospel means for selfish ends. The person may well suppose he can go west by going east. The divine abundance manifested through you is given you for ministry to others. You can neither receive it indolently nor retain it selfishly. If you attempt either, the flow of divine oil will be stopped.

In Christ, or in the consciousness of the indwelling divine Spirit, we know that every man and woman is our father and mother, brother and sister; that nothing is our own, but all is God's because all is God.

And because we know this, we give as we work without thought or hope of return because God flows through us to others. Giving is our only safety valve. Abundance is often a snare to those who know not God, the indwelling One, who is love. But the abundance that is manifested from within outward is only the material clothing of perfect love and cannot bring selfishness. "The blessing of the Lord makes rich, and he adds no sorrow with it" (Prov. 10:22).

Will God, being manifest as our abundant supply, foster idleness? A thousand times, no! We shall then, more than ever, be co-workers with God, working but not laboring, working always for others. Work is labor only when it is for self. Labor, not work, brings weariness, sorrow, and sickness. Labor not for any good to yourself. Working as God works does not weary, for then the current of unlimited divine life is always flowing through us anew to bless others.

"There is a river whose streams make glad" (Ps. 46:4), but we must always keep the stream flowing *from within*—the source of its uprising—*outward* if it is to make glad. When we work in harmony with divine law, we have with us the whole force of the stream of living waters to carry us along.

Better than he knew, spoke the poet when he said, "Earth has no sorrow that heaven cannot heal."

Not the faraway heaven after death, when a whole lifetime has been spent in sorrow and trouble, but the kingdom of heaven is here, now, today. The mortal, human, earth part of you has no sorrow that cannot be healed, overcome, wiped out at once and forever by this ever-indwelling divine Spirit.

If anyone would hasten the day of everyone's deliverance from all forms of human sorrow and want, let that person at once begin to withdraw himself from outside sources and external warfare and center his thoughts on Christ, the Lord within.

"Great in your midst is the Holy One" (Is. 12:6).

"Acquaint now thyself with him, and be at peace: thereby good shall come unto thee" (Job 22:21 KJV).

"Prove me now ... if I will not ... pour you out a blessing, that there shall not be room enough to receive it" (Mal. 3:10 KJV).

Let us prove Him. "Ponder it on your beds, and be silent" (Ps. 4:4). Be still and know. Be still and trust. Be still and expect.

"For God alone my soul waits in silence, for my hope is from him" (Ps. 62:5).

175

Chapter 7
GOD'S HAND

There is but one hand in the universe. It is God's hand. Whenever you have felt that your hand was empty, it has been because you have believed yourself separate from God. Have you at times felt a great desire to give to others something they needed or wanted, yet have not been able to give? Have you said many times within yourself: "Oh, if I only had money, how I would relieve anxiety and distress! If it were only in my power, how quickly I would give a lucrative position to this one needing work, freedom to that one wanting release from material bondage," and so forth? Have you often said, "If I could only afford it, I would gladly give my time and service to others with no thought of return"?

From where, do you suppose, comes this desire to give? Is it from the mortal of you? No, it is the voice of the Giver of all good gifts crying out through you. It is God's desire to give through you. Cannot God afford to give whenever and wherever God will, and not be made poorer, but richer, thereby? Your hand is God's hand. My hand is God's hand. Our Father reaches out through these, His only hands, to give His gifts. We have nothing to do with the supply. Our part is to pass out the good gift, freely and without ceasing. This we can do only by making a complete consecration (so far as our consciousness goes) of our hands, our entire being, to the service of God, the All-Good. When we have given anything to others, we no longer consider it our own, but recognize it as belonging to them. So this conscious consecration of our hands to God helps us to recognize them as God's hands in which is (no longer "shall be") the fullness of all things.

When first the full recognition of there being but one hand was given to a certain woman, it was so real that for hours whenever she looked at her right hand she seemed unable to close it, so full of all good things did it seem. She said to herself, "Then if this be true, I have, in my hand, health to give the sick, joy to give the mourning, freedom to give those in bondage, money to give those needing it; it only needs that I keep the hand open for all good gifts to flow out." To all who came to her that day in need of anything, she said mentally: "Here is just what you desire; take it and rejoice. All my gifts are in my hand to give; it is God's hand."

And the result of that day's work almost startled her, with such marvelous swiftness did the external manifestations of the heart's desire come to everyone to whom she gave the word. One aged man, who for five years had been in external bondage and exile in a foreign land, held there by the machinations of another, and in which case no external law had been of avail to free, was set into perfect liberty with the most complete vindication of character and consequent public congratulations and rejoicings, by the word of liberty spoken for him through this woman that day. Recognizing her hand as God's hand, she only said, "Then in this hand are that man's freedom papers," and mentally extending to him her hand she said: "Here is your freedom. It is God's gift; wake up and take it; get up and go forth; you are free." Then she committed the whole matter to Him who invariably establishes the word spoken in faith, and He brought to pass the physical outpicturing of freedom.

"You open your hand, satisfying the desire of every living thing" (Ps. 145:16). Would you like to be able to do this? Then keep the hand open. Refuse to be hindered by fear of poverty, fear of want, fear that you will not be appreciated or justly dealt with. Go right on giving aid to all who need anything. "Only speak the word" (Mt. 8:8) of giving. It is God's word spoken through your lips, and has He not said, "My word ... shall not return to me empty, but it shall accomplish that which I purpose" (Is. 55:11)?

We cannot afford to withhold from giving our time, our intellect, our love, our money to those who need, for the law is that withholding makes poorer. "There is that scattereth, and yet increaseth; and there is that withholdeth more than is meet, but it tendeth to poverty" (Prov. 11:24 KJV), said Solomon.

The supply is inexhaustible. Its outflow can be limited only by demand. Nothing can hinder the hand that is consciously recognized as God's hand from being refilled, except, as was the case when the widow's oil was multiplied through Elisha: "There is not a vessel more" (2 Kings 4:6 KJV). Let not the seeming emptiness of your hand at times stagger your faith for a moment. It is just as full when you do not see it as when you do. Keep right on recognizing it as God's right hand in which are all good gifts now, thus you will prove Him who said: "Prove me now herewith, saith the Lord of hosts, if I will not open you the windows of heaven, and pour you out a blessing, that there shall not be room enough to receive it" (Mal. 3:10 KJV).

God is surely calling us to "move up higher" (Lk. 14:10). To all those who are earnestly seeking Truth for Truth's sake, and not for the loaves and fishes, nor that they may be able to "give a sign" to those seeking signs, He is saying loudly: "Therefore do not worry, saying, 'What will we eat?' or 'What will we drink?' or 'What will we wear?' ... Your heavenly Father knows that you need all these things. But strive first for the kingdom of God and his righteousness, and all these things will be given to you as well" (Mt. 6:31-33).

"Freely ye have received, freely give" (Mt. 10:8 KJV). "Love your enemies, do good, and lend, expecting nothing in return. Your reward will be great, and you will be children of the Most High" (Lk. 6:35). God is forever giving, giving, giving, with no thought of return. Love always thinks of giving, never of receiving. God's giving is the spontaneous outflow of perfect love. The higher we rise in recognition and consequent manifestation of the Divine, the more surely we think always of the giving, not of what we shall receive.

We know now that money, houses, lands, and all material things can be made to come to us by our holding them in our thoughts as ours, but that is not the *highest* that God has in store for us. "What no eye has seen, nor ear heard, nor the human heart conceived, what God has prepared for those who love him" (1 Cor. 2:9). What? Self? No, but "who love him"—who love Good more than self. Jesus said, "Everyone who has left houses ... for my name's sake, will receive a hundredfold" (Mt. 19:29). They that have forsaken, they that have forsaken self, they that dare let their hands be forever open to their brothers, doing good and lending, hoping for nothing again, to them is the promise of a hundredfold even in this life.

God has called us to be His stewards. He has chosen us as vessels to carry good to others, and it is only while carrying to others that we can be filled. The law is "give, and it will be given to you. A good measure, pressed down, shaken together, running over, will be put into your lap" (Lk. 6:38). Give without thought of return.

"But," says one, "am I to give my time, my money, my best thoughts to others and not require of them something in return? It is not fair." Give as God gives. He knows no *mine* and *yours.* He says, "All that is mine is yours" (Lk. 15:31).

Look only to God for supply. If anything is returned to you through the one to whom you give, render thanks for it. If nothing visible is returned, give thanks just the same, knowing that no man can stand between you and the inexhaustible supply; that it is he that withholds who is impoverished thereby, not he from whom anything is withheld.

"Agree with God, and be at peace; in this way good will come to you.... If you return to the Almighty, you will be restored, if you remove unrighteousness from your tents, if you treat gold like dust, and gold of Ophir like the stones of the torrent-bed, and if the Almighty is your gold and your precious silver, then you will delight yourself in the Almighty, and lift up your face to God" (Job 22:21, 23-26).

When we have learned that God is our supply and that from Him comes all our help, we shall no longer care whether or not "pay" is rendered for our services. We shall simply know that all things are ours now, and out of the fullness of love, we shall give freely. God's hand is sure. Your hand is God's hand now, today. It is full now. Give out of it mentally to all who call on you, whatever they need. "Trust also in him; and he shall bring it to pass" (Ps. 37:5 KJV).

Chapter 8
IF THOU KNEWEST

It would seem almost childish, almost an insult to the intelligence of one's readers, to assert that the sunlight coming into a darkened room will annihilate the darkness. The merest child knows this, even if he does not understand the *modus operandi* of such fact. The sunlight does not have to make an effort to do this; it does not have to combat the darkness or wrestle or strain to overcome it; in fact, it does not change its course or its natural action in the least. It just goes on calmly radiating itself as usual. And yet the darkness is annihilated the instant it is touched by the light. Why? Because the darkness is not an entity having a reality of its own. It is no thing. It is simply the absence of a positive, real something. When there is made a way for the something to rush in and fill to fullness the empty space, the no thing then is the nothing, the darkness annihilated, destroyed, healed; all there is left is the something, the light.

Where did the darkness go? It did not go anywhere because it was not; it had not existed. It was simply the lack of something, and when the lack was filled, there was no longer any lack. So it is with all negation, with all that is not good, not light, not love, not health, not wholeness. They are each and every one the absence of the Real, and they are all annihilated or healed by letting in a something, a real substance that fills the vacuum.

Remembering that the things that are seen are the temporal and the unreal, which pass away, while the things that are not seen are the eternal, the Real, let us carry this thought of the "no thing" a little further. Unhappiness is not a reality because it is not eternal; it belongs in the category of things that pass away. Envy, selfishness, jealousy, fear, and so forth are not real entities in our lives. Each is a lack of love, its positive opposite. Lack of temporal goods, lack of health, lack of wisdom—these things do not belong to the kingdom of the Real because they are all temporal things that will, as the philosopher Epictetus said, pass away. Nothing is Real except the eternal, that which is based on the real substance—God—that which can never be changed or made less by any external circumstances whatever.

Does this not make a little clearer and more acceptable, a little less antagonistic, the oft repeated statements, "There is no evil; sickness is not real; sin is not real," and so forth? I repeat, nothing is real that is not eternal, and all conditions of apparent evil, of sickness, poverty, fear, and so forth, are not things, not entities in themselves, but they are simply an absence of the opposite good, just as darkness is the absence of light. In the deepest reality there is never an absence of the good anywhere, for that would mean absence of God. God as life, wisdom, love, substance, fills every place and space of the universe or else God is not omnipresent. Who shall dare say God is not? Eventually our best healing of wrong conditions and human suffering is done when we recognize and affirm this great whole of Truth, the omnipresence of God, refusing absolutely to recognize anything else. The only "absence" that exists is in our consciousness or lower senses. But in order to bring this matter to the human understanding piecemeal, to break the bread so that each shall have the portion which he is able with his present growth to take, let us take up a little detail.

Your friend is to all appearances very ill. God is life—all the life there is in the universe. Is your friend's illness an entity, a "Real" thing (that is, an eternal thing)? No, it is rather like the darkened room, needing only the light to heal, an absence of perfect life in the body. Would not the incoming of newness of life—this perfect life—to all the diseased atoms heal and renew and make alive? Of course. Well, how are we to let in this fullness of life? We shall see later.

Take another example, for bodily illness is one of the least of the woes of blinded humanity with which we have to deal. A mother's precious son is going all wrong. He drinks, steals; he breaks his mother's heart with his unkindness and his dissipation. She weeps, rebukes, entreats, lectures, finally nags. What is all this that is killing the mother? It is *no thing*, nothing at all. It is not real because it is not eternal. It is the absence of love, that is all. A perfect flood of love permeating and saturating that boy's being would heal all his diseases, both moral and physical, because he is simply manifesting a great selfishness that is absence of love—the darkened room again. How are we to get the remedy, fullness of love, let in and thus applied to the root of the disease? We shall see.

Poverty belongs among the no things, the nothings. It is not Real, for only the eternal things are Real, and poverty is temporal. It is an absence of substance, and it is only permanently healed by an inflow of substance to fill the empty space. Sin is not Real, for it is not eternal. It is failure to reach the mark. It is a blind, ignorant outreaching of the human for something not possessed, the sinner desiring and hoping thereby to gain happiness. This empty void, this awful outreaching that resulted in failure, is only satisfied and healed by the incoming flood of Good that fills the lack, as the sunlight fills the darkness.

In overcoming undesirable conditions in our life, there are two ways of arriving in our consciousness at the realization of the omnipresence of God—the great, comprehensive Truth, which heals all manner of diseases and which makes free. First, we persistently deny the Reality of all seeming evil; second, we let in the substance of all good.

Everything undesirable passes away if we refuse to give it recognition by word, deed, or thought as a Reality. This we can do more easily when we remember that nothing is Real except the eternal. Paul said, "Do not make room for the devil [evil]" (Eph. 4:27). It has no existence whatever, any more than has the darkness that often causes us fear and suffering. It has no more Reality (remembering what is Real) than the fiction of dreams. When one awakens from an unpleasant dream, some moments of assertion to oneself that it was only a dream, not real, are required before the heart's normal action returns and the natural breathing is restored. Even with one's eyes wide open, the dream seems strangely real, but we all know that it was a delusion of the senses, nothing else; it has no substance, no reality. So the physical and material troubles are not Real, and they will disappear if we refuse to give them any life or reality by our word or thought. Let us rejoice in words of thanksgiving that this is one of God's ways, simply that evils are not. This is our first step.

Now for the second step. Had a person any true conception of the gift of God to him, nothing in the created world would be able to withstand his power. We speak of a person's "gift" without realizing how truly we are speaking. We say he is gifted in this way or that, as though he were in possession by nature of some remarkable ability inherited from parents, or created by peculiar environment. While many of us are ready to acknowledge in a general way that "every generous act of giving, with every perfect gift, is from above, coming down from the Father of lights" (Jas. 1:17), even we are not prepared for the reception of the marvelous truth of endowment from the Source. When a glimpse of it comes, it makes one almost breathless with wonder and astonishment.

"If you knew the gift of God" (Jn. 4:10)—what is this inestimable gift? What, indeed, but that He has given the veritable Son of God to be forever within us. This is the marvelous way of creation and also of redemption from all human lack and suffering, Christ-in-you. "For in him [in this Christ, this Son of God] the whole fullness of deity dwells bodily, and you have come to fullness in him" (Col. 2:9-10)—fullness of life, love, wisdom, substance yes, of the very substance of everything this human can need or desire. We can truly know that "Christ himself, in whom are hidden all the treasures of wisdom and knowledge" (Col. 2:2-3), "from his fullness we have all received" (Jn. 1:16).

To have created man thus seemed wise to Infinite Wisdom, and the one object in this life should be with us as it must be in the Mind of God, to make manifest this son of God. "Each of us was given grace [power, love, life, wisdom, substance] according to the measure of Christ's gift" (Eph. 4:7), not that God's giving is with partiality. Make no mistake here. The Creator of the universe is no respecter of persons. There are no favorites in God's creation. All the "fullness of deity" is embodied in His Son, this indwelling Christ. But this power, life, wisdom, this "all" that makes up the "fullness of deity," is manifested only in proportion as we recognize this Christ as the Source of the good that we desire, look to Him for it, acknowledge Him as All, and affirm persistently in the face of all opposition that the Son of God is now made visible through us.

Each of us is small or great, gifted or otherwise "according to the measure of Christ's gift" (Eph. 4:7) we receive consciously. There must be an incoming of this divine Son of God to our conscious mind. The incoming will depend on our faithfulness in acknowledging the Source and affirming its manifestation. We cannot idly drift into it. We must speak the words of Truth before Truth will become manifest. John said, "The Son of God was revealed ... to destroy the works of the devil [evil]" (1 Jn. 3:8). Precisely so, just as the light is manifested to destroy the darkness by filling it full. Let us take and definitely use, day after day, this statement of Truth: *The Son of God in me is now manifested, made visible in my body and all my affairs. He comes not to destroy, but to fill full.*

Chapter 9
TRUSTING AND RESTING

There is a perfect passivity that is not indolence. It is a living stillness born of trust. Quiet tension is not trust. It is simply compressed anxiety.

Who is there among those who have learned the law of good and have tried to bring it into manifestation, who has not at times felt his or her physical being almost ready to snap with the intensity of "holding to the Truth." You believe in omnipresent life. You attempt to realize it for others. Someone comes to you for help, one who is always in a hurry for results, always wanting to know how much more time will be required, and so forth. The person's impatience and unbelief, together with your great desire to prove the law to him, stimulate you, after a few treatments, to greater efforts; and almost immediately you find yourself thinking frequently of the person when not treating and trying to throw more force into the treatment when the person is present.

Then, after giving a treatment, you find a sense of fullness in your head that is very uncomfortable; and very soon, what at first was a delight to you becomes a burden, and you almost wish the patient would go to someone else. You cannot help wondering why the person improved so perceptibly with the first few treatments, and afterward, even with your increased zeal, seemed to stand still and get worse. Let me tell you why. When you first began to treat, you, so sure of the abundance of divine life, calmly and trustingly spoke the Truth to your patient. When the person got in a hurry, you, beginning to take on responsibility that was God's, not yours, grew anxious and began to cast on him your compressed anxiety. You were no longer a channel for divine life, sweet, peaceful, harmonious, to flow through, but by your intensity and hurry, you completely shut off the divine influx and were able only to force on the person, out of your anxious mortal mind, a few strained, compulsory thoughts that held him as in a vise and exhausted you.

Some healing and other demonstrations of power are brought to pass in this way, but it is always the stronger mortal thought controlling the weaker and is always wearing to the one thus working. This plane is entirely one of mental suggestion, a mild form of hypnotism.

In the matter of God as our supply or any other side of the divine law that we, from time to time, attempt to bring into manifestation, the moment we begin to be anxious, our quiet becomes simply the airtight valve of tension or suppressed anxiety that shuts out the very thing we are trying to bring about and so prevents its manifestation.

This way of holding with intensity to a thought, be it mental argument for healing or looking to God for material supply, recognizing that we have power by such firmness of thought to bring what we want into manifestation, is one way of obtaining results, but it is a hard way. We therefore give out what is within us, and it is helpful so far as it goes, but by some mental law, this intensity of thought seems to cut off our consciousness from the Fountainhead, thus preventing inflow and renewal from God, resulting in the quick exhaustion and the burdened feeling.

We need to rise above this state of tension to one of *living trust.* There is such a thing as an indolent shifting of our responsibility to an outside God, which means laziness, and which never brings anything into manifestation. But there is also a state of *trustful passivity* into which we must enter to do the highest work.

There are some things that we are to do ourselves, but there are others that God does not expect us to do. (When I speak of ourselves as something apart from God, I simply mean our *conscious* selves. We are always one with God, but we do not always consciously realize it. I speak of ourselves as the conscious part of us.) They are His part, and our greatest trouble lies in our trying to do God's part, just because we have not learned how to trust God to do it. We are, with our conscious thought, to speak the words of life, of Truth, of abundant supply, and we are to act as though the words were true. But the "bringing it to pass" is the work of a Power that is higher than we, a Presence that we do not see with these mortal eyes, but which is omnipotent and will always rush to our rescue when we trust it.

From the smallest thing of our everyday life to the rolling away of the largest stone of difficulty from our path, this Presence will deliver us. But its working depends on our trusting, and trusting means getting still inside.

In our effort to bring into manifestation the good that we know belongs to every child of God, it is when we get beyond the point where we try to do it all ourselves and let God do His part that we get the desires of our heart.

After we have done our part faithfully, earnestly, we are told to "stand still, and see the salvation of the Lord, which he will shew to you today .... The Lord shall fight for you, and ye shall hold your peace" (Ex. 14:13-14 KJV). See the conditions here imposed. This invisible Presence will remove from your path the difficulties, which look to your mortal vision to be almost insurmountable, only if you stand still. The Lord will fight for you if you hold your peace. But there is no promise of deliverance for you while you preserve a state of unrest within. Either a state of internal unrest, or a forced external quiet, which simply means compressed anxiety, prevents this invisible omnipotent force from doing anything for your deliverance. It must be peace, peace; possess your soul in peace, and let God work.

Marvelous have been the manifestations of this power in my life when the "bringing to pass" has been left entirely to it. Ask not, then, when or how or why. This implies doubt. "Be still before the Lord, and wait patiently for him" (Ps. 37:7).

When, in the reign of Jehoshaphat, king of Judah, the Ammonites, Moabites, and others—a great multitude—came against the king in battle, he, in great fear, called the people together, and they sought counsel of the Lord, saying: "We are powerless against this great multitude that is coming against us. We do not know what to do, but our eyes are on you" (2 Chron. 20:12). Then the Spirit of the Lord came upon Jahaziel, and he said: "Listen, all Judah ... Thus says the Lord to you: 'Do not fear or be dismayed at this great multitude; for the battle is not yours but God's.... This battle is not for you to fight; take your position, stand still, and see the victory of the Lord on your behalf....' Tomorrow go out against them, and the Lord will be with you" (2 Chron. 20:15, 17).

My friend, the battle you are trying to fight is not yours, but God's. You are trying to heal; you are trying to hold vigorously to the law of good in that very trouble at home that the world knows not of, but which at times nearly overwhelms you. Be still. Let go. The battle is God's, not yours, and because it is God's battle through you, God desiring to manifest through you, victory was on your side before the battle began (in your *consciousness*, for that is the only place where there is any battle). Can you not calmly—even with rejoicing—claim the victory right now, because it is God's battle? You need no longer fight this battle, but "stand still," right where you are today, in the struggle to overcome material things, and "see the victory of the Lord on your behalf."

Does some doubting Thomas say, "Yes, but I must have money today" or "I must have relief at once, or this salvation will come too late to be of use, and besides I do not see how"? Stop right there, dear friend. You do not have to see how. That is not your business. Your business is to "stand still" and proclaim, "It is done."

God said to Jehoshaphat, "Tomorrow go out against them"; that is, they were to do calmly and in order the external things that were in the present moment to do, but at the same time, they were to stand still or be in a state, mentally, of trustful passivity, and see God's saving power. Jehoshaphat did not say, "But, Lord, I do not see how" or "Lord, I must have help right away or it will be too late, for already the enemy is on the road." We read: "They rose early in the morning ... and as they went out, Jehoshaphat stood and said, 'Listen to me, O Judah ....! Believe in the Lord your God and you will be established' " (2 Chron. 20:20). And then he appointed singers, who should go forth before the army, singing, "Give thanks to the Lord, for his steadfast love endures forever" (2 Chron. 20:21).

All this, and not yet any visible sign of the promised salvation of the Lord! Right into the very face of battle against an army mighty in number, singing, "Give thanks to the Lord."

Are you any nearer than this to the verge of the precipice in this material condition that you are trying to overcome? What did Jehoshaphat do? Did he begin to think or pray hard and forcibly? Did he begin to send strong thoughts of defeat to the opposing army and exhaust himself with his efforts to hold on to the thought until he should be delivered? Did he begin to doubt in his heart? Not at all. He simply remembered that the battle was God's and that he had nothing to do with the fighting, but everything to do with the trusting. Further on we read: "As they began to sing and praise, the Lord set an ambush against the Ammonites, Moab, and Mount Seir, who had come against

Judah, so that they were routed" (2 Chron. 20:22).

It was only after they began to sing and to praise that the Lord made the first visible move toward the manifestation of His promised salvation. It may be so with you. You may be at the very verge of apparent failure and the overthrow of the cherished principle. Your "friends" are already beginning to speak disparagingly to you of your foolish trust saying, "You must do something in this matter." Fear not. Just try to realize that the battle is God's through you; that because it is God's battle, it has been victory from the start and can never be anything else. Begin to sing and praise God for deliverance; and assuredly as you do this, giving no thought to the when or the how, the salvation of the Lord will be made visible, and the deliverance as real as it was in Jehoshaphat's case, even to the gathering of unexpected "spoils" will follow. For this narrative of Judah's king further says:

"When Judah came to the watchtower of the wilderness, they looked toward the multitude; they were corpses lying on the ground; no one had escaped. When Jehoshaphat and his people came to take the booty from them, they found livestock in great numbers, goods, clothing, and precious things, which they took for themselves until they could carry no more. They spent three days taking the booty, because of its abundance" (2 Chron. 20:24-25).

So God delivers when fully trusted—perfectly, fully, even beyond anything we have asked or thought; adding good that we have never dreamed of, as though to give double assurance of God's favor and love to any who will trust God. This is the "victory of the Lord on your behalf" when you "stand still."

We must learn that the *time* of help coming to us is not our part, but God's. We do know that in all the accounts in Scripture of those who realized God's special deliverance from their troubles—from Abraham's going forth to sacrifice his son, to the time when Jesus put out his hand to save the sinking and faith-less Peter, and even after this in the experience of the Apostles—this invisible Power came to hand just at the *right time* always, never a moment too late.

The promise is "God will help it when the morning dawns" (Ps. 46:5) or, as the Hebrew reads, "at the turning of the morn-ing," which means the darkest moment before dawn. So if, in whatever matter you are trying to exercise trust in your Father, the way grows darker and the help goes further away instead of coming into sight, you must grow more peaceful and still than ever, and then you may know that the moment of deliverance is growing nearer with your every breath.

In Mark's account of that early morning visit of the women to the tomb of Jesus, when bent on an errand of loving service, they forgot the immense stone lying across their path until they were almost at their journey's end, and then one exclaimed in momen-tary dismay: " 'Who will roll away the stone for us from the entrance to the tomb?' When they looked up, they saw that the stone, which was very large, had already been rolled back" (Mk. 16:3-4). Is not "very large" full of meaning? The very greatness of the difficulty that made it impossible for the women to remove it was the more reason why it was done by this invisible Power.

"Man's extremity is God's opportunity." The more we are cut off from human help, the greater claim we can make on divine help. The more impossible a thing is to human or mortal power, the more at peace we can be when we look to the Lord for deliv-erance, for the Lord said, "My ... power is made perfect in weakness" (2 Cor. 12:9). And Paul, realizing that when he placed less confidence in the mortal, he had more help from the Divine, said, "Whenever I [the mortal] am weak, then I am strong" (2 Cor. 12:10).

Trusting means resting confidently. We are to rest confidently, saying: "God is my strength; God is my power; God is my assured victory. I will trust in Him, and He will bring it to pass."

"Take delight in the Lord,
and he will give you the desires of your heart."
—Psalm 37:4

"It is better to take refuge in the Lord
than to put confidence in princes."
—Psalm 118:9

"Those of steadfast mind you keep in peace—
in peace because they trust in you."
—Isaiah 26:3

Chapter 10
THE SPOKEN WORD

"Without him [the Word] not one thing came into being" (Jn. 1:3).

"In the beginning ... God created the heavens and the earth."

How?

Listen: "The earth was a formless void and darkness covered the face of the deep ....

"Then God said, 'Let there be light'; and there was light....

"And God said, 'Let there be a dome in the midst of the waters ....' And it was so....

"And God said, 'Let the waters under the sky be gathered together into one place, and let the dry land appear.' And it was so....

"Then God said, 'Let the earth put forth vegetation ....' And it was so....

"Then God said, 'Let us make humankind in our image, according to our likeness' " (Gen. 1:1-3, 6-7, 9, 11, 26).

God, Infinite Power, might have thought about all these things till doomsday. He might have wished during an indefinite time that they were formed and made visible. Nothing would ever have been created in visible form had there not been the spoken word put forth into the formless ether. It took the definite positive "let there be," to bring forth order out of chaos and to establish in visible results the thoughts and desires of even an infinite, omnipotent Creator.

To create is to bring into visibility, to form something where before there was nothing, to cause to exist or to take form that which before was without form and void. To exist (from *ex*, out from, and *sistere*, to stand) is to stand out. Being always is; existence (from Latin, *existere*, to stand forth, emerge, appear) is that which stands forth as a visible entity.

God creates. Because man was created or brought into the visible universe in the image and likeness of God, he, spiritually, has like powers with God: he has the power of creating, of bringing into visible form that which before did not exist. As God created by the spoken word, without which "not one thing came into being," so man can create by his spoken word. In fact, there is no other way to bring into existence the visible conditions and the things that we want.

Today scientists agree (material as well as spiritual) that there is but one universal substance out of which all things are made. This substance is divine stuff that, though invisible and intangible, is lying all about us, as is the atmosphere. This divine substance is without form and void, as is also this same physical atmosphere. It is waiting, forever waiting, for us to form it as we will by our spoken word.

What is liquid air? It is compressed invisibility, is it not? It is invisible, formless substance pressed into form by a definite and continued process until it becomes visible and tangible. This God stuff, divine substance, is likewise subject to the pressure of our thought and word.

There are three realms in the universe: the spiritual, the mental or psychic, and the physical or material. These three, while in a way distinct, are so blended into one that it is difficult to know where one ends and another begins. All created things have Spirit, soul, and body. All things that we desire are now in being in the spiritual or invisible. But, as someone has said, thought and the spoken word stand between the invisible and the visible. By the action of these two—thought and the spoken word—is the invisible made visible.

When we desire anything—I use this word *anything* advisedly, for did not the Master say, "Whatever you ask for in prayer" (Mt. 21:22)? We must take our thought off the visible world and center it on God. We begin, as God began in creation, by speaking out into this formless substance all about us with faith and power, "Let there be so and so (whatever we want). Let it come forth into manifestation here and now. It does come forth by the power of my word. It is done; it is manifest." We continue this with vehemence a few moments and then let go of it. This should be repeated with firmness and regularity and definite persistence, at least in the morning and in the evening. Continue it, regardless of any evidence or want of evidence. Faith takes hold of the substance of the things hoped for and brings into evidence the things not seen.

The moment one takes cognizance of circumstances, that moment he lets go of faith.

Our spoken word first hammers the thing desired into shape. Our continued spoken word brings this shaped substance forth and clothes it with a visible body. The first action brings that which is desired from the formless toward the external as far as the psychic; the continued action brings it forth still further and clothes it with visible form or material body.

This was illustrated to me a few years ago. A woman had been for days vigorously "speaking the word" for something she much desired. She had no confidante and recognized no human help.

One day she wrote an ordinary business letter to a friend in the country. This friend, on receipt of the letter, immediately replied, saying: "What is this strange thing about this letter of yours? When I took it from the post office, it had the appearance to me of being covered with so and so [the very thing which the writer had been shaping in the invisible by her spoken word]. I opened the letter," she continued, "and for some minutes the opened letter took the form, to my sight, of a 'horn of plenty,' pouring out in unlimited quantity this same thing. Have I gone crazy or what does it mean?"

The word spoken by the woman, alone in the silence of her own room, had shaped and brought forth toward the external, as far as the psychic realm, the thing desired. The vibrations of her thought had permeated, all unknown to her, everything that she had touched. The friend, having psychic power, saw, plainly surrounding this letter, the shape that the woman had created, though it was yet invisible to the natural eye. It is needless to say that the continued word very soon brought this shape forth into the visible world as a solid manifestation of exactly what the woman desired.

In this process, there are two things you must do. One is, do not talk with anyone about what you are doing. Talk scatters and wastes all this precious divine Substance; and what we want to do is to *focus* it. Much needless talk diffuses and wastes all of one's power. One might as well pierce full of holes the boiler of a steam engine, letting the steam ooze at dozens of pores, and then expect any power in the engine to draw the train. It is impossible to both diffuse and focus at the same time.

The other important thing you must do is continue with the spoken word. "Let us not grow weary in doing what is right, for we will reap at harvesttime, if we do not give up" (Gal. 6:9).

Chapter 11
UNADULTERATED TRUTH

There is a straight white line of absolute Truth upon which each one must walk to have demonstration. The slightest swerving in either direction from this line results in nondemonstration, no matter how earnest or intense one may be.

The line is this: *There is only God; all seeming else is a lie.*

Whoever is suffering today from sickness, poverty, failure—any kind of trouble—is believing otherwise.

We talk largely about Truth and quote with ease and alacrity the words of the Master: "The Truth will make you free" (Jn. 8:32). Free from what? Free from sickness, sorrow, weakness, fear, poverty. We claim to know the Truth, but the question is, are we free from these undesirable things? And if not, why not?

Let us be practical about this matter. We talk much about the omnipresence of God. In fact, this is one of the basic statements upon which rests New Thought. *God is omnipresent, omnipotent, omniscient.* When I was a child in spiritual things, I thought as a child and understood as a child. I believed that God was here, there, and everywhere, within hailing distance of every human being, no matter whether under the sea or on the mountaintop, in prison or outside, in a hospital or at the wedding feast. In any and all places, God was so near that in an instant God could be summoned to help. To me this was God's omnipresence. Then God's omnipotence meant to me that while sickness and poverty, sorrow, the evil tongue of jealousy or slander, and so forth, had great power to make one suffer, God had greater power. I believed that if God were called on to help us, God surely would do it, but it would be after a fierce and prolonged combat between the two powers of good and evil, or of God and trouble.

I wonder if there are others today whose real, innermost thoughts of God's omnipresence and omnipotence are much like this. Are you one of those who believe in God and something else? God and sickness? God and poverty? God and something unpleasant in your life that you are daily trying to eliminate by applying a sort of plaster of formal statements of Truth over the sore place of your trouble, while at the same time you are giving in your own mind (if not also in your conversation) almost equal power to the remedy and the disease? While you remain in this, you will never escape from your bondage, whatever it may be.

Try for a moment to think what is meant by omnipresent Spirit, remembering at the same time that what applies to your body applies equally to all other forms of human affairs or conditions.

Each little atom of one's physical body, taken separately, is completely filled, permeated by Spirit, Substance, Life. This must be true because there could be no external form to the atom without first the *sub-stans*, that which stands under or as the basis of all material things. The Spirit permeating each atom is now, always has been, and always will be absolutely perfect, because it is God, the only life in the universe. These atoms are held together each moment by the same Spirit. They work together in perfect harmony because the Spirit pervading them is one Spirit and not several spirits. Not one of these atoms can change into a diseased or imperfect atom, even for a moment; because if it did, that would be one place where, for a time, there would be lack of God, perfect life. One place for one instant without God would break up the entire law of omnipresence, which cannot be.

Jesus said, "The truth will make you free" (Jn. 8:32). But he prefaced this statement by the words "you will know the truth." It is, then, knowledge of the Truth that sets free. We are free now but we do not know it. You may be the child of a king, but if you do not know it, you may live in poverty and squalor all your life. We are all, today, this very hour, free from all sickness, because God, who is perfect life, unchangeable and indestructible, abides within and completely fills every atom of our bodies. If God, divine Substance, fills every part, every place and space, as the atmosphere fills the room, there is certainly no lack of life in any part. Then if today we are manifesting sickness, it is because we have believed the lie about ourselves and have reaped the results of the lie—that is, apparent lack of health—in our consciousness.

All that *is*, is good. But lack of God in any part is not; that is, does not exist. Such a thing is a mortal impossibility.

Many people are greatly puzzled by this. They are told that "there is no evil; all is good because all is God," and so forth. When they find themselves or others suffering pain, sickness, lack of money, and so forth, they are staggered in faith, and begin to say: "Surely this is not good; lack of health is not good; sin is not good; poverty is not good. What is this?" For an answer they are often told, "Oh, yes, this is good, for there is nothing but good (God) in the universe. This is unripe good, like the green apple."

Now the truth is that all which is not good (God) is no thing. It is the lie, and has only to be characterized as such in order to disappear. What is the wild beast that sits on your chest with such overwhelming weight when you have a nightmare? Is it "unripe good"? Is it something that, after a few days or weeks or right thoughts, you can manipulate into good? Not at all. From beginning to end it is nothing, no thing but a vagary, a deception of the mortal brain and senses. Had it at any time any sort of reality whatever? Surely not. It is all a lie, which, at the time, seems so real that it requires almost superhuman efforts to throw it off, even after you realize that it is only a nightmare.

"There is one God, the Father, from whom are all things" (1 Cor. 8:6), said Paul. And again: "For from him and through him and to him are all things" (Rom. 11:36).

If God, then, is the substance of all things visible and invisible, and is omnipresent, there is no such thing as lack of God or lack of substance in any place in this universe. Sickness would be lack of life in some part of the body. Impossible! Poverty would be lack of substance in the circumstances. Impossible! Foolishness, ignorance, insanity, would be lack of God, Divine Mind, omniscience in man. Impossible! These things cannot be.

Do you not see, then, how all these negatives are nothingness, not true, the lie? And how, instead of recognizing them as something to be overcome, we should put them at once and at all times into their real place of nothingness?

Let us go back to our straight, white line of absolute Truth: *There is only God.* All that is not God is no thing, has no existence—is simply the nightmare. If we walk on this white line where we refuse to see or acknowledge anything but God, then all else disappears. In dealing with the everyday problems of life, we shall succeed in becoming free, in proportion as we cease to parley with apparent evils as though they were entities. We cannot afford to spend a moment's time agreeing with their claim, for if we do, we shall be the overcome instead of the overcomers. We must rise to the highest, most sweeping statements of Truth that we know. Our great statement must be: *There is only God.* Whatever is not God (good) is a lie. And this lie must be instantly and constantly crushed on the head as a viper the moment it appears in our mentality. Hit the hydra-headed monster (the lie) as soon as it appears, with the positive statement: *You are a lie. Get to where you belong. There is no truth in you. There is only God, and God is fullness of good, life, joy, peace, now and forever.*

The absolute Truth is that there is no real lack anywhere, but a waiting abundance of every kind of good that we can possibly desire or conceive of. Stop believing the lie. Stop speaking it. Speak the Truth. It is the spoken Truth that makes manifest.

In the domain of Spirit, there is neither time nor space. What is to be and already is must be spoken into visibility. Practice thinking and realizing omnipresence, that is, practice realizing that all good that you desire is here now, all-present; it is not apart from you, and its coming to you does not require time. There is no time or space.

There is not God *and*—a body.

There is not God *and*—circumstance.

There is not God *and*—any sort of trouble.

There is only God through all things—in our bodies, in our seemingly empty purses, in our circumstances—just waiting as invisible Substance for us to recognize and acknowledge Him, and Him only, in order to become visible. All else is a lie.

God is.

God is all.

God is manifest, because there is nothing else to manifest.

Chapter 12
ONENESS WITH GOD

Ralph Waldo Emerson said: "Prayer that craves a particular commodity, anything less than all good, is vicious. Prayer is the contemplation of the facts of life from the highest point of view. It is the soliloquy of a beholding and jubilant soul. It is the Spirit of God pronouncing His works good. But prayer as a means to effect a private end is meanness and theft. It supposes dualism and not unity in nature and consciousness. As soon as the man is [consciously] at one with God, he will not beg."

True prayer then is just a continual recognition and thanksgiving that all is good and that all good is ours now as much as it ever can be. Oh, when will our faith become strong and steadfast enough to take possession of our inheritance here? The Israelites entered not into the Promised Land because of their unbelief. Their inheritance was real and was awaiting them then and there, but it could not do them any good nor give any enjoyment until they took hold of it by faith, after which and as a result of which, would have come the reality. It is this taking by faith that brings something into actuality and visibility.

Why do our mortal minds postpone the acceptance of all good as our rightful inheritance for this life? The heir of material wealth must accept his inheritance before he can possibly come into its possession or use. So long as he rejects it, he is as poor as though nothing had been provided for him. All things are ours now—fullness of love, of life, of wisdom, of power—even more than these, fullness of all good, which means abundance of all things, material as well as spiritual. "Every generous act of giving, with every perfect gift, is from above, coming down from the Father of lights, with whom there is no variation or shadow due to change" (Jas. 1:17).

Many of God's children are ceasing to look at the things of God from the objective standpoint and are learning to contemplate the facts of life from the subjective, or higher side—even pronouncing all things good, as God does, until everything else but the thought of good drops out of mind and only the good is manifest.

How marvelous are the little glimpses we from time to time obtain of things as God sees them! To what high points of privilege are we, God's children, being lifted so that it is possible for us to see things from the standpoint of pure intelligence, perfect wisdom! "Truly I tell you, many prophets and righteous people longed to see what you see, but did not see it" (Mt. 13:17).

One instant's view of the facts of life from the subjective side (God's side) makes all our carnal aspirations and struggles, all our ambitions, all our boasted wisdom and pride sink into utter nothingness. We see instead "the wisdom of this world is foolishness with God" (1 Cor. 3:19). All other objects in life fade into insignificance beside the one of getting more into conscious oneness with the Father, where, at all times, we shall pray the true prayer of rejoicing and thanksgiving that all good is the only real thing in the universe. When we come into perfect recognition of unity instead of duality, then, indeed, shall we know prayer to be but the *soliloquy of a beholding and jubilant soul*, and we shall cease forever to pray the prayer as a means to effect a private end.

The nearer we approach to God and the more we grow into the realization of our true relationship to Him, our Father, the more surely are all personalities, all divisions lost sight of; our oneness with all people becomes so vivid and real to us that a prayer for "private ends" becomes impossible to us. All desires of the little self are merged in the desire for universal good, because we recognize but One in the universe, and ourselves as part of that One.

How can we most quickly and surely attain this conscious oneness with the Father, which will enable us to see things as He sees them—all good?

Instantly flashes into the intuition, out from the stillness of the invisible, a voice saying, "Return to God." Return, turn away from the mortal, away from people, from human ways; turn *within* and look to God.

Seek the light from the interior, not from external sources. Why always seek to interpose human help between our soul and God? Emerson says: "The relations of the soul to the divine spirit are so pure that it is profane to seek to interpose helps.... Whenever a mind is simple and receives a divine wisdom, old things pass away—means, teachers, texts, temples fall. Let us not roam, let us stay home with the cause."

Constant reading, discussions, interchange of opinions are all external ways of reaching the Truth from the intellectual side. These are a way, but "I am the way, and the truth, and the life" (Jn. 14:6) said the voice of the Father through the Nazarene. "The anointing that you received from him abides in you, and so you do not need anyone to teach you" (1 Jn. 2:27). "When the Spirit of truth comes, he will guide you into all the truth ... he will declare to you the things that are to come" (Jn. 16:13).

When will we cease running after Truth and learn to "be still, and know that I am God!" (Ps. 46:10)?

In order that we may hear the inner voice and may receive the highest form of teaching, which alone can open the eyes of our spiritual understanding, the mortal self must cease its clamoring even for Truth; the human intellect must become absolutely still, forgetting to argue or discuss. The Father can lead into all Truth only when we listen to hear what He will say—not to what others will say. We must learn to listen—not anxiously and with strained ears, but expectantly, patiently, trustingly. We must learn how to wait on God in the attitude of: "Speak, Lord, for your servant is listening" (1 Sam. 3:9) if we would know Truth.

Jesus said, "Unless you change and become like children [that is, teachable and trusting], you will never enter the kingdom of heaven" (Mt. 18:3) or the kingdom of understanding of Truth. And again he said, "I thank you, Father ... because you have hidden these things from the wise and the intelligent and have revealed them to infants" (Mt. 11:25).

We must put aside all preconceived opinions of Truth, either our own or any other person's, and with receptive minds opened toward the source of all light, say continually, "Lord, teach me." We must become as babes in human wisdom before we can enter into the deep things of God.

But believe me, the revelation that the Spirit of Truth will make to you when you have withdrawn from all outside sources and learned to listen to the voice in your own soul, will be such as to make you know—no longer believe—your oneness with the Father and with all His children. They will be such as to fill you with great joy. "I have said these things to you so that my joy may be in you, and that your joy may be complete" (Jn. 15:11).

The great God of the universe has chosen you and me through whom to manifest. "You did not choose me but I chose you" (Jn. 15:16). Shall we forever limit this manifestation by making ourselves into a little, narrow mold of personality that will shape and size the Divine, or worse still, shall we run here and there to borrow some measure our neighbor has made of himself and hold it as our measure under the great rushing waters of infinite wisdom and love, thereby saying: "This full is all I want; it is all there is to be had, all that thou art"?

Away forever with such limitations!

> There's a wideness in God's mercy,
> Like the wideness of the sea:
> There's a kindness in His justice,
> Which is more than liberty.
> For the love of God is broader
> Than the measure of man's mind;
> And the heart of the Eternal
> Is most wonderfully kind.
> —Frederick W. Faber

Would you, then, know God, "whom to know aright is life eternal"? Go not abroad looking for the Divine. "Stay at home within thine own soul." Seek earnestly, calmly, trustfully, the source of all good. Know at once and forever that only therein will you find Truth and only thereby will you grow to be what you desire—centered, poised. Let go your narrow thoughts of the Divine, cease to desire anything less than the fulfillment of God's will in you. God's thoughts are higher than ours as the heavens are higher than the earth. Let nothing short of the perfect fulfillment of God's thought in and through you satisfy you.

Do you comprehend this in its fullness—the desire of infinite love and pure intelligence being fulfilled (or filled full) in you and me?

How quickly and far recede the cankering cares of life, the frets and fumes, the misunderstandings and the being misunderstood! How sure we are when we have consciously—and by effort if need be—swept away all limitations of personal desire and are saying: "Here I am, infinite Father, great Fountainhead of all good. I have no desire. You are fulfilling Your highest thoughts in me, unhindered by my consciousness; You are now pouring Yourself through this organism into visibility; You are thinking Your thoughts through this intellect; You are loving through this heart with Your own tender Father-Mother love, which thinks no evil, endures all things, bears all things, and seeks not its own; You are manifesting Yourself in Your own way through this organism into the visible world."

I say, when we thus burst the bonds of personal desire and rise to a willingness that the Father's will be done through us every moment, how sure we are of the fatherly care that will clothe us with the beauty of the lilies and feed us as the birds of the air. Indeed, with even a more lavish abundance of all good things than He gives to either of these, for "you are of more value than many sparrows" (Mt. 10:31).

Do you fear to break loose from teachers, from human helps? Fear not. Trust to the great and Mighty One that is in you and is limitless to manifest as Truth to you and through you. There will be no failure, no mistake. Spend some time daily alone with the Creator. In no other way will you come into the realization that you desire. Learn to sever yourself from those around you. Practice this, and soon you can be as much alone with God in the street or in a crowded room as you could be in the wilds of a desert. A little book called *The Practice of the Presence of God,* by Brother Lawrence, tells how he, for years, kept himself consciously in the glory of divine Presence, even while at the most humble daily tasks, by keeping the thought: *I am in His presence.* All things that were not divine in the man died out and dropped away, not because he fought them or resisted the uprising of the natural man, but because he persistently practiced the Presence (or thought of the Presence) of God, and in that Presence, all other things melted away like snow before a spring sun.

This is the only way of growth of overcoming. "Let the same

mind be in you that was in Christ Jesus" (Phil. 2:5). We do not have, by some supreme effort, to draw this Mind into us, but simply to let it come into us. Our part is to take the attitude consciously of receiving, remembering first to enter the "inner chamber" of our own soul and to shut the door on all thought but that of divine Presence.

Each individual has his own salvation to work out—that is, his own true Self to bring into visibility. This is not to be done by some intense superhuman effort, but by each one dealing directly with the Father.

So long as anyone clings to another, just so long will the manifestation of the real Self, God, remain weak and limited. Wait only on God for the light you desire. He will tell you how to act, what to do. Trust your own inspiration; act on it, though all the world sit in judgment on it, for when any man puts aside selfish aims and desires only to manifest the Highest, his life then becomes the perfect One manifesting through him.

When you learn to let God manifest through you, it will not be like the manifestation through anyone else. You will think and speak and do without previous thought or plan. You will be as new and surprising to yourself as to anyone else. For it will not be you speaking, but the Spirit of your Father speaking in and through you.

Oh, what supreme tranquillity we have when we are conscious that our thought is God's thought through us; our act, our word, God's act and word through us! We never stop to think of results; that is God's care. We are quietly indifferent to criticism of lesser minds (mortal thought), for we know whom we have believed. We know that what we speak and do is right, though all the world be made wrong thereby. "What I must do is all that concerns me, not what the people think," says Emerson. Then God in you becomes a law to you, and you no longer have need of external laws. God becomes wisdom to you, ever revealing to you more of Himself, giving you new and clear visions of Truth, and indeed "you do not need anyone to teach you" (1 Jn. 2:27). You no longer have use for external forms, which are but the limitations of Truth and not Truth itself. Then God shall be to you, and through you to others, not only wisdom and understanding, but love and life and the abundance of all things needful.

Then shall you have at all times something new to give to others, instead of looking to them to receive; for you will stand in the very storehouse of all good with the Master of the house, that through you, the Master may pass out freely the bread and water of life to those who are still holding up their empty cups to some human hand to be filled—not yet having learned to enter into all the fullness of good.

Believe me, you who seek Truth, who seek life and health and satisfaction, it is nowhere to be found until you seek it directly from the Fountainhead who gives to all.

Begin at once to put aside all things that you have previously interposed between your own soul and the Great Cause of all things.

Cease now and forever to lean on anything less than the Eternal. Nothing less can ever give you peace.

GOD A
PRESENT
HELP

BOOK THREE

God a Present Help was first published in 1908 by Roger Brothers in New York. It was published again in 1912 by R. F. Fenno & Company in New York and copyrighted by H. E. Cady. *Unity Magazine* published it in installments in 1940, and the first Unity Book edition came out that same year. There have been eleven printings through 1985.

Chapter 1

GOOD TIDINGS OF GREAT JOY

"Come to me, all you that are weary and are carrying heavy burdens, and I will give you rest."

—Jesus[1]

Suppose some dear lifelong friend in whose ability, resources, and faithfulness you have the utmost confidence should come to you today and say: "Friend, rejoice; I have brought you some good news, almost too good to seem true, but true nevertheless. From this day all things in your life may be changed. You have inherited a large fortune. In fact, I have come to bring it to you, together with a message of love and goodwill. Everything that money can buy is now yours for the taking."

What do you think would be the effect of such news upon you?

At first, the glad tidings might seem too good to believe; but if this messenger friend reiterated his statement, giving not only verbal assurances but tangible evidence of its truth, do you think you would hesitate and question and quibble about taking the proffered gift? I think not. Instead, your very heart would leap within you with great and inexpressible joy as you began to realize all that this good news meant, if true. It would mean relief from pressing care, cessation of the gnawing anxiety about mak-

1. Matthew 11:28.

217

ing ends meet, ability to gratify your lifelong craving for the beautiful in art and literature, time to read, think, travel, live; and above all else, it would mean the ability to help hundreds of others who are struggling with the problems of sickness, poverty, and discouragement.

Then suppose that before you had mentally quite taken in the new situation, this messenger of good news should say, "Friend, in addition to this, I have found a physician who has never failed to cure every kind of bodily disease from which you are suffering, and if you will come with me to him, he assures me that he can cure you." How long would any sane person stand undecided about accepting these two gifts? How long would anyone hesitate while he argued with the messenger about his doubts and fears, his unworthiness, or his lack of ability to use these gifts properly?

Yet this is exactly what we as Christians do with God our Father. A messenger has been sent with a definite, positive message: "Good news of great joy for all the people" (Lk. 2:10). The good news is this: "The kingdom of heaven has come near" (Mt. 3:2), here, now. We have read and heard the story since childhood, with varying emotions. At first, with a child's understanding and simple trust, we imagined that it meant just what it said. But as we went on in the Christian life, we found ourselves losing the child's idea and coming to believe that the message does not mean at all what it says. The very simplicity of it made our older, wiser minds recoil from taking it as it reads, and this in spite of the truth uttered by Jesus: "Unless you change and become like children, you will never enter the kingdom of heaven" (Mt. 18:3).

Jesus' first sermon of which we have any record was preached in Nazareth.

"When he came to Nazareth, where he had been

brought up, he went to the synagogue on the sabbath day, as was his custom. He stood up to read, and the scroll of the prophet Isaiah was given to him. He unrolled the scroll and found the place where it was written:

'The Spirit of the Lord is upon me,
because he has anointed me
to bring good news to the poor.
He has sent me to proclaim release to the captives
and recovery of sight to the blind,
to let the oppressed go free,
to proclaim the year of the Lord's favor.'
And he rolled up the scroll, gave it back to the attendant, and sat down. The eyes of all in the synagogue were fixed on him. Then he began to say to them, 'Today this scripture has been fulfilled in your hearing.' "

—Luke 4:16-21

In other words, the Lord God hath sent me, Jesus Christ, and I am now this day here present with you "to comfort all who mourn;" to deliver the captives from prison, to give sight to the blind, to heal the sick, "to give them a garland instead of ashes, the oil of gladness instead of mourning, the mantle of praise instead of a faint spirit" (Is. 61:2-3). This is the good news I have come to bring to you from God your Father.

As time went on, Jesus sent out twelve men whom he chose to spread this good news, giving to each the same power and the same commission, that is, the power to heal the sick, to cast out devils, and so forth, and to preach this practical gospel:

"As you go, proclaim the good news, 'The kingdom of heaven has come near.' Cure the sick, raise the dead, cleanse the lepers, cast out demons" (Mt. 10:7-8).

When John the Baptist sent two of his disciples to ask Jesus if he really was the Christ or if they should look for another, he said, as evidence that he really was the messenger sent from God:

"Go and tell John what you hear and see: the blind receive their sight, the lame walk, the lepers are cleansed, the deaf hear, the dead are raised, and the poor have good news brought to them" (Mt. 11: 4-5).

After Jesus had risen and as he was about to part from his disciples, he told them that their future mission in this world was to be exactly what his had been: "As the Father has sent me, so I send you" (Jn. 20:21).

In other words, as the Father has sent me to preach the good news that the kingdom of heaven is right here now, that the sick can be healed now, that the blind can receive sight at once, that the brokenhearted can be made to rejoice, that all this spirit of mourning and sorrow and heaviness can be changed into joy and praise, so send I you into the world to preach the same glad tidings to them that sit in darkness and discouragement to tell all people that God is their Savior, their genuine right-at-hand-this-moment deliverance.

As Jesus continued in the ministry of such a gospel, his heart was wrought upon as he saw how ignorant the people were of the real truth of God's desire toward them, and we read:

"After this the Lord appointed seventy others and sent them on ahead of him in pairs to every town and place where he himself intended to go. He said to them .... 'Cure the sick ... and say to them, "The kingdom of God has come near to you." '

"The seventy returned with joy, saying, 'Lord, in your name even the demons submit to us!' He said to them ... 'See, I have given you authority to tread on snakes and scorpions, and over all the power of the enemy; and nothing will hurt you. Nevertheless, do not rejoice at this, that the spirits submit to you, but rejoice that your names are written in heaven.' "

—Luke 10:1-2, 9, 17-20

In other words, rejoice not so much because you are able to make these marvelous demonstrations of power as because your spiritual eyes have been opened to the real relations between God your Father and yourself.

Jesus Christ did many marvelous works in the material world; and in thus appointing others to help him in his work among men—in increasing members as the work enlarged—and giving to them the power to manifest the same mastery over untoward material conditions, he showed conclusively that at least part of the gospel deals directly with God's deliverance of His children from sickness, poverty, and all manner of human suffering. The early Christians for three hundred years following the Resurrection of Jesus believed this and did the mighty works that he said should be done in His name. Then they lapsed into worldliness and the power was lost.

Every Christian recognizes today that the work of Jesus in the world was to establish a kingdom of righteousness, peace, and love; to teach us a higher law than the one we had known, that of "an eye for an eye and a tooth for a tooth" (Mt. 5:38). But many entirely overlook the fact that in addition to teaching us a higher way of living, Jesus also proved to us by daily ministering among the sorrowing and sick—"he ... healed those who needed to be cured" (Lk. 9:11)—and by giving the same power and commission to those whom he sent out to continue the work in His name and stead that God is in His world to do both; that is, to help His children live a better life and also to be to them life, health, comfort, all material things needed.

There is no record that Jesus Christ ever said to the sick who came to him that continued suffering would develop in them greater spiritual virtues. He did not say to the leper: "Your disease is the result of sensuality. I will not heal you, because if I do, you will continue in the same way of sin." He only said, "Do you want to be made well? ... Stand up, take your mat and walk" (Jn. 5:6, 8).

He did not say to anyone who came for healing or for any other deliverance, "Yes, I will heal you, but the healing will not become manifest for several months—just to test your faith." Nor did he say to anyone who came, "I heal many; but it is not God's will for you to be healed, and you must be submissive to His will." Oh, the deadening effect of this kind of submission! Who but knows it!

He did not let the people go hungry, saying it was their own carelessness not to have provided bread and they must not expect a miracle to be wrought to encourage such carelessness. He first fed them with spiritual food, to be sure; but immediately following that he ministered with equal ease and alacrity to their physical hunger, even though the lack may have been their own fault. When the widow of Nain, with heartbreak such as only a mother can know, followed the bier upon which lay dead her soul's pride, her beautiful and only son, Jesus did not simply comfort her with platitudes or even by bringing some superhuman joy in the place of sorrow. She wanted her boy back, and he gave her what she wanted.

Peter lacked money for the taxgatherer. Did Jesus say: "Peter, the gift of God is spiritual riches. Do not ask for worldly money, for God has nothing to do with that. If you have no money for taxes, be patient and work it out someway"; and then did he leave Peter to anxiety and care? Not at all. He instantly supplied the thing that was needed.

Jesus Christ came to show us the Father, to reveal to us the will of the Father toward us. Did he not say: "Whoever has seen me has seen the Father.... The words that I say to you I do not speak on my own; but the Father who dwells in me does his works" (Jn. 14:9-10)? Then how can we in our minds separate God from His world as we do? Most of us confine Him to His spiritual kingdom alone. We know that He wants to give us purity and spiritual grace. Every Christian believes this. But do we know or believe that He wants us to have the other desires of our heart as well? Do we believe He wants to heal our bodies, provide our taxes, feed our hunger? Do we believe that Jesus Christ really is "the same yesterday and today and forever" (Heb. 13:8)? Do we believe that He is God not of the dead, but of the living" (Mt. 22:32); that the kingdom of heaven is here at hand this moment, only that our eyes are so held by sense conditions we do not see it?

He said, "You will know the truth, and the truth will make you free" (Jn. 8:32). Then if we are not free, we do not yet know the Truth but are believing in a lie, or in the lack of Truth at least. Is this not so?

Is dumb, hopeless submission to suffering a spiritual grace? I do not believe it is. Jesus Christ never taught that it is. He taught us nonresistance to evil itself; that is, not to fight the evil thing as an entity. But he also taught us how to obtain absolute victory over and deliverance from evil of whatever form by coming into living and vital touch with Christ. This he declared to be God's will toward us, and he demonstrated it continually by delivering all who were bound in any manner by sin, sickness, suffering, or sorrow.

An earnest Christian mother related to me a few years ago a story of her little boy, who had the whooping cough. The mother had taught the boy to pray, and whenever he felt one of the dreaded coughing spells approaching, he instantly ran and fell on his knees, exclaiming, "Oh, Mamma, let me pray, let me pray quickly so God will keep this cough away!" The mother told of the difficulty she had had in explaining to the child that while it was good to pray, yet he must not expect God to stop the cough, because when one has the whooping cough, it is natural to cough! Now, according to Jesus' teachings and his dealings with people here on earth, is this not just what the boy might and ought to have expected God to do? "Unless you change and become like children, you will never enter the kingdom of heaven" (Mt. 18:3).

> "Call on me in the day of trouble;
> I will deliver you."
> —Psalm 50:15

This is the gospel, the "good news of great joy for all the people." This is something of what he meant when he said, "The kingdom of heaven has come near." Surely he meant more than we can ask or think when he said, "Come to me" (Mt. 11:28).

Chapter 2
THE WILL OF GOD

"Is there anyone among you who, if your child asks for a fish, will give a snake instead of a fish? Or if the child asks for an egg, will give a scorpion? If you then, who are evil, know how to give good gifts to your children, how much more will the heavenly Father give the Holy Spirit to those who ask him!"

—Jesus[1]

God's will for us is not sorrow, poverty, loneliness, death, and all the other forms of suffering that we usually associate with the expression "Thy will be done."

"That creature in which the Eternal Good most manifests itself, shines forth, works, is most known and loved, is the best."[2]

Paul expresses the same idea when he says, "For in him all the fullness of God was pleased to dwell" (Col. 1:19). This means fullness of love, fullness of life, fullness of power, fullness of joy, fullness of all good; and Christ abides in you. "From his fullness we have all received" (Jn. 1:16). "And you have come to fullness in him" (Col. 2:10).

God is not death; He is life. God is not hate and sorrow; He is

1. Luke 11:11-13.

2. *Theologia Germanica*, Pantheon Books, Inc., New York, 1949, p. 122.

225

love and joy. God is not weakness and failure; He is power and success.

When Jesus Christ was here on earth, he said he came to represent the Father, that is, to be to us as the Father would be; to do to us and for us what the Father would do: "Whoever has seen me has seen the Father" (Jn. 14:9). "Very truly, I tell you, the Son can do nothing on his own, but only what he sees the Father doing; for whatever the Father does, the Son does likewise" (Jn. 5:19). Jesus never gave sorrow or sickness to anyone. Did he not say, "I have said these things to you so that my joy may be in you, and that your joy may be complete" (Jn. 15:11)? Did he not definitely say, "I came that they may have life, and have it abundantly" (Jn. 10:10)?

It has been urged by many good people that Jesus meant only spiritual life. Well, he did not say so, and "the common people" who "heard him gladly" (Mk. 12:37 KJV) were not desiring or seeking spiritual life. They wanted at that time health for their sick ones, and in that day, life meant just what the common people would understand today by life. Oh, how the human intellect in its ignorance and egotism has twisted and turned and distorted the plain, simple words of the Master in order to make them conform to its darkened understanding!

Truly "the light shines in the darkness, and the darkness did not overcome it" (Jn. 1:5).

"Jesus must have meant so and so, because we do not see how he could have meant otherwise," says the intellect of man. What a pity that we should have grown so far away from the very simplicity of the "good news of great joy for all the people" (Lk. 2:10).

Truly, "those who are unspiritual do not receive the gifts of God's Spirit, for they are foolishness to them, and they are unable to understand them because they are spiritually discerned" (1 Cor. 2:14).

Jesus gave physical health for physical sickness and "healed those who needed to be cured" (Lk. 9:11). He gave life where there had been physical death, as to the daughter of Jairus; he gave power and courage to the disciples where weakness and fear had existed, so that the once cowardly Peter became a very rock of courage and strength forever after; he gave joy for sorrow, as when he restored to Mary and Martha the brother who had left them.

All of the conditions from which the human heart so shrinks he changed for the mere asking. He did not have to be begged and besought for weeks and months. He changed the conditions. How? Not by merely giving the suffering one a spirit of submission, which is but another word for a state of absolute benumbment and discouragement, but by removing the cause of the sorrow and restoring life, joy, power; by giving back something to fill to fullness the very gap that existed. "If you then, who are evil, know how to give good gifts to your children, how much more will the heavenly Father give the Holy Spirit to those who ask him!" (Lk. 11:13). "Every generous act of giving, with every perfect gift, is from above, coming down from the Father of lights, with whom there is no variation or shadow due to change" (Jas. 1:17).

Throughout all the ages of the biblical record, it was the experience and teaching of prophets, priests, and kings unto God that more of God in one's life meant more of good.

Life is good, and we all desire more of it. "I am ... the life" (Jn. 11:25), said Jesus Christ. "I came that they may have life, and have it abundantly" (Jn. 10:10), more life because of His indwelling.

"In your presence there is fullness of joy" (Ps. 16:11). "I have said these things to you so that my joy may be in you, and that your joy may be complete" (Jn. 15:11). There is fullness of joy because of His joy in us.

"Peace I leave with you; my peace I give to you. I do not give to you as the world gives" (Jn. 14:27). "The peace of God, which surpasses all understanding" (Phil. 4:7), alone is able to keep our hearts and minds overflowing with joy.

"You will receive power when the Holy Spirit has come upon you" (Acts 1:8); that is, after more of the Spirit of God comes into your life. Greater power is only more of God, of All-Power.

"My servants shall eat ... my servants shall drink ... my servants shall rejoice ... my servants shall sing for gladness of heart .... They shall build houses and inhabit them" (Is. 65:13-14, 21).

The Christ, the Son of God, speaking through Jesus of Nazareth ("the word that you hear is not mine, but is from the Father who sent me" [Jn. 14:24]), in his prayer of thanksgiving to our Father said: "As you, Father, are in me and I am in you, may they also be in us .... I in them and you in me, that they may become completely one" (Jn. 17:21, 23).

Marvelous way, is it not, in which the creature is to be made perfect and known and loved and great, simply letting God's will be done in us and in our circumstances and surroundings? Yet heretofore one's saying, "Thy will be done," has been associated in mind only with death and suffering and failure and with a forced submission to these ungodlike conditions, as though God were the author of them. "God is a God not of disorder but of peace" (1 Cor. 14:33). Oh, how in our ignorance, we have mistaken and misunderstood God, in consequence of which we are today ants when He wanted to make us giants in love and health and power by manifesting more of Himself through us! We would not let Him, because we have been afraid to say, "Have Your way in me; manifest Yourself through me as You will."

If then it is God's will to give us all these good gifts, how is it that as good and sincere Christians, really and truly God's children, we so often lack them all and cry in vain for help? It is because we have not known how to deal with the things that are contrary to His will, and how to take that which God has freely given.

How are we to deal with the things that we know are contrary to the Father's will as it was revealed by Jesus Christ?

Take sickness, for instance. We are to remember that Jesus repeatedly spoke of it as not of God but rather of Satan. An instance is the case of the "woman with a spirit that had crippled her for eighteen years. She was bent over and was quite unable to stand up straight" (Lk. 13:11). Of her, he said: "Ought not this woman, a daughter of Abraham whom Satan bound for eighteen long years, be set free from this bondage on the sabbath day?" (Lk. 13:16)

On another occasion, "they brought to him a demoniac who was blind and mute; and he cured him, so that the one who had been mute could speak and see" (Mt. 12:22). When the Pharisees, who knew Jesus as a son of David, saw this and accused him of working by the power of Beelzebul, the prince of devils, he said: "If Satan casts out Satan, he is divided against himself; how then will his kingdom stand?... But if it is by the Spirit of God that I cast out demons, then the kingdom of God has come to you" (Mt. 12:26, 28).

Let us then recognize, as Jesus did, that according to the will of God, we ought to be loosed from our infirmities. Let us meet the issue fairly and squarely without a moment's fear or hesitation, acting in His name and by His authority. "And these signs will accompany those who believe: by using my name they will cast out demons" (Mk. 16:17). Let us boldly say: "Get you behind me, Satan! You are a lie and the father of all lies. Sickness is not of God, and I will not submit to it. God is life. He is almighty, and His will is to manifest life more abundant through me. Christ does and shall reign in this body. His will is done." This is the attitude of mind we must take.

· How are we to deal with our Father's will? Exactly as with any other will.

What should we do if some friend left a will giving something very desirable to us? We should first make sure by probate that it was his will; then we should not leave a stone unturned in having it executed. If we met with some opposition and delay, we should push the harder and with more determination to obtain that which by right of inheritance belonged to us.

Shall we not, ought we not, do the same as regards the will of God our Father? This will was made ages ago, giving to whoever will "whatever you ask for in prayer." This latter clause in the will and testament of God is the only limitation He has placed on any human being. "Whatever you ask for in prayer with faith, you will receive" (Mt. 21:22). "If in my name you ask me for anything, I will do it" (Jn. 14:14).

"Put me to the test, says the Lord of hosts; see if I will not open the windows of heaven for you and pour down for you an overflowing blessing" (Mal. 3:10).

God has already done His part in full. In Judges 18:10, it is written,"God has indeed given it into your hands—a place where there is no lack of anything on earth"; that is, of anything the human heart desires. Jesus said, "You will receive, if you have faith" (Mt. 21:22 RSV). God has said, "The right of inheritance is thine" (Jer. 32:8 KJV); that is, whatever you desire is yours by right of inheritance because you are His children, and the children are the natural and rightful heirs to all that the Father has. Also "the redemption is thine" (Jer. 32:8 KJV); that is, in the redemption wrought out by Christ, we have become "heirs of God and joint heirs with Christ" (Rom. 8:17). For we are all sons and daughters of God, through faith in Christ Jesus. He has thus assured us that all things are ours by right, and:

"God is not a human being, that he should lie,
or a mortal, that he should change his mind.
Has he promised, and will he not do it?
Has he spoken, and will he not fulfill it?"
—Numbers 23:19

Now it only remains for us to prove the will by affirmation and trust, to prove Him and see if He will not do all that He has promised. The Holy Spirit alone is the executor of God's will, but even this executor can do nothing for us unless we take the right attitude.

"Come," He says, "Do not be slow to go, but enter in and possess the land" (Judg. 18:9). Thus there is something definite for us to do. In proving God, there must be no meek submission to the things coming upon us that we know are contrary to His will for us, as that will was revealed by Jesus Christ.

Did Jesus ever tell anyone that it was God's will for him to suffer lack or be sick or be a failure in any way? If any such vision of God's will is in your mind, rise up instantly, and in the name of Christ, put it forever out of your thoughts as unworthy of a loving Father, and doubly unworthy of yourself, His offspring. When any of these things come upon you, arise at once and claim your rightful inheritance. "I am thy part and thine inheritance" (Num. 18:20 KJV), says the Lord. Remember what God is, who says to you, "I am ... thine inheritance." He is life, wisdom, peace, joy, strength, power. Remember that He has given it into your hands, although to you, it may not yet be visible: a place where there is no want of anything.

When God said to Moses, "I AM," it was as though He said: "I am this moment to you anything that you have the courage to claim Me for, but you must prove Me. I am the supply of every lack in your life, but you must take Me for it, and then stand still and see the salvation that I will work for you."

To us in our spiritual impotence, Jesus says today, as he did to the infirm man at the Pool of Bethzatha, "Do you want to be made well?" (Jn. 5:6) That is, "Do you will it, and not simply languidly desire it? Are you determined to have that executed which you are satisfied is God's will for you? Well, then I will it too," and it is done.

Listen! "If you will" brings no visible answer to prayer. But a definite, positive will-not-be-put-off attitude, a determined "I will have Your will done in this matter" is a force that always brings results into manifestation.

Chapter 3
LIFE MORE ABUNDANT

"I came that they may have life, and have it abundantly."
—Jesus[1]

All life is the breath of God. When God created man, He "breathed into his nostrils the breath of life; and the man became a living being" (Gen. 2:7).

Life then, that mysterious something that man has tried in vain to analyze, to weigh, and to measure, even to produce; life, I say, is the breath of God. "The spirit of God has made me, and the breath of the Almighty gives me life" (Job 33:4). Is it any wonder that man tries in vain to catch this life principle, to harness it, to produce it?

There is but one kind of life in the universe. All life is divine; all life is the breath of God. All life is God made manifest, and the manifestation varies according to the degree, so to speak, in which God, the breath of life, comes forth into visibility through the various forms, "according to the measure of Christ's gift" (Eph. 4:7). In the rock, an invisible something holds the atoms from flying off from one another, as would be their natural bent. Natural science calls this the force of cohesion. Cohesive force is but another name for the breath of God pervading the atoms of the rocks. Life in the vegetable, the grass, the tree, is all one and

1. John 10:10.

the same life manifested in larger measure than in the rock. Man is the fullest, highest form of God manifested as life.

We read that "in the beginning" this mysterious something, which we cannot see, feel, or handle but which is plainly stated to be the "breath of life," was breathed into clay man and "man became a living being." Has the manner of creation changed any since the "first beginning"? Is it not "the beginning" for every new creation today? Is not the life of every being the very breath of God today just as much as it ever was? Are not we all equally His children, His offspring by inheritance? Yea, verily.

God's breath is what God is; that is, it is of the same nature and substance. If God is life, His breath is life. If God's breath is our life, that life must be like God, eternal in every child He creates. Without that breath of God given individually, none of us could exist today. Neither the soul of man nor the body of man has life in itself. Both are made alive and kept alive momently by the Spirit that is God pervading and permeating them. "The Spirit gives life" (2 Cor. 3:6). "For you have died, and your life is hidden with Christ in God" (Col. 3:3).

Jesus came that we might have life and that we might "have it abundantly." He came to show us our true relation to the source of all life and to teach us how to draw consciously upon God our Father for more abundant life as we need it. This does not mean spiritual life alone but life for the entire being. Is our heart cold, and is our love dead? We cannot analyze love; we cannot work it up at will, but we know that God is love and love is God. What we need is more of God, love, breathed into our hearts until we are surcharged and transformed into new creatures by divine love. "He breathed on them and said to them, 'Receive the Holy Spirit' " (Jn. 20:22). Something was given by His breathing on them.

Do we lack wisdom? It is not more laborious study that we need in order to obtain it, but a fresh supply of Omniscience—

All-Knowledge, All-Wisdom—breathed into this intellect by Him who "gives to all generously and ungrudgingly" (Jas. 1:5). It is more of the breath of the living God we need.

If we are weak and unstable in character; if we are failures mentally, spiritually, or physically; if we feel ourselves in any way bound or limited, it is because we need more of this mysterious breath of God, which is power, life, freedom. "He is God not of the dead, but of the living" (Mt. 22:32), said Jesus.

Health is more life. Drugs will not give life. Travel and change of scene, so often resorted to in illness of mind and body, will not give life except in so far as they tend to relax the tense, rigid mind and body and permit God—who is always in process of outgoing as life toward us His children—to flow in to fill the lack. We do not have to beseech God. Life more abundant rushes into the souls and bodies of men, as air does into a vacuum, the moment they learn how consciously to relax and, turning toward God, let it.

People who are persistently ill or unsuccessful in any way say they are tired of it all and want to die. They know not what they say. They do not understand. It is not death they want but more life. This breath of the Almighty is to us the only health and strength, the only power and success of either mind or body. "With you is the fountain of life" (Ps. 36:9). "Whoever finds me finds life" (Prov. 8:35). "In him [Christ, this very Christ who now lives within each of us] was life, and the life was the light of all people" (Jn. 1:4). "If the Spirit of him who raised Jesus from the dead dwells in you, he who raised Christ from the dead will give life to your mortal bodies also through his Spirit that dwells in you" (Rom. 8:11).

Life is God's gift. The outer life is but the outflowing of the inner life, and that inner life is momentarily fed from the fountain of life through Christ at the center of our being. God gives His own life freely to all who can receive it.

If this be true, that the breath of the Almighty is the only health of mind or body, why look elsewhere?

What then are we to do?

Change our minds. Turn around. If through ignorance of the only and unfailing source of all life, we have turned our backs upon God and our faces toward human helps, like drugs, change of environment, and the like, let us halt, face about!

"Yet you refuse to come to me to have life" (Jn. 5:40), says the Christ of God today as much as He did through the lips of the Master nineteen hundred years ago. "He came to what was his own, and his own people did not accept him" (Jn. 1:11). "I am the resurrection and the life" (Jn. 11:25), says this same Christ within you today. Notice that it is "I am," not "I will be," present tense, not future. "Those who believe in me, even though they die, will live" (Jn. 11:25). It is as though He said, "He that believeth on Me as the source of his life and turns away from human ways to Me as the Way, even if he seems to be at the very last gasp of his soul, body, or circumstances, I say he shall be made alive by the same power that was able to raise Jesus from the dead."

God's gifts are alike to all; but we have to learn how to receive freely that which He gives, how to open ourselves to the inflow of divine life through the Christ at the center of our being, exactly as we would open ourselves to the warm rays of the sun. "But to all who received him, who believed in his name, he gave power to become children of God" (Jn. 1:12).

Elsewhere we have said that all conscious taking or receiving from God is a mental process. The human mind believes itself, in the matter of life, cut off from God, a separate being, something apart from God. This belief is not correct. The wire of communication between the Creator and His creations is never cut, the channel of inflowing divine life never closes. Each blade of grass receives its life, its springtime renewing force, as directly from the fountain of all life as though it were the only thing in the universe. Each sparrow draws its life directly from the same source. "You are of more value than many sparrows" (Mt. 10:31).

How can man by mental process stimulate and increase this inflow of divine life? How can even the least of us consciously draw upon the inexhaustible Fountain for the life more abundant that we need for soul, body, and circumstances?

"The words that I have spoken to you are spirit and life" (Jn. 6:63), said the Master. Words. Is there any power or life in words? Let us see. "But only speak the word, and my servant will be healed" (Mt. 8:8), said the centurion. That was all that was done; but a little further, we read: "The servant was healed in that hour" (Mt. 8:13).

> "He sent out his word and healed them,
> and delivered them from destruction."
> —Psalm 107:20

> "So shall my word be that goes out from my mouth;
> it shall not return to me empty,
> but it shall accomplish that which I purpose."
> —Isaiah 55:11

All words of Truth are alive with an invisible energy that has power to work miracles. Truth is mighty to accomplish results, but in order to do so it must be spoken into activity. It must be put into words. The same Christ who said, "I am the life," said also, "I am the truth." Life, Truth, Christ are one. The words of Truth that you and I speak in the name and spirit of the Master become His words, full of life and health. Such words set into motion the invisible energy that accomplishes results, and nothing is accomplished when it is quiescent.

Speaking definite, positive words of assurance to oneself or to another has marvelous power to lift and transform, power to fill the fearful, trembling heart and the suffering body with a consciousness of the real living presence of God. There is wondrous life-giving power in definitely and vigorously compelling oneself to "sing to the Lord a new song" (Ps. 96:1), even making it a song of praise and thanksgiving for benefits. Everyone has power through his will, apart from any feeling if need be, to follow the prophet's advice: "Take words with you and return to the Lord" (Hos. 14:2). No matter how deep or poignant his misery, a person can compel himself by mere willpower to look up to God and say:

> "Bless the Lord, O my soul,
>   and do not forget all his benefits—
> who forgives all your iniquity,
>   who heals all your diseases,
> who redeems your life from the Pit,
>   who crowns you with steadfast love and mercy,
> who satisfies you with good as long as you live."
>   —Psalm 103:2-5

No matter whether you feel like it or not, say it. Put it into words. Out of the depths of misery begin sincerely and earnestly to speak words of praise and thanksgiving, and soon you will find yourself involuntarily saying: "I fear no evil; for you are with me .... My cup overflows" (Ps. 23:4-5).

This is God's way of working to deliver us out of our troubles. Thus He comforts us and gives newness of life through our first "speaking comfortably" to ourselves and to Him the words of Truth. Such words have power to free the channel between our own centers of life and the fountain of all life—channels that may have become clogged by our selfishness or igno-

238

rance—so that a great, surging influx of new life can take place. "You shall call your walls Salvation, and your gates Praise" (Is. 60:18). Praise and thanksgiving open wide the gates to salvation.

You may say, "Of what avail is all this except to uplift my thought, making it easier for me to bear my trouble, illness, sorrow? It cannot change the real, visible conditions." Yes, it can and does. Lazarus was as dead as he ever could be and there was no faintest stirring of life when Jesus lifted his eyes and said, "I thank you, Father" (Mt. 11:25). Jesus understood that the gates in the wall of salvation from this death would fly wide open at the paean of praise. Every instant that our hearts are thus uplifted in the spirit of gratitude (which, remember, is aroused by our first beginning to speak *words* of gratitude for benefits received) this mighty energy that we have spoken of and that is none other or less than the Spirit of the living God, is working to change, restore, and heal the very trouble that seems about to destroy us.

Oh, how many times this has been proved by those of God's children who, in some degree at least, have come to know the way of the Father's working even as Jesus knew it. How many times they have proven that the solution of the problem, the healing of the illness, depended not upon human effort but entirely upon taking the thought altogether off the distress and centering it, by main force of will if need be, upon thanking and blessing God for all His benefits. "Not by might, nor by power, but by my spirit, says the Lord of hosts" (Zech. 4:6) is the work accomplished. This is a spiritual law, infallible and unchangeable, a law that works; and many times it is the only thing that does work.

No one is so weak in will but that he can thus compel himself to "take words ... and return to the Lord" (Hos. 14:2), even as he would take hold of a mighty lever to lift a heavy weight.

"Let anyone who wishes take the water of life as a gift" (Rev. 22:17).

Chapter 4
CHRIST IN YOU

Though Christ a thousand times in Bethlehem be
    born,
If He's not born in thee, thy soul is all forlorn.
          —Johann Scheffler

Man is a threefold being composed of Spirit, soul, and body
so intermingled, so blended into one that it is beyond the finite
mind to say where one ends and the other begins. We read that
when man was created, he was made in the image and likeness
of God. No intelligent person can make the mistake of supposing
that God has parts like the human body or that the external man
is in any way the image and likeness of God.

God is Spirit, God is life, God is love and wisdom and power.
God is a combination of all good. Can anyone tell me the active
principles composing life? Can anyone analyze love for me?
Can anyone weigh or measure wisdom? Can anyone catch and
box up, see, or handle Spirit? Nay, verily. God is Spirit, and the
real man made in His image is Spirit also. Spirit is substance.
Substance (from Latin *sub*, under, and *stare,* to stand) is that
invisible, intangible but real something which as its indestructible core and cause stands under, or at the center of, every visible thing.

That there is but one substance of which all things visible and
invisible are made is conceded by all scientists, whether spiritual

or material. This one substance is Spirit, forever invisible but indestructible. "The worlds were prepared by the word of God, so that what is seen was made from things that are not visible" (Heb. 11:3). God is not only the creative cause of every visible form of intelligence or life at its beginning, but at each moment of its existence. He lives within every created thing at its very center as the life, the ever-renewing, re-creating, upbuilding cause of it. This is not pantheism, which declares that the visible universe, taken or conceived of as a whole, is God. No, far from it. God expresses Himself in visible ways. Man is His fullest, most complete expression. God is the living, warm, throbbing life that pervades our being. He is the quickening intelligence that keeps our minds balanced and steady throughout all the vicissitudes of life. He never is and never can be for a moment separated from His creation. "We are the temple of the living God; as God said, 'I will live in them and walk among them' " (2 Cor. 6:16). "Do you not know that you are God's temple and that God's Spirit dwells in you?" (1 Cor. 3:16) "The king of Israel, the Lord, is in your midst" (Zeph. 3:15); not in the midst of the community at large but in the midst of you individually.

God is the Father of our spirit, of our real Self. We are His offspring, His children. "There is one body and one Spirit ... one God and Father of all, who is above all and through all and in all" (Eph. 4:4, 6). God has made all His children alike. He has no favorites. The Spirit of man always has been and always will be in His image while creation continues, no matter what the external man does to hide that image. More than once, Jesus gave public recognition to the fact of our oneness with himself as sons of God—even as He is the Son—and joint heirs with Him. "Our Father," he prayed, with thousands about him. "Go to my brothers and say to them, 'I am ascending to my Father and your Father, to my God and your God' " (Jn. 20:17), said he to Mary. "Call no one your father on earth, for you have one

Father—the one in heaven" (Mt. 23:9).

The moment we recognize God as the Father of the spirits of men, and therefore the Father of all men, that moment we recognize a new and vital relationship of all men to one another; we say "our Father" with new depth and meaning. That moment we step out forever from all narrow, selfish loves, all "me and mine," into the broad universal love that encompasses the whole world, exclaiming as did the Christ when looking around on the multitude, "Here are my mother and my brothers!" (Mt. 12:49)

We are made in the image of God. Then is this eating, drinking, sensuous creature we see the image of God? Not at all. But the divine spark at the center of our being, the ever-renewed breath of God, which is the life, the intelligence, of this person, be it full or limited, is God's image, is very part of God Himself. Is the ugly, rough piece of marble, with only a nose or a mouth visible, a statue? No, but it will be when the sculptor has finished with it. The perfect statue is there, but hidden, awaiting the touch of the master's hand to bring it forth.

Jesus primarily taught men how to live, to repent of their sins, to turn from all wrongdoing, to love others even to the laying down of their lives for their enemies if necessary. Toward the last of his ministry, he said: "I still have many things to say to you, but you cannot bear them now. When the Spirit of truth comes, he will guide you into all the truth; for he will not speak on his own, but will speak whatever he hears, and he will declare to you the things that are to come" (Jn. 16:12-13). Jesus had been to them a visible savior. He had shown them that he had power on earth to forgive sin, to heal the sick, and raise the dead. He had called Himself the life, the door, the way. But after it all, he said he had not told them all he knew as yet; they could not bear it then. "It is to your advantage [not mine] that I go away, for if I do not go away, the Advocate will not come to you" (Jn. 16:7). "And I will ask the Father, and he will give you another

Advocate, to be with you forever.... Because he abides with you, and he will be in you" (Jn. 14:16-17).

Thus Jesus recognized that a personal savior to whom people could go, outside of themselves, was not enough; such a scheme of salvation had its limitations. There must be an inner spiritual birth to each one, a consciousness of an indwelling Christ ever present within him to be his guide and teacher when he, Jesus, was no longer visible. "I will not leave you orphaned," he said to his disciples, "I am coming to you.... On that day you will know that I am in my Father, and you in me, and I in you" (Jn. 14:18, 20). In all of Paul's early teaching, he spoke only of the son of man, Jesus, who had been crucified and was risen. But in later years, as he grew in grace and in the knowledge of Truth, he spoke to his spiritual children: "I am again in the pain of childbirth until Christ is formed in you" (Gal. 4:19)! He also spoke of "the mystery that has been hidden throughout the ages and generations but has now been revealed to his saints.... Which is Christ in you, the hope of glory" (Col. 1:26-27).

What did Jesus mean? What did Paul mean? Is there then a higher, fuller birth than the one that many Christians know, that of following after the crucified Jesus, the son of Mary, who is and ever must be a personality outside ourselves?

Surely there is. It is not easy to explain the relation that Jesus, the Man of Galilee, bears to the Christ of God who is to be formed in us; scarcely possible by words to explain the mystery "which is Christ in you, the hope of glory." It cannot be put into words. It comes to one as a revelation, and thus coming, is as real as one's very existence. It was not the man Jesus, the personality, the son of man that was to be the Savior, for that part of Jesus was human. He spoke of it as such. "I can of mine own self [mortal self] do nothing" (Jn. 5:30 KJV). "The Father who dwells in me does his works" (Jn. 14:10). "The Son can do nothing on his own" (Jn. 5:19). It was the Christ, the Anointed, the very divine at the center of his being who came forth and did the works through Jesus. The Comforter that he promised was to be "the Holy Spirit, whom the Father will send in my name" (Jn. 14:26). The very Spirit of this same Father who abode in Jesus was to abide within them and us. This same Spirit, this Christ, to whom is given all power, is formed by a spiritual birth at the center of your being and mine and abides there. He who "is the image of the invisible God" becomes "the firstborn of all creation" (Col. 1:15); that is, He is the first coming forth of the invisible Father into the visible creature. He abides within us first as a "babe" (or in small degree); but as He grows and increases in stature in proportion as we recognize Him there, with encouragement and a sort of wooing, so to speak, we make room for the "Babe in the Inn."

There comes to be in this sweet and holy relation a living touch, an intimate sort of intersphering of our whole being with the divine source of all good and all giving. We become conscious of a new relationship between the living, indwelling Christ, unto whom is given all power, and the creature whose needs are unlimited. The very mind of Christ that was in Jesus is in you. You get to know that the infinite supply for soul, body, and circumstances is someway right at hand in this indwelling Christ, "in whom are hidden all the treasures of wisdom and knowledge" (Col. 2:3). "In him the whole fullness of deity dwells bodily" (Col. 2:9). "From his fullness we have all received" (Jn. 1:16). "And you have come to fullness in him" (Col. 2:10). What a marvelous, almost incomprehensible relationship!

How are we, in our entirety, soul and body, to be made perfect? By striving and effort? By lopping off branches of the old tree here and there? By cutting off this habit and that habit? Not at all. None of these is the way laid down by Christ. He said, "I am the way" (Jn. 14:6). He said, "I in them and you in me, that they may become completely one" (Jn. 17:23). We are perfected then by His perfect life dwelling within the imperfect life and filling it with His own fullness. We are made perfect, entire, by this I-in-them coming forth into visibility, because of our waiting upon Him in recognition of His indwelling presence and our continued affirmation that He does now manifest Himself as the perfect One through us. "He must increase, but I must decrease" (Jn. 3:30).

Chapter 5
FAITH

"Ask, and it will be given you; search, and you will find; knock, and the door will be opened for you. For everyone who asks receives, and everyone who searches finds, and for everyone who knocks, the door will be opened."

—Jesus[1]

What could Jesus have meant when, speaking as one having authority, he made such a sweeping, and to the poor human mind almost incomprehensible, statement as that quoted above?

We pray, we ask, believing that we are going to receive, but we receive not. Again and again this happens until we grow sick, and our courage fails because of our unanswered prayers, and we begin to say: "God does not answer. I don't have sufficient faith or the right kind of faith." Because of repeated failures, we are benumbed, and though we still pray, we seldom expect an answer. Is not this so?

Where is the trouble?

Many Christians mistake hope for faith. Hope expects an answer sometime in the future; faith takes it as having already been given. Hope looks forward; faith declares that she has received even before there is the slightest visible evidence. Our

1. Matthew 7:7-8.

way is to declare something done after it has become obvious to the senses; God's way is to declare it done before there is anything whatever in sight. "God ... calls into existence the things that do not exist" (Rom. 4:17). This declaring, "It is finished," when there is still no visible evidence has power to bring the desired object into visibility. "The worlds were prepared by the word of God [God's declaring that it was done], so that what is seen was made from things that are not visible" (Heb. 11:3). That is, things that are seen were not made of visible but of invisible substance by the spoken word of God. If we expect anything from God, we must conform to His way of working.

Listen to Paul's definition of faith: "Faith is the assurance of things hoped for, the conviction of things not seen" (Heb. 11:1). In other words, faith takes right hold of the invisible substance of the things desired and brings into the world of evidence or visibility the things that before were not seen. There is but one substance from which the real of all things is made. This substance is ever present but invisible. It is all around us and fills the universe as the atmosphere we breathe covers the earth. In it, we live and move and have our being, for it is the divine Presence, or substance. It is the unseen but real and eternal that always "stands under" and "within" the seen but temporal.

Faith upon which depends all answer to prayer is not, as many earnest, sincere people suppose, a sort of will-o'-the-wisp mental condition that it is difficult to catch and hold. If this were so, the child of God might well despair. But there is a faith that might be called understanding faith that is based upon principles as unerring as those of mathematics. It was of this faith that the man of Galilee spoke when he said: "All things can be done for the one who believes" (Mk. 9:23).

Jesus invariably spoke as one having authority. He had proved that whereof he spoke, and he knew positively. He knew that all God's dealings with man were based upon an immutable law, a law that if complied with is bound from its very nature to work out certain results, no matter who or what manner of man it is that complies with that law. He never went into details as to how or why God's laws work; but positively, in a few concise words, he spoke the law and left the working of it to be proved by "whosoever will."

What is this understanding faith upon which the literal fulfillment of all God's promises rests?

There are some things which God has so indissolubly joined together that it is impossible for even Him to put them asunder. They are bound together by fixed, immutable laws; if we have one of them, we must have the other.

This may be illustrated by the laws of geometry. For instance, the sum of the interior angles of a triangle is equal to two right angles. No matter how large or small the triangle, no matter where we find it or who finds it, if we are asked the sum of its angles, we can unhesitatingly answer that it is just two right angles. This is absolutely certain. It is certain, even before the triangle is drawn by visible lines; we can know it beforehand, because it is based on unchangeable laws, on the truth or reality of the thing. It was true just as much before anyone recognized it as it is today. Our knowing it or not knowing it does not change the fact. Only in proportion as we come to know it as an eternally true fact can we be benefitted by it.

It is a simple fact that one plus one equals two; it is an eternal truth. You cannot put one and one together without two resulting. You may believe it or not; that does not alter the fact. But unless you do put the one and one together, you do not produce the two, for each is eternally dependent on the other.

The world of spiritual things is governed by law just as unalterable and unfailing as is the law governing the natural world. The so-called supernatural is not beyond law by virtue of being above natural law. It is simply the working of a higher law than any that we, with our limited understanding, have heretofore known; and it is because it operates in a higher realm that we have not understood. When we come into harmony with this higher law, we instantly have all the power of God working with us for the very thing we pray for, and we get it. Sometimes a soul comes into this harmony by childlike intuition, and he receives answer to prayer. But we can know the law and put ourselves consciously in harmony with it.

The promises of God are certain, eternal, unchangeable Truths that always have been and always must be true, whether in this age or another, whether on the mountaintop or under the sea. A promise, according to *Webster's* dictionary, gives reason to expect something. It is a declaration that gives to the person to whom it is made the right to expect, to claim, the performance of whatever is promised. God has bound Himself to His children by promises innumerable, and He has magnified His word above all His name.

> "I bow down toward your holy temple
> and give thanks to your name for your steadfast love
>   and your faithfulness;
> for you have exalted your name and your word
> above everything."
> —Psalm 138:2

"When God made a promise to Abraham, because he had no one greater by whom to swear, he swore by himself …. Human beings, of course, swear by someone greater than themselves, and an oath given as confirmation puts an end to all dispute. In the same way, when God desired to show even more clearly to the heirs of the promise the unchangeable character of his purpose, he guaranteed it by an oath, so that through two unchangeable things, in which it is impossible that God would prove false, we who have taken refuge might be strongly encouraged to seize the hope set before us" (Heb. 6:13, 16-18).

God is our all-sufficiency in all things. He is the infinite supply, above all that we ask or think, of all that the finite creature can possibly need or desire. The promises are already given. The supply, though unseen by mortal eyes, is at hand. "Before they call I will answer" (Is. 65:24).

"My God will fully satisfy every need of yours according to his riches in glory" (Phil. 4:19). But "he that cometh to God must believe that he is, and that he is a rewarder [and the reward as well] of them that diligently seek him" (Heb. 11:6 KJV).

Here are the two fundamental principles on which rests the whole secret of understanding faith:

First, the supply forever awaits the demand.

Second, the demand must be made before the supply can come forth to fill it.

To recognize these two statements as Truth and affirm them persistently is to comply with the law of God's giving. Faith has nothing to do with visible circumstances. The moment one considers circumstances, one lets go of faith.

When Jesus recognized the unchangeable fact that the supply of every want awaits us just at hand, though unseen, and said, "Everyone who asks receives" (Mt. 7:8), He was simply stating a truth as unalterable as that of cause and effect. He knew that there need be no coaxing or pleading, for God has answered before we ask.

"Whatever you ask for in prayer, believe that you have received it, and it will be yours" (Mk. 11:24). "Believe that you have received it"—present tense! Ah, this is the hard part. Believe that you will (future) receive them. Yes, this is easier. But to say a thing is done when there is no sign of it anywhere— can we do this? Yes, we can, and we must if we would obtain an answer to our prayer. This is the faith on which all receiving depends—calling that which is not as though it were—simply because God has said so, and holding to it unwaveringly by positive and continued affirmation that it is done. This is our part of the contract. This is complying with God's law of supply. God said, "I AM," not, "I will be," when He gave His name to Moses. He says, "I AM" to each of us today, and then He leaves us to fill in whatever we pray and ask for. I AM health, I AM strength, I AM supply, success, anything we dare take Him for.

How are we to take that which we desire?

This taking is purely a mental process. When Jesus went to the tomb of Lazarus to perform the mighty miracle, he did not plead for help, but he lifted up his eyes and said, "Father, I thank you for having heard me. I knew that you always hear me" (Jn. 11:41-42). So remembering God's law of supply and demand, we begin to thank Him that He has made Himself our abundant supply and that before we have called, He has provided that for which we are about to ask. We continue to thank Him that we *do have* (not shall have) the petition desired of Him; and in confidence, but silently and positively, we affirm over and over again that we have it in possession. We must be persistent and unyielding. God said to Joshua, "Every place that the sole of your foot will tread upon I have given to you" (Josh. 1:3). And He says it to us in every act of prayer. Every place that you stand firmly and determinedly upon in affirmation, that have I given you. Dare to claim it; put your foot firmly upon your claim, and you shall have it. Have faith in what you are doing, because you are working with God's own unfailing, unchangeable law, and you cannot fail.

Even in the midst of illness calmly and confidently affirm: *God is in me, my full abundant health now, in spite of this appearance*; for has He not said "I AM"? Jesus said, "Do not judge by appearances, but judge with right judgment" (Jn. 7:24). In lack of whatever kind, ask and believe that you receive; that is, ask and begin immediately to affirm, even in the absence of any visible evidence: *God is (not will be) my supply right here and now.* Be determined about it; He will surely manifest Himself according to His promise.

"Whatever you ask for in prayer" is the only stipulation governing the relations between us and His I AM. Expecting that anything *will* be given tends to keep it forever a little in the future, just ahead of the now. Hard though it may be mentally to do it, we must step right over the dividing line and say, "It is done." As far as God's part is concerned, everything has already been given us in Christ, who is "the whole fullness of deity ... bodily." Christ is here present, not far off. Though it is invisible to our mortal eyes, all we are capable of desiring is here now. "For in him every one of God's promises is a 'Yes.' For this reason it is through him that we say the 'Amen' " (2 Cor. 1:20); which means that they are all fulfilled now in Him. All things are in Christ, and Christ is in you. "You have come to fullness in him" (Col. 2:10). Then can we not say in faith, "All things are mine here and now"?

Persistent, unwavering affirmation that it is done and is made visible now brings into manifestation whatever one asks or desires.

Chapter 6

GIVING AND FORGIVING

"For if you forgive others their trespasses, your heavenly Father will also forgive you; but if you do not forgive others, neither will your Father forgive your trespasses."

—Jesus[1]

We have become so familiar with the sayings of Jesus that at times they seem to have lost all meaning to us. He said: "So when you are offering your gift at the altar, if you remember that your brother or sister has something against you, leave your gift there before the altar and go; first be reconciled to your brother or sister, and then come and offer your gift" (Mt. 5:23-24). This was equivalent to saying that anyone coming to God in prayer must simply let go of all ill will toward his brother or sister if he desires or expects any conscious fellowship with God.

"Those who say, 'I love God,' and hate their brothers or sisters, are liars; for those who do not love a brother or sister whom they have seen, cannot love God whom they have not seen" (1 Jn. 4:20).

"... whenever our hearts condemn us; for God is greater than our hearts, and he knows everything.... If our hearts do not condemn us, we have boldness before God; and we receive from

---

1. Matthew 6:14-15.

him whatever we ask" (1 Jn. 3:20-22).

Jesus once said, "If you do not forgive others, neither will your Father forgive your trespasses." He was then, as at all times, speaking in full recognition of the great law governing God's dealings with His children. We are not for an instant to understand by this that God, in an I-will-give-you-back-as-good-as-you-send spirit, refuses us forgiveness when we do not forgive others. Neither are we to understand that because we fail, He is angry with us and turns in an unforgiving mood away from us. Not at all. God is not an overindulgent parent who gives a reward for well-doing and punishes in anger for failing to do well. Such a conception of Him is belittling and is unworthy of the thought of any intelligent person.

Let us see if we can find out the law of God's working in this matter of *for*giving as well as in the matter of giving. Our first step is to remember how we are related to God and to our fellow human beings. God is in Christ, and Christ is in us and in all persons. God, the infinite, unfailing source, the great spring and reservoir of All-Good, is forever desirous of outflowing and ever in process of outflowing to His children through Christ. We, God's children, His offspring, are made alive and kept alive by His breath continually renewed in us, and thus in the deepest reality, we are never separated from Him for an instant: Him— the life, the love, the mind that is in us, the only power through which we can do anything. If Jesus said, "I can of myself do nothing," how much more must every human being say the same.

Of ourselves, if in reality we are separated from God, we are nothing and can do nothing. "But we have this treasure [Christ] in clay jars, so that it may be made clear that this extraordinary power belongs to God and does not come from us" (2 Cor. 4:7). Christ in us and God in Christ says, "I am ... the life" (Jn. 11:25): "The words that I say to you I do not speak on my own;

but the Father who dwells in me does his works" (Jn. 14:10). (It is the Father speaking thus in Christ.) With every breath, we draw in anew this life of God, which is God. And there must be a continual renewal. The breath of yesterday or an hour ago does not suffice for this moment. When we breathe in but little of this breath of life, we are only half alive, so to speak. Yet our "life is hidden with Christ in God" (Col. 3:3) just the same, waiting for us; and it is not His fault if we take but little of it. No matter how sinful we are or how completely our life is covered and hidden by worldliness or indifference, still the source of our life remains unchanged.

So it is with our inner light, the light of all persons: wisdom, judgment, knowledge, and so forth. This comes into us momentarily from God through Christ, "in whom are hidden all the treasures of wisdom and knowledge" (Col. 2:3). "The life was the light of all people" (Jn. 1:4). "The true light, which enlightens everyone, was coming into the world" (Jn. 1:9). To whom was this referring? A few Christians? A few in this church or that church? No, but He is the "light which enlightens everyone."

Now if God in Christ is the life of all life, if He is the light of all light, the force of all forces, how is it that some are suffering from lack of life, some are sitting in darkness, some are handicapped by weakness of character and body?

Listen! We are not automatons. We are made in the image and likeness of God, and like Him, we have the power of choice, the power of deciding for ourselves: "There is one God, the Father, from whom are all things and for whom we exist, and one Lord, Jesus Christ, through whom are all things and through whom we exist" (1 Cor. 8:6), to be sure. There is but one force, but we each have the power of opening ourselves to this force or closing ourselves against it, whichever we choose. The force lives on whichever we do. "But to all who received him, who believed in his name, he gave power to become [consciously] children of

God" (Jn. 1:12).

The inner light comes to "everyone ... coming into the world"; but we may close ourselves to this light either through ignorance or willfulness—the result is the same—and live in darkness. The light within every man goes right on shining just the same, whether he accepts it or rejects it. "The light shines in the darkness, and the darkness did not overcome it" (Jn. 1:5). In this case, the light is shut off through ignorance. "And this is the judgment, that the light has come into the world, and people loved darkness rather than light because their deeds were evil. For all who do evil hate the light and do not come to the light, so that their deeds may not be exposed. But those who do what is true come to the light, so that it may be clearly seen that their deeds have been done in God" (Jn. 3:19-21). Thus is the light voluntarily or willfully shut out, again as a matter of man's choice. Both conditions are dependent on the mental attitude of man. In the first instance, he is not conscious that there is light within himself—"the darkness did not overcome it." In the second instance, he stubbornly refuses to come to the light because he hates the light.

The power that is in us is divine. It is all from God, who is omnipotent, but we are given the choice of using or directing this power for either good or evil. The light that is in us is good. It is Christ, but we may elect to use this light for our guidance or for our destruction.

All our relations to God our Father, as we are taught by Jesus, whether we are conscious of it or not, depend on our own mental attitude and not on any changeable attitude of God toward us. From His very nature, God is forever in process of giving, just as the sun from its very nature is forever in process of radiating, of shedding abroad, light and heat. The sun does not have to be coaxed and urged to shine. It simply cannot for an instant cease to shine while it remains the sun. The only way we can escape from the direct oncoming of the sun's rays is to interpose something between ourselves and the sun, an act, as you see, that is entirely our own and not that of the sun. Even the sun will continue undisturbed to give forth alike "on the righteous and on the unrighteous" (Mt. 5:45) what it has and is, and let whosoever will take.

So it is with God. He is forever in the process of giving out what He is and has. Nothing can hinder our receiving unless we, consciously or unconsciously, interpose some condition, some mental obstacle between God and ourselves that completely shuts God out.

If we expect to receive anything from God, "who gives to all generously and ungrudgingly" (Jas. 1:5), we must turn our faces toward Him like little children and open our entire being to His incoming. We must not shut Him out by either a tense, rigid, mental condition of anxiety or by an unforgiving spirit. When Jesus said, "Forgive ... so that your Father in heaven may also forgive you your trespasses," he understood perfectly that just as we freely direct this divine force toward others, so by our own words and mental attitudes, we likewise direct this force toward and through ourselves. In other words, this indwelling Christ is as obedient to us as we are obedient to the Christ. "By your words you will be justified, and by your words you will be condemned" (Mt. 12:37). "For with the judgment you make you will be judged, and the measure you give will be the measure you get" (Mt. 7:2).

No one can possibly radiate darkness while he is full of light. "Whoever says, 'I am in the light,' while hating a brother or sister, is still in the darkness. Whoever loves a brother or sister lives in the light, and in such a person there is no cause for stumbling. But whoever hates another believer is in the darkness, walks in the darkness, and does not know the way to go, because the darkness has brought on blindness" (1 Jn. 2:9-11).

The everlasting light abideth in us, but if we shut it off so others cannot receive it, we by the same mental act shut it entirely out of our own consciousness. When we withdraw ourselves from our fellow human beings in any way, particularly when we retain toward anyone an unforgiving spirit (no matter how he may have injured us), we cut off by strangulation, as it were, all the invisible arteries and nerves through which constantly flow into us life, light, love from God, the source. It is like ligating an artery between the heart and an extremity. The heart goes right on, but the extremity withers and dies because the source of its nourishment has been cut off.

When by our own acts we thus cut ourselves off from God, we become, as someone has said, "a mere bundle of strained nerves, trembling and shaking with fear and weakness and finally dying" because by our own mental attitude, we shut off God's life and love, which is ever springing up within us, seeking to flow out through us anew to the world.

We all know what Jesus said to Peter in answer to his question whether one should forgive another seven times: "Not seven times, but, I tell you, seventy-seven times" (Mt. 18:22). By this Jesus meant: "Always be in a mental attitude of forgiving, never any other way; and if this is the way God is toward you, how much more should you be so toward your brother." Read the parable on forgiveness that he spoke as it is recorded in Matthew 18:23-35.

Again, this matter of forgiveness demands a mental attitude much more definite than a simple feeling of indifference toward the offending one. To pardon means simply to remit or wipe out the penalty and let the offender go free, but to forgive means much more than this. It means to give "for"; that is, to give some definite positive good in return for the evil received. Is this "a hard saying"? One often hears this phrase: "I can forgive, but I cannot forget." That is not God's way of forgiving. "I will not remember your sins" (Is. 43:25) is what He says. Why? Because He keeps right on giving "for," giving us good for our evil.

Nothing else so surely clears out all remembrance of wrongs suffered as definitely and positively as to "give for" the offending one.

If you think you have been wronged by anyone, sit down quietly in your own room and speak out to this person silently. Tell him that you forgive him for the sake of the Christ in him. Tell him that you give him love, love, love in return for anything he may have given you. Keep telling him you love him until you begin to feel what you are saying. Believe me, he, a thousand miles away, will hear your message and be melted by it, for it will travel to him via heaven, and it cannot miss the way.

If you have ill will toward anyone, if you are prejudiced against anyone, if you have accused anyone even in your silent thought of injustice, or if you have criticized anyone, sit down alone at night before retiring and mentally ask him to forgive you. Calling him by name, silently confess to him what you have done and ask his forgiveness, telling him as you do the others, over and over again, that you love him and are sure there is nothing but God's perfect love between you. Never retire until you have thus definitely "cleaned the slate" as regards yourself and every other human being, definitely *for*given—given love "for"—everyone. Keep at this until all the tightened cords that have been cutting off the free flow of God's love and life through you are loosened; until a habit of forgiving is established within you.

This is what Jesus meant by "seventy-seven times." This spirit of perfect love and forgiveness will often heal the worst disease by opening the channel for omnipresent love and life to flow through unobstructed.

Chapter 7
POWER IN THE NAME OF JESUS CHRIST

"Very truly, I tell you, if you ask anything of the
Father in my name, he will give it to you."
—Jesus[1]

That the name of Jesus Christ is a real, practical, wonder-
working, result-producing power there is no doubt.

In The Acts of the Apostles, we find that, immediately following the death and Resurrection of Jesus, Peter and John one day
instantly healed "a man lame from birth .... People would lay
him daily at the gate of the temple called the Beautiful Gate so
that he could ask for alms" (Acts 3:2). This healing was done
through Peter by the spoken word: "In the name of Jesus Christ
of Nazareth, stand up and walk" (Acts 3:6).

We further read that "immediately his feet and ankles were
made strong. Jumping up, he stood and began to walk, and he
entered the temple with them, walking and leaping and praising
God. All the people saw him walking and praising God, and they
recognized him as the one who used to sit and ask for alms at the
Beautiful Gate of the temple; and they were filled with wonder
and amazement at what had happened to him....

"When Peter saw it, he addressed the people, 'You Israelites,
why do you wonder at this, or why do you stare at us, as though

---

1. John 16:23.

263

by our own power or piety we had made him walk? The God of Abraham, the God of Isaac, and the God of Jacob, the God of our ancestors has glorified his servant Jesus .... By faith in his name, his name itself has made this man strong' " (Acts 3:7-10, 12-13, 16).

The following day when the rulers of the Jews, the high priests and others, were gathered together, they set Peter and John (whom they had arrested the night before for preaching and healing in this name) in their midst and began to ask: " 'By what power or by what name did you do this [meaning the healing of this man]?' Then Peter, filled with the Holy Spirit, said to them, 'Rulers of the people and elders ... let it be known to all of you, and to all the people of Israel, that this man is standing before you in good health by the name of Jesus Christ ... whom God raised from the dead.... There is salvation in no one else, for there is no other name under heaven given among mortals by which we must be saved' "(Acts 4:7-8, 10, 12).

Later on in the ministry of Peter, we read of his healing Aeneas, who had been in bed eight years, sick of palsy: "Peter said to him, 'Aeneas, Jesus Christ heals you; get up and make your bed!' And immediately he got up" (Acts 9:34).

Paul, in the same way, instantly healed a woman possessed with a "spirit of divination" (Acts 16:16). "Paul, very much annoyed, turned and said to the spirit, 'I order you in the name of Jesus Christ to come out of her.' And it came out that very hour" (Acts 16:18).

When Isaiah prophesied the coming of the Savior, he said: "Look, the young woman is with child and shall bear a son, and shall name him Immanuel" (Is. 7:14). *Immanuel* means God with us. The Hebrew name *Jesus* means savior, *Christ* means the anointed of God; Jesus Christ, the Savior anointed of God; Immanuel, God with us.

When the Christ, the Anointed, the very Son of God, came to

abide in Jesus, the result was the fullest conscious expression of the invisible Father that had ever occurred; and the very names that contain all power were given to this child by those devout souls who were open enough to receive them by direct illumination of the Spirit.

The name of Jesus Christ holds all power within it.

We know that all sensations, all impressions, either mental or physical, that reach us from without or within reach us through vibrations of one sort or another. We also know that different words spoken produce different effects. If one doubts this, let him speak out into the formless ether the word *power* repeatedly. Then let him by way of experiment take the word *weakness* and do the same for a day; or take the words *love* and *hate*, or any other opposing words, and watch the results. As we ascend from the outer or lower region, the physical, to the higher or more spiritual self living at the center, the vibratory movements by which all information or help is given become finer and subtler but infinitely more powerful.

The name, the words *Jesus Christ*, with all their original meaning behind them and embodied in them, produce spiritual vibrations of infinite fineness and power. The Master of spiritual things understood this, and many times as he was about to leave his humble disciples and was giving them last instructions, he tried to impress upon them the truth that there is power in His name to accomplish things.

"Very truly, I tell you, if you ask anything of the Father in my name, he will give it to you. Until now you have not asked for anything in my name. Ask, and you will receive, so that your joy may be complete" (Jn. 16:23-24).

And again: "I will do whatever you ask in my name, so that the Father may be glorified in the Son. If in my name you ask me for anything, I will do it" (Jn. 14:13-14).

Jesus Christ is a revelation of God in us. He is invisible God made visible. Jesus Christ is God-with-us made visible. This is exactly what we all need and desire, did we but know it. This same Christ abiding within you and me is God come forth to center or focus Himself in humanity. "We have this treasure in clay jars, so that it may be made clear that this extraordinary power belongs to God and does not come from us" (2 Cor. 4:7). "For we are the temple of the living God; as God said, 'I will live in them and walk among them, and I will be their God, and they shall be my people' " (2 Cor. 6:16).

Because of this intimate relationship, we may each become in Christ's name and stead a savior, always remembering however that the "extraordinary power belongs to God and does not come from us." Of ourselves, we can do nothing. All the power we have comes to us and through us from the Spirit of God. "Each of us was given grace [free gift of wisdom, power, and so forth] according to the measure of Christ's gift" (Eph. 4:7).

When a person is given authority to speak or act in the name of a king or of a chief executive, his speaking or acting carries with it the full power vested in the ruler together with that of the entire government behind him. When using the name with full authority, we speak in the name of Jesus Christ, the anointed Son of God, the Savior unto whom has been given "all authority in heaven and on earth" (Mt. 28:18); we become even as He is, in this world, and we set in motion a mighty though invisible force to accomplish that whereto our word is sent.

Is your way so hedged in by difficulties that you do not know which way to turn?

Jesus Christ says, "I am the way." Take His name and use it. There is surely power in it to open ways that the finite mind never dreamed of. Let your silent affirmation constantly be: *Christ is the way now; Christ is the way made visible, for Christ is God-with-us made visible, or the invisible way made visible.*

Let go all external ways and see the marvelous way that will appear before you when you trust this word spoken in His name.

Do all the doors of escape from physical or mental bondage in your daily life seem closed to you?

Jesus Christ says, "I am the door." Stand still and see the salvation that He will work for you when you begin to say: *Christ is the door, the open door made visible this moment. God-with-me is my Savior and deliverer.* Says the Christ within us this very day, right in the midst of our seeming bondage of environment or circumstances, "I have set before you an open door, which no one is able to shut" (Rev. 3:8). Jesus Christ is the open door. By it—this door—we may enter into visible possession of the good that He has for us. We must first stop all external planning for escape and then enter by faith and by continual affirmation that Christ is now the open door made visible.

Does your life seem dark and gloomy, covered by a thick, black darkness wherein is no light? Remembering that Jesus Christ is God-with-us made visible, recall what He said: "I am the light of the world. Whoever follows me will never walk in darkness but will have the light of life" (Jn. 8:12). It is God speaking to you. Take up the name and remember that whatever you ask in His name, He will do. Your darkness will soon glow with "the true light, which enlightens everyone" (Jn. 1:9).

Does sickness reign in your body?

Still, God-with-us made visible is the remedy.

"For just as the Father has life in himself, so he has granted the Son also to have life in himself" (Jn. 5:26).

Is your illness a desperate one?

"I am the resurrection and the life. Those who believe in me, even though they die, will live" (Jn. 11:25). Your case is not quite so bad as "dead," is it? Even if it is, just let go of everything else and take up the all-powerful, all-prevailing name: *Jesus Christ is my life. Christ is God made visible. The life more abundant is this same Christ within me made visible now. He that believeth on this name (the power of the name), though he were dead yet am I his resurrection.* "If the Spirit of him who raised Jesus from the dead dwells in you, he who raised Christ from the dead will give life to your mortal bodies also through his Spirit that dwells in you" (Rom. 8:11).

"Until now you have not asked for anything in my name. Ask and you will receive, so that your joy may be complete" (Jn. 16:24). This is the message coming out of the silence from the invisible Father to His children: "Ask and you will receive, so that your joy may be complete" (Jn. 16:24). This is a marvelous message indeed!

Christ in us is our all-sufficiency in all things. *Is.* It is a finished condition as far as He is concerned; but we must bring it forth into the material world of manifestation by claiming it (speaking the word of it in His name) and sticking to it through thick and thin no matter what the appearance is. "Do not judge by appearances" (Jn. 7:24).

There is a marvelous power for protection and deliverance in this name when it is simply and earnestly spoken. In times of great mental disturbance or of lack of wisdom, in times when peace and harmony seem to have fled from the home, or when one is in the presence of impure-minded persons or of any false teaching or association, just quietly repeating within one's own heart the sacred and all-powerful name of Jesus Christ will not only keep one's mind in perfect peace ["Thou wilt keep him in perfect peace, whose mind is stayed on thee" (Is. 26:3 KJV)] but it will radiate marvelous and living power from the indwelling divine Presence. And all that is not of Christ flees away as did the devil-possessed men who cried out, "What have we to do with thee, Jesus, thou Son of God?" (Mt. 8:29 KJV)

"The name of the Lord is a strong tower;
the righteous run into it and are safe."
—Proverbs 18:10

"Some take pride in chariots, and some in horses,
but our pride is in the name of the Lord our God."
—Psalm 20:7

Seek often to retire from the world of noise ["go into your room and shut the door" (Mt. 6:6)] to find revelation of the Christ in your own soul. Sit down quietly and alone and with closed eyes begin to say: *Jesus Christ is now present. He is within me.* Say the words. Say them. You do not need to say anything else, just repeat the name. It will bring wonderful realization of the divine Presence. One moment's real conscious communion with the Son of God is of more worth than a thousand worlds.

Chapter 8
LIFE, A MINISTRY

> "Whoever wishes to become great among you must be your servant, and whoever wishes to be first among you must be slave of all. For the Son of Man came not to be served but to serve, and to give his life a ransom for many."
>
> —Jesus[1]

Looked at from a purely commercial standpoint, the life of Jesus Christ was a failure. His place in the world was obscure, His occupation a humble one. The work of his hands commanded only the usual recompense. From the world's point of view, his contribution was merely that of an average man.

Even after his public life began, he seemingly failed just as notably as before. He made himself no reputation among men. In the field where his greatest visible success lay, the delivering of men from sorrow and trouble, he sometimes failed. "He saved others; he cannot save himself" (Mt. 27:42), they cried when deriding him. All the way to his ignominious death, he stood before self-satisfied men, chief priests, and Pharisees as a failure. Why? Because he and these men lived from entirely different standpoints. Men lived largely from the external; Jesus lived from within. Men reckoned success then as the world reck-

---

1. Mark 10:43-45.

271

ons success today, largely in terms of numbers and figures and the possession of external things.

After two thousand years, we can see that the life of Jesus Christ, lived so obscurely, so unostentatiously, really was not the failure it seemed, that he was living a life that in the long run was the only successful one. For today, when his contemporaries have passed away and are forgotten, his life stands forth as the inspiration of all love and all goodness, the inspiration of all success.

"The Son of man came not to be ministered unto, but to minister" (Mt. 20:28 KJV), and all Godlike living is the spirit of ministry unto others. Someone has given the following definitions:

> Selfishness: mine, not thine.
> Justice: mine and thine.
> Love: thine, not mine.

We speak of love as unselfish or selfish. There is no such thing as selfish love. Such a thing would be a paradox indeed. Love always gives; selfishness always expects to receive. The law of love must be the law of giving, the law of ministration to others, not from sense of duty but from spontaneity and delight. What mother ministers to her children from duty? What father makes daily provision for his children because he is their father and the law says he must? Why, the very heart of parenthood springs out spontaneously and with joy supreme to minister to the child in every possible way even before he or she can ask or think what he or she wants.

Pure love always asks, "What can I give?" never "What shall I receive?" God is pure love. Parenthood is a little of God, so to speak, come forth into manifestation, the offspring of God.

God, the source of all life spiritual and physical, God, the only source of real success and joy, abides in Christ within us.

God gives without thought or hope of return. So do we as soon as we become conscious of an indwelling Christ; we cease to expect or desire to be ministered unto.

If we would live the life of real success, real joy, real Christlikeness, we must keep the current turned to flow from within outward instead of in the opposite direction.

God says: "If you offer your food to the hungry and satisfy the needs of the afflicted, then your light shall rise in the darkness and your gloom be like the noonday. The Lord will guide you continually, and satisfy your needs in parched places, and make your bones strong; and you shall be like a watered garden, like a spring of water, whose waters never fail" (Is. 58:10-11). Of course, if you offer yourself, it could not be otherwise. All drawing out of the soul is a drawing out directly from the Fountainhead within, from Him who is all life, all light, all good, to minister Him unto others. And as the water of life flows through you to minister to others, it must first refresh you with new life and light and joy.

Oh, how we have mistaken and misunderstood Him who is the Way! How we have missed the joy of service by letting our ministry to others be from a sense of duty, thus striving to satisfy the conscience, in a way, by afflicting our souls and feelings that such a sacrifice was acceptable to God and in some way an aid to our growth in grace.

"Is not this the fast that I choose: to loose the bonds of injustice, to undo the thongs of the yoke, to let the oppressed go free, and to break every yoke? Is it not to share your bread with the hungry, and ... when you see the naked, to cover them ...? Then your light shall break forth like the dawn, and your healing shall spring up quickly; your vindicator shall go before you, the glory of the Lord shall be your rear guard. Then you shall call, and the Lord will answer; you shall cry for help, and he will say, Here I am" (Is. 58:6-9).

No one can live to himself and not be a failure both spiritually and physically. Such living causes the stream of life and light to form backwater, and the body as well as the soul shrivels for want of new supplies from the Fountainhead. It is only when you draw out your soul that your healing shall spring forth speedily, because health is nothing less than the life more abundant that the immanent Christ made manifest through the body. "I am ... the life," said Jesus Christ. "The life" thus implies His recognition of only one life. God does not live unto Himself. His greatest desire is to get into expression, into visibility, as life, love, joy, all good.

The divine Father of us all is forever trying to manifest Himself in what the dear Scottish minister, George MacDonald, called "a reckless extravagance of abundance." He might have manifested Himself in a few flowers; but instead He fills to overflowing the very brooksides, the unused and often unseen valleys with a perfect wealth of foliage and beautiful blossoms. He gives from the very joy of giving. What He has given in nature without our interference is truly an "extravagance of abundance." Can this desire to get into expression as the fullness of all that He is—not of all that He has—be less than it is in nature when it comes to His highest creation, humankind? Surely not.

Imagine a great reservoir fed inexhaustibly from ever-living springs within itself. Leading out from this reservoir but never separated from it are innumerable little streams, each ending in a fountain. A fountain is simply a receiving and distributing station; it is never self-existent or self-feeding. Each one of the fountains is an individual center for distributing the water it receives. It is constantly renewed from the one great source without any effort on its own part. Its sole business is to distribute what it receives. At its external extremity, each little fountain is separate and distinct from all the others, but at its inner extremity, at the center, it is one with them all.

This is exactly God's relation to His children. He is the reservoir; we are the receiving and distributing stations; He is the vine; we the branches. He is the "one God and Father of all, who is above all and through all and in all" (Eph. 4:6). "We too are his offspring" (Acts 17:28). "Call no one your father on earth, for you have one Father—the one in heaven" (Mt. 23:9).

There is no obstruction between this great reservoir and any individual fountain except what we put there. Each one is, as Emerson says, the inlet, and may become the outlet of all there is in God. But each one must keep his own fountain free for the great stream to flow through. He must not let it get dammed up by selfishness. There must be a constant outflow in order to keep water pure, cold, and invigorating. No one need plead with the water in a spring to flow. It is bound by its very nature and "desire" to make room for the pressure of new waters, which are ever crowding up from its living center to flow wherever they can find a free outlet. If one outlet becomes obstructed, the water simply seeks more room through another, for flow it must by the law of its being.

New life, new wisdom, new love and joy and power, more than we can ask or think, are waiting every instant to flood our being from the great reservoir God: "What no eye has seen, nor ear heard, nor the human heart conceived, what God has prepared for those who love him" (1 Cor. 2:9).

Either consciously or unconsciously, we close up the outlet when we refuse to give out to others what we receive—"What do you have that you did not receive?" (1 Cor. 4:7). By mentally living unto ourselves alone; by sharply, shrewdly looking out for number one first, last, always; by feeling that it isn't our duty to minister unto others without return, then in the name of worldly wisdom we repress the God-given loving impulse to distribute freely and without thought or hope of return what we receive. If we turn the current in the opposite direction by seeking what we can get from the world instead of what we can give to it—then we so choke up the living stream of good that God Himself is powerless to pour into us the very things for which we may be praying.

Christ is the light of the world. Christ is within us. This light is ever fed from the great fountain of all light, the Father in Him: "I in them and you in me" (Jn. 17:23). God made each one of us to be a radiating center, constantly shining outward toward others in a spirit of ministry and giving. If you draw out your soul to satisfy the afflicted, "then your light shall break forth like the dawn .... And your gloom be like the noonday" (Is. 58:8, 10).

But if you put a covering over your light by harboring the thought of not letting your neighbor receive from you anything for which he makes no return, you will simply find yourself walking in the darkness. "If then the light in you is darkness, how great is the darkness!" (Mt. 6:23) As Christian Gellert said, "Whoever in the darkness lighteth another with this lamp [Christ] lighteth himself also; and the light is not of ourselves, it is of Him who appointeth the suns in their courses."

The Spirit of Christ is ever the spirit of ministration. We are not called upon to give that which we have not, but only that which we have. When Peter and John were going into the Temple and saw a certain lame man lying at the gate of the Temple, where he daily asked alms, Peter said to him, "Look at us." Acts says: "He fixed his attention on them, expecting to receive something [some money] from them. But Peter said, 'I have no silver or gold, but what I have I give you; in the name of Jesus Christ of Nazareth, stand up and walk' " (Acts 3:4-6). Who shall say that Peter did not give more than any amount of money or alms? "Give, and it will be given to you. A good measure, pressed down, shaken together, running over, will be put into your lap; for the measure you give will be the measure you get back" (Lk. 6:38).

Jesus knew the immutable law when he said this. He knew that "every perfect gift, is from above, coming down from the Father of lights" (Jas. 1:17). He also knew that all giving tends to larger receiving.

> "Some give freely, yet grow all the richer;
> others withhold what is due, and only suffer want."
> —Proverbs 11:24

> "Freely ye have received, freely give."
> —Matthew 10:8 KJV

A BRIEF GLOSSARY OF TRUTH TERMS

NOTE: The terms *Truth* (capitalized) and *Unity* are used to designate the principles taught by Unity School of Christianity and presented to the public through its literature. The term *Truth* (capitalized) means that which is the fundamental and ultimate reality of anything. Truth may transcend fact. For instance, to a Unity student a person's illness is fact, not Truth; he believes that the Truth about the person is wholeness; he believes that wholeness is God's will for His children and that wholeness is the fundamental and ultimate reality of each person's being.

Being—God; Deity.

being—finite existence.

consciousness—sum total of inner awareness.

demonstrate—to bring forth; reveal; prove.

demonstration—outward expression; proof.

Divine Mind—God.

manifest—to bring into form; to make evident to the senses; prove; give evidence of.

manifestation—that which has been brought forth as evident to the senses; expression.

meditate—to contemplate or ponder; to dwell in thought.

metaphysics—that division of philosophy that includes the science of being or reality, or the science of the fundamental causes and processes in things.

principle—basic law.

reality—that which is absolute or ultimately true.

realization—clear, vivid knowing; understanding.

the silence—state of stillness, relaxation, and receptivity wherein one may experience the presence of God.

Spirit—God; Deity.

spirit—life; the principle.

spiritual consciousness—inner or intuitive awareness of the things of Spirit.

substance—the spiritual essence out of which all things are made.

Afterword
DR. H. EMILIE CADY:
AUTHOR WITH AUTHORITY

When I came to work at Unity World Headquarters, one of the persons whom I wanted most to meet—and thought I never would—was Dr. H. Emilie Cady.

"She doesn't live here," I was told.

"Where does she live?"

"In New York City."

"What is her address?"

"Oh, that's not available."

"She must have an address."

"Of course, but we cannot give it to you."

"Why not?"

"We promised not to give it out to anyone."

What seemed to be a profound mystery had like many another, a simple explanation. As any Unity student would know, next to the Bible itself, Dr. Cady's *Lessons in Truth* is Unity's primary textbook. So many readers had asked for her address and had taken advantage of the information to call on her, that it had proved to be very wearing on her, and she had asked that her address no longer be given out.

I suppose if I had made an issue of the matter, I could have obtained the address from Lowell or Charles Fillmore, but it seemed too petty a matter to pursue. If I were supposed to know

Dr. Cady personally, a meeting would come about, in the right time, the right way.

It did, in a most delightful way, but eight years were required to bring it about.

Unity School was invited by CBS to present a service on its Columbia *Church of the Air*. Charles and Lowell did not want to do it so Lowell brought the invitation to me.

I accepted. It was, to my knowledge, the first Unity national network broadcast from Kansas City. It was so well received that further invitations followed; the final one, (before management was assigned to a council of churches) my seventh, took place in 1939 over KNX in Los Angeles.

It was after one given on April 6, 1935, that a letter came from the director of Radio Talks, Edward R. Murrow, which read in part, "I believe your broadcast was among the first two or three this year on the *Church of the Air* series that drew over one thousand letters." But it brought another letter that pleased me more—an invitation from Dr. Cady to visit her next time I was in New York.

So a few months later I arrived at her modest apartment on West ll9th Street, a copy of her *Lessons in Truth* deluxe edition in hand, prepared for a ten-minute meeting—which extended to more than an hour.

She greeted me cordially as I entered her living room. "I already know you," she said, with the winning smile that would charm any visitor. "My radio was turned on the day of your broadcast. I did not know of the program in advance, so you can imagine my surprise and joy to hear a service from Unity Headquarters. I felt as if I could just look through the little opening in the speaker and see you all and talk with you. I don't remember a thing you said, but I was deeply impressed by the religious feeling, the devotion in your voice."

This, I soon learned, was characteristic of Dr. Cady. She was intensely but very sanely religious in her approach to Truth. "When praying, I like to say not just 'in the name of Christ' but 'in the name of *Jesus* Christ,' " she told me.

She hoped sometime to visit Unity Headquarters, "But I shall never appear on a public platform, and I do not like crowds," she warned. "You do not reach people, to know them, that way."

"I feel as if I know you very well," I said.

"And I you!"

We talked of Myrtle Fillmore and Charles, of Lowell and Alice. She remembered a visit from Frank B. Whitney, founder of Unity's *Daily Word*. She recalled Charles Fillmore's astonishment that in her twelve years' continued residence in the same place, she had not become acquainted with her neighbors.

A friend who was a member of a traditional church lived with her. "I do not talk to her about Unity or ask her to read from it to me, because it troubles her," Dr. Cady confided. "She has a right to her opinion as I have to mine. Had I been reared in a Catholic family, I probably would be a Catholic ..."

"And you would have found the Truth in it," I ventured.

"Yes, there is good in all religions. I see little difference. It is what you use that brings you close to God that really counts."

The walls of her rooms were lined with pictures, mostly reproductions in color of the scenes and the masters that she had seen in travels through Europe, a street scene from Amalfi, the terrace of a monastery where she had slept twice in one of the little cells, another of Scottish heather. "See how the artist has caught the reflections of its purples and reds in the overhanging mist?"—a detail from Michelangelo's frescoes in the Sistine Chapel, a Raphael madonna. "They keep fresh in my mind the joys of my travels," she commented.

"And help to enrich the present," I offered.

She flashed a smile in assent.

Time was going by. I did not want to wear out my welcome.

Hesitantly I ventured, "I've brought a copy of your much-loved book with me. Would you autograph it for me?"

"Are you married?" she asked.

"No. What difference does that make?"

"I want to put a little love in the inscription," she responded with a smile.

I have the copy before me now as I write: "With warm affection, H. Emilie Cady, June 4th, 1935."

Following my article in *Youth* magazine about my visit, I had a long letter from her which reads in part:

Dear Mr. Wilson:

I cannot quite tell why you are so much in my mind today. I can almost hear your voice and touch your hand, you are so close.

I want to thank you for the wise and sensible way you "wrote me up"—no fulsome praise, which I so thoroughly abhor—just a few plain, unvarnished facts, outside of the "picture covered" walls at 420. If ever you come again, which I devoutly hope you will, I shall realize I am being visited by a reporter ... and be careful what I say! Anyway, thanks for being so kind to me in your writing.

I am longing for the day when I can take up your books and read them myself without my intervening mentality. That time doesn't seem quite yet, though I have tried so long and earnestly.

God surely gave me the vision—such a vision as in the past prophets, priests and kings have longed to see and have not been able.... It seems inexplicable that this lack of physical vision should be my greatest trial. Does not it seem so to you?

I wonder, Mr. Wilson, if you have ever felt the "aloneness" of Jesus Christ? Do you know what it is? Must not every soul know it and feel it at times as that soul goes on.

My kindest regards to Lowell, and you.

H. Emilie Cady

She told me that friends who were studying with her in the early years demurred against her practice of medicine, accusing her of inconsistency. She was much troubled as to what she should do about it.

Finally she went to her desk, buried her head in her hands—as she talked to me she did this—and asked God to tell her what to do. She said He told her to keep on doing as she was doing. From that time on she never questioned her course, and she felt that results obtained during the years that followed justified this decision. Hundreds of persons came to her for help. She would prescribe for them, and then she would ask perhaps, 'What is the trouble in your home?"

Then out would come some story of inharmony, misunderstanding, or needed adjustment.

Dr. Cady would say, "Take these tablets three times a day, and three times a day sit down quietly and close your eyes and say silently (you need not attract attention by speaking aloud), 'God loves me.' Think of Him." If the trouble was inharmony in the home, she would admonish the seeker to remember the love of her husband in the days of their courtship and to feel now the deeper, wiser love of God.

Often patients would question this procedure. "What has this to do with my illness?" they would protest.

"You have come to me for help. Do what I say because you trust me even though you do not understand. You do not know what these tablets will do for you. I do. You take them because you believe that I know. Do this other thing for the same reason.

"They seldom made more than three calls," said Doctor Cady. "They would come back with a puzzled look and say, 'I feel so much better—and do you know, what you said seemed to help me more than the medicine. I don't think I need any more tablets.' "

Simplicity and directness describe Dr. Cady and her style of writing. "The only value of Truth is what is incorporated into our daily living," she said. She liked the term *intersphered* as suggesting the relationship of Jesus Christ to the indwelling Christ.

Photographs of Dr. Cady that I have seen do not do her justice, as is so often the case with persons of strong physical characteristics. She was above average height, of matronly build, with the large hands and spatulate fingers that are often seen on surgeons. There was a kind of inner radiance, an inner beauty the camera did not reveal, that softened her features. Her voice, though strong and definite, had a warm, friendly intonation.

She has often been described as a homeopathic physician who became a disciplined Truth student. Her book *How I Used Truth*, which many students find easier to understand and apply in their personal lives than the more widely acclaimed *Lessons in Truth*, is, as she confesses, the record of her personal problems and their solution through applied metaphysics. Gradually in her medical practice, she found she seemed to be helping patients more through counseling than through prescriptions.

Born in the town of Dryden, New York, in 1848, she was eighty-seven years of age when I first met her. Both in appearance and in spirit, she belied the years.

It was not until 1939 that I had an opportunity to see her again. She had had a fall on the iron stairs in the building where she lived and sustained a hip injury that was causing her some discomfort. But I found her spirit to be as vigorous and forthright as ever.

We had a prayer together, and as I was preparing to leave, she clasped my hands in hers and said she felt that this might be our last meeting on this plane.

She did, however, write to me again before her transition, following another *Church of the Air* broadcast from Los Angeles in 1939 in which I referred to her, her writings, and her influence on the Unity movement. In this final letter, she reached past the intimation of transition in our last visit in New York. It reads in part:

I very much appreciate the tribute you paid me in your radio talk, and am deeply grateful for the notes in response ... I shall never forget the precious visit you paid me last year, and ... I shall be more than glad to see you when you come again to New York. I am not quite up to writing to you myself just now and have asked Miss S. to do it for me.

As ever your faithful friend,
H. Emilie Cady, per M. S.
September 19, 1940

—Ernest C. Wilson
1979

ABOUT THE AUTHOR

Dr. Harriet Emilie Cady was born on September 12, 1848, on a farm near Dryden, New York. Very little is known about her personal life. She never married, and she started her professional life as a teacher in a little school in Dryden. Dr. Cady left to study homeopathic medicine and probably was one of the first women doctors in New York.

Early in her career as a physician, she discovered that her patients' ills were too deep for outer remedies to cure. In accord with the tenets of homeopathy, she began treating her patients as spiritual beings, helping them find within themselves the source of health for mind and body. She became convinced that God was always the healer.

Dr. Cady's openness to Truth ideas led her to become a student of Emma Curtis Hopkins, the New Thought pioneer. She wrote a booklet called *Finding the Christ in Ourselves*, which fell in the hands of Myrtle Fillmore, Unity's co-founder along with her husband Charles. They were so impressed with the author's spiritual discernment, they wrote Dr. Cady and invited her to write for them.

The first of several articles in *Unity Magazine* appeared in January 1892 ("Neither Do I Condemn Thee"). Her articles met with instant approval of the readers, many of whom asked her to write a simple course of lessons on the principles of divine healing. At first she was doubtful, then she consented. From the appearance of the first lesson "Statement of Being" (*Unity*

Magazine, October 1894), these lessons met with an extraordinary response. Continued demand for extra copies of the magazines in which the lessons were printed led Charles Fillmore to have them reprinted in three booklets, four lessons in each booklet. In 1903 *Lessons in Truth* came out in book format and has since been translated into eleven languages and sold over a million and a half copies.

An impressively tall woman with strong features and a hearty voice, Dr. Cady did not meet the Fillmores until 1927 when they visited her in New York. As part of her belief in not emphasizing the personality, she never visited Unity Village. She died in her home in January 1941 at the age of 92.

H. Emilie Cady was a woman who proved God within her life. The fruits of her life, her writings, are so full of light and life that they continue to inspire readers today. Certainly, the works of Dr. Cady are of the caliber of a spiritual classic, some of the very best the movement of metaphysical Christianity has yet produced.

Printed U.S.A

100-1013-15M-5-95